THE INEQUALITY PARADOX: GROWTH OF INCOME DISPARITY

James A. Auerbach
and Richard S. Belous

Editors

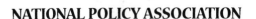
NATIONAL POLICY ASSOCIATION

BLK 0158-5/1

The Inequality Paradox:
Growth of Income Disparity

NPA Report #288

Price $19.95

ISBN 0-89068-143-0
Library of Congress
Catalog Card Number 98-65107

The Inequality Paradox: Growth of Income Disparity

◆

James A. Auerbach and Richard S. Belous
Editors

Acknowledgments

◆

THE NATIONAL POLICY ASSOCIATION held a major conference on "The Growth of Income Disparity" in Washington, D.C., on April 10, 1997. Speakers at this conference included key leaders from government, business, and labor and noted academic experts. This book is based on the papers delivered at the conference plus several other chapters that were written and submitted following the conference. The remarks of the conference moderators are excerpted in the "Introduction" to the separate Parts of this volume. The editors wish to express their appreciation to the contributors to this book and to those who participated in the conference that preceded it.

Funding for the conference and the publication was provided by the Charles Stewart Mott Foundation and The Annie E. Casey Foundation. Additional conference support was provided by the Friedrich Ebert Foundation.

About the Authors and Editors

◆

James A. Auerbach is Senior Vice President of the National Policy Association (NPA) and Director of the Income Disparity Project. He is also director of NPA's Committee on New American Realities and of NPA's Food and Agriculture Committee as well as Managing Editor of *Looking Ahead*, NPA's flagship quarterly journal. He is an Adjunct Instructor at the University of Virginia and at the U.S. Department of State, Foreign Affairs Training Institute. Mr Auerbach is coeditor of *Aging and Competition: Rebuilding the U.S. Workforce* and *The Future of Labor-Management Innovation in the United States*.

Morton Bahr became the third President of the Communications Workers of America (CWA) in 1985. Before accepting the CWA presidency, Mr. Bahr served for 16 years as CWA Vice President and Head of District 1, the union's largest district, covering New York, New Jersey, and New England. Mr. Bahr also serves as a Vice President of the AFL-CIO. He is a member of the Labor Advisory Committee on Trade Negotiations for the U.S. Trade Representative, the Federal Commission on Public Employment Policy, and the Labor Advisory Committee to the National Administrative Office, which oversees the NAFTA labor side agreement.

Richard S. Belous is Vice President and Chief Economist of the National Policy Association. He is North American Director of the British-North American Committee, of which NPA is the U.S. sponsoring organization, and also Director of NPA's Global Economic Council. Dr. Belous has been an advisor to several presidential commissions and has written or edited 14 books and numerous articles in the fields of international economics, human resources, technological change, and economic growth. He is also an Adjunct Professor of economics at George Washington University.

Vernon M. Briggs, Jr., is Professor of Labor Economics at the New York State School of Labor and Industrial Relations at Cornell University. Before coming to Cornell in 1978, Dr. Briggs was a member of the faculty of the University of Texas at Austin. From 1977 to 1987, he was a member of the National Council on Employment Policy and Chairman of the Council from 1985 to 1987. Dr. Briggs has written extensively on topics such as human resource economics and public policy, including the preparation of workers for employment, immigration, direct job creation policy, rural labor markets, and apprenticeship training.

Gary Burtless is a Senior Fellow in the Economic Studies Program at the Brookings Institution. Currently, he serves on the Panel on Privatization of Social Security of the National Academy of Social Insurance. Before joining Brookings in 1981, he was an Economist in the office of the U.S. Secretary of Labor and in the office of the Assistant Secretary for Planning and Evaluation, U.S. Department of Health, Education, and Welfare. Dr. Burtless has consulted extensively for the World Bank on reforming social security policy in countries such as Egypt, Mexico, and Russia.

Sheldon Danziger is Professor of Social Work and of Public Policy at the University of Michigan. He is also Director of the Research and Training Program on Poverty, the Underclass, and Public Policy. Prior to his work at Michigan, he was on the faculty of the School of Social Work and the Institute for Research on Poverty at the University of Wisconsin. Dr. Danziger's research focuses on trends in poverty and inequality and the effects of economic changes, demographic shifts, and government social programs on disadvantaged groups. He has written and edited numerous books and articles and often consults for government agencies and Congress.

Dieter Dettke has served as Executive Director of the Washington Office of the Bonn-based Friedrich Ebert Foundation since 1985. He oversees the U.S. activities of the Foundation, including more than 60 conferences, seminars, and workshops throughout the United States, Canada, and Germany each year. Dr. Dettke lectures widely in the United States and works to foster cooperative projects between American and German institutions as well as among individuals.

Barbara J. Easterling was elected Secretary-Treasurer of the Communications Workers of America (CWA) in 1992, the first woman to serve in CWA's second highest office. In 1995, she became the first woman to serve as Secretary-Treasurer of the AFL-CIO. Ms. Easterling is responsible for managing CWA's finances and physical facilities, as well as overseeing the government relations and political affairs department.

Walter C. Farrell, Jr., is Professor, Department of Education Policy and Community Studies, School of Education, and Professor, Graduate Program in Urban Studies, University of Wisconsin-Milwaukee. He is a National Research Affiliate with the Urban Investment Strategies Center at the Frank Hawkins Kenan Institute of Private Enterprise at the University of North Carolina at Chapel Hill. Dr. Farrell has published more than 150 journal articles, scholarly essays, and book chapters dealing with economic/business development, urban poverty, education, and race discrimination.

Gail Fosler is Senior Vice President and Chief Economist of The Conference Board, where she directs the Economics Research Program that produces major studies on economic policy issues. She recently initiated a major program examining issues of productivity and living standards on a global basis. Ms. Fosler also developed a study group on the Consumer Price Index to extend the work of the Boskin Commission. Before joining The Conference Board in 1989, she was Chief Economist and Deputy Staff Director of the Senate Budget Committee.

Lynn Franco is Associate Director of The Conference Board's Consumer Research Center. She produces the monthly Consumer Confidence Index, termed a leading economic indicator. She analyzes major consumer and economic trends and produces a wide variety of reports focusing on demographic trends and consumer spending patterns and buying behavior.

Richard B. Freeman holds the Ascherman Chair of Economics at Harvard University. He is also Program Director of the National Bureau of Economic Research Program in Labor Studies, and Executive Director of the Program in Discontinuous Economics, Center for Economic Performance, London School of Economics. Dr. Freeman has been a recent member of the U.S. Secretary of Labor and Commerce Commission on the Future of Worker-Management Relations. He has published more than 250 articles and 16 books dealing with youth labor market problems, higher education, trade unionism, transitional economies, high skilled labor markets, economic discrimination, social mobility, and income distribution and equity in the marketplace.

Peter Gottschalk is Professor of Economics at Boston College. He is currently a Research Affiliate for the Institute for Research on Poverty at the University of Wisconsin-Madison, and was previously a Russell Sage Foundation Visiting Scholar and a Brookings Economics Policy Fellow. Dr. Gottschalk's main area of research is labor economics, with a special emphasis on income distribution and poverty issues. His current work focuses on cross-national comparisons of inequality and changes in economic mobility in the United States.

James P. Harris is Senior Vice President of Exxon Chemical Company, a division of Exxon Corporation. Prior to being named to his current position in 1997, he had been General Manager of Corporate Planning since 1995. From 1991 to 1994, Mr. Harris served as President of Exxon Chemical International in Belgium, and in 1994 he was named Executive Assistant to the Chairman and President of Exxon.

Reiner Hoffmann is Director of the European Trade Union Institute in Brussels, Belgium, a position he has held since 1994. He is also Editor of the journal *Transfer*, a European review of labor and research. Mr. Hoffmann began his career as a foreign trade merchant with Hœschst AG. In 1983, he served as Assistant to the Economic and Social Committee of the European Community, and from 1984 to 1994, he was a researcher and department head at the Hans-Böckler-Stiftung. He has written and edited numerous publications on a variety of issues affecting the global economy.

James H. Johnson, Jr., is the E. Maynard Adams Distinguished Professor of Business, Geography, and Sociology and Director of the Urban Investment Strategies Center at the Frank Hawkins Kenan Institute of Private Enterprise at the University of North Carolina at Chapel Hill. His research interests include the study of interregional black migration, interethnic minority conflict in advanced industrial societies, minority-owned business development, and workforce diversity issues. He has published more than 100 scholarly research articles and has coedited four theme issues of scholarly journals on these and related topics.

John T. Joyce has been President of the International Union of Bricklayers and Allied Craftworkers since 1979. He is a Vice President of the AFL-CIO and First Vice President of the AFL-CIO Building Trades Department. He is also Co-Chair of the International Masonry Institute, a labor-management trust that he helped establish to carry out labor-management relations, apprenticeship and training, market development, and research and development. Since 1983, Mr. Joyce has been a member of the U.S. delegation to the International Labor Organization Construction Committee conferences.

Lynn A. Karoly is a RAND Senior Economist and Director of the RAND Labor and Population Program. Since joining the RAND Corporation in 1988, she has focused her research on analyzing the demographic, economic, and technological factors underlying the changing wage structure and the growing income inequality among U.S. individuals and families. Currently, Dr. Karoly is also a Research Associate with the Institute for Research on Poverty at the University of Wisconsin-Madison. She is the author and coauthor of numerous publications on income distribution.

Robert B. Reich is University Professor and the Maurice B. Hexter Professor of Social and Economic Policy at Brandeis University and its Heller Graduate School. Mr. Reich served as the 22nd Secretary of the U.S. Department of Labor during the Clinton administration's first term. Before heading the Labor Department, Mr. Reich was on the faculty of Harvard University's John F. Kennedy School of Government. He is the author of seven books, including *The Work of Nations,* as well as more than 200 articles on the global economy, the changing nature of work, and the importance of human capital.

Isabel Sawhill is currently a Senior Fellow occupying the Johnson Chair at the Brookings Institution and was formerly a Senior Fellow at the Urban Institute. She is also President of the National Campaign to Prevent Teen Pregnancy. She was Associate Director at the Office of Management and Budget from 1993 to 1995. Before joining the Clinton administration, Dr. Sawhill directed several large projects at the Urban Institute. She has served as the Director of the Children's Roundtable and as a Visiting Professor at Georgetown Law School. Dr. Sawhill is the author or editor of numerous publications.

Timothy M. Smeeding is Professor of Economics and Public Administration at the Maxwell School of Citizenship and Public Affairs, Syracuse University. Dr. Smeeding is also Director of the Luxembourg Income Study project, which he founded in 1983. Since 1994, he has been serving as the Director of the Maxwell Center for Policy Research. Dr. Smeeding has written extensively on the topic of inequality and poverty.

Janet L. Yellen is Chair of the White House Council of Economic Advisers. Before her appointment in 1997, Dr. Yellen was the Bernard T. Rocca, Jr., Professor of International Business and Trade at the Haas School of Business at the University of California at Berkeley, where she had taught since 1980. Previously, Dr. Yellen served as an Economist with the Federal Reserve's Board of Governors and a Lecturer at the London School of Economics.

Setting the Stage—
The Inequality Paradox:
Growth of Income Disparity

by James A. Auerbach and Richard S. Belous

CHARLES DICKENS' OPENING SENTENCE in *A Tale of Two Cities* ("It was the best of times; it was the worst of times") describes the current American economic landscape. In recent years, the growth of the U.S. economy has resulted in many positive trends; however, some disturbing side effects such as the growth of income disparity remain on the scene.

In many ways, the U.S. economy is the marvel and envy of the world. Not only is America experiencing its sixth year of economic expansion, but it is also enjoying healthy economic growth of roughly 3 percent a year. The United States ended fiscal year 1997 with the smallest deficit since 1974. Unemployment has dropped well below 5 percent to its lowest level in a quarter of a century. Inflation has remained low, and labor costs are showing only minor increases. Further, median U.S. household incomes increased in 1996 for the second consecutive year.

But not all Americans are enjoying the benefits of the current economic expansion. Those at the bottom are not fairing well, with real median income for the poorest 20 percent of families falling in 1996. Recent data also show a continuing increase in the number of individuals who lack health insurance.

CHILLING LESSONS

As *The New York Times* noted in an editorial on current U.S. Census Bureau data on income: "Mr. Clinton is right that the recovery is beginning to pay off, though modestly, for the middle class. But the chilling lesson from the census data is that even a healthy economy leaves the poor firmly in a depressing place."[1] *The Washington Post* commented on the same data: "The numbers showed no improvement in what many economists consider one of the most disturbing trends in recent years—the huge disparities between rich and poor. The gap has been widening for nearly two decades."[2]

The problem of income inequality is an increasingly contentious topic. To explore this significant national issue, the National Policy Association held a major conference on "The Growth of Income Disparity" in Washington, D.C., on April 10, 1997. Speakers included key leaders from government, business, and labor and noted academic experts. This book is based on the papers delivered at the conference plus several chapters that were submitted following the conference.

THE AMERICAN MODEL

When communism failed and capitalism triumphed, several different models of capitalism became contenders on the international economic scene. The American version of capitalism favors a relatively small public sector, and the presumption is usually in favor of the private sector. The American model—to a greater degree than the other models—allows market forces to work through labor markets. The supply and demand for different forms of labor and the different wage rates and benefit packages are mainly (although not exclusively) determined by Adam Smith's "invisible hand." The European model tends to have much greater reliance on the state sector, and it has many more restrictions on how labor markets operate. The Asian model is based on long-term relationships that often do not follow short-term market forces.

During this decade, the European model has frequently generated the undesirable side effects of relatively high unemployment and slow economic growth. The Asian model, on the other hand, had positive results for most of the 1990s. However, in light of the problems in Asian markets in 1997, Asian capitalism is being critically examined.

Because of the problems facing the European and Asian models, the American model of democratic market economies is viewed very favorably by many analysts. Or as *The Wall Street Journal* recently noted: "Trying to keep score in the continuing Asian financial crisis? Here's an early call: Wall Street won. . . . The American system . . . may have some shortcomings, but it is doing far better than the alternative."[3]

By allowing market forces greater sway in the world of work, U.S. labor markets can better solve major periods of disequilibrium than can other industrialized economies. The rise of the contingent workforce in the United States (i.e., the growth of temporary, part-time, and subcontracted workers) has generated considerable flexibility in American labor markets.[4]

A flexible labor market that responds to shifting market forces produces a number of positive results. It has been a key factor in contributing to the improvement of U.S. competitiveness in global markets. It has helped the United States achieve relatively low unemployment and inflation rates and improve productivity. But a flexible labor market has also meant that wage differentials have increased, with more rewards going to the top one-fifth of the nation relative to the bottom one-fifth. This has produced benefits for the American economy, but it has also generated costs. While the American model has been able to cope with many of the economic realities of the 1990s, it has been unable to respond to the negative side effects caused by growing income disparity.

In general, the authors in this publication point to three main factors leading to the increase of income disparity in the United States:

- *labor market forces*—including shifts in the world of work created by technological changes and globalization, shifts in the relative demand and supply of different types of labor, and the decline of unionization;

- *a growing diversity in the composition of households*—including the rise of single-parent families and families with dual earners; and

- *political policy changes*—including changes in the tax structure and in social welfare programs.

The most important factor appears to be changes in the world of work, followed by shifts in household structures. However, the rise in income inequality probably would have occurred even without the more conservative policies of the 1980s.

DIRECTIONS AND VIEWS

The 14 chapters examine the following:

1. Robert B. Reich, Brandeis University and former U.S. Secretary of Labor, examines the "inequality paradox." He notes that, "Almost two decades ago,

inequality of income, wealth, and opportunity . . . began to widen, and today the gap is greater than at any time in living memory. All the rungs on the economic ladder are farther apart than they were a generation ago, and the space between them continues to spread."

2. Janet L. Yellen, White House Council of Economic Advisers, maintains that economic disparity has shown some modest declines in recent years, although there is still work to be done in this area. While stressing that decades of social policies have not been futile and do not need to be completely overturned, she outlines policy responses that would help mitigate the economic and social consequences of income disparity.

3. Richard B. Freeman, Harvard University, National Bureau of Economic Research, and London School of Economics, examines the key economic, political, and social variables that are regarded as major contributors to the rise of income inequality. According to Dr. Freeman, the message from the basic facts is clear: "U.S. economic success is marred by one great failure—the maldistribution of the fruits of that success."

4. Morton Bahr, Communications Workers of America, points out the strong correlation between unionization rates and income distribution. In general, economies that have high unionization rates also have relatively lower rates of income inequality. Mr. Bahr contends that the decline of unionization has contributed significantly to the rise of income inequality in the United States.

5. Gail Fosler and Lynn Franco of The Conference Board examine the complex issue of income disparity from different perspectives. They note that even though there has been significant economic progress in the United States during the past two and one-half decades, the earnings of the average worker have fallen, due in part to the changing mix of personal income. They point to the use of price deflators as creating even more distortion in the income picture. The better educated baby boomers as well as a radically changed family and household structure have led to the growth of economic inequality. They conclude that, "When all the factors are considered, the widening income gap is due as much to the dramatic demographic and social changes America has experienced . . . as to the forces of the economic system."

6. Gary Burtless, Brookings Institution, examines the impact of technological change and international trade in shaping income distribution. Dr. Burtless concludes that neither international trade nor technological change is the major reason for the rise of income disparity. Other factors play a larger role, including changes in the technology of production, new patterns of immigration, and the dwindling influence of unions.

7. Peter Gottschalk of Boston College and Sheldon Danziger of the University of Michigan explore family income mobility in the United States. They find that although there is substantial income mobility, the extent of mobility has not increased in recent years—and in fact may have declined somewhat. "As a result, the gaps between those at the top and those at the bottom have widened and have remained at least as persistent as they were in the 1970s. . . . The hope that mobility is sufficiently large or growing fast enough to offset the rise in inequality is inconsistent with the data."

8. Vernon M. Briggs, Jr., Cornell University, looks at the impact of immigration on income disparity. He concludes, "The fact that prevailing immigration policy is linked to mounting income disparity within the populace and that it is associated with declining union membership should provide additional support for its overhaul. Immigration reform is an issue that will not go away."

9. James H. Johnson, Jr., University of North Carolina, and Walter C. Farrell, Jr., University of Wisconsin-Milwaukee, explore the nature and depth of income inequality in the inner cities and minority populations, with a focus on metropolitan Los Angeles.

10. Reiner Hoffmann of the European Trade Union Institute discusses the increase of income disparity throughout Europe. He concludes that "new poverty" and the "working poor" are labels that can no longer be applied just to the situation in developing countries or in the United States. As a result of radical and far-reaching structural changes in European labor markets, the European Union is faced with permanently high levels of unemployment and 50 million people already reduced to poverty.

11. Timothy M. Smeeding, Syracuse University, presents a cross-national comparison of income inequality. He finds that while income inequality has tended to rise in all developed countries, the rise has been the sharpest in the United States.

12. Richard B. Freeman, Harvard University, National Bureau of Economic Research, and London School of Economics, believes that growing economic disparity could prove to be the "Achilles' heel" of the American economy. He argues that Americans should be deeply concerned about income inequality and should seek policies to reduce existing disparities.

13. John T. Joyce, International Union of Bricklayers and Allied Craftworkers, explains why "the fabric of collective bargaining in the United States must be rebuilt" and how this process will lead to improved income distribution in America.

14. Lynn A. Karoly, RAND Corporation, highlights potential policy goals to narrow the income and wage gap. Dr. Karoly outlines a range of policy options to help achieve these objectives.

By itself, economic growth so far has not solved the problems produced by income disparity. It would clearly be beneficial if a higher gross domestic product could erase the difficult challenges raised by the authors of these chapters. However, sensitive and compassionate public and private sector efforts appear to be in order if the American economy is to remain an equitable, dynamic model of the post-Cold War era.

NOTES

1. "The Tide Is Not Lifting Everyone," *New York Times*, October 2, 1997.

2. Barbara Vobegda and Clay Chandler, "Household Incomes Rise Again: Women Catching Up; Rich-Poor Pay Gap Continues to Widen," *Washington Post*, September 30, 1997, p. A1.

3. Alan Murray, "New Economic Models Are Fading While America Inc. Keeps Rolling," *Wall Street Journal*, December 8, 1997, p. A1.

4. For more on contingent workforces, see "The Rise of the Contingent Workforce: Growth of Temporary, Part-Time and Subcontracted Employment," by Richard S. Belous, *Looking Ahead*, Vol. XIX, No. 1 (June 1997); and Dr. Belous's forthcoming full-length study on *The Contingent Workforce* (NPA, 1998).

PART I
OVERVIEW

Chapter 1

The Inequality Paradox

◆

by Robert B. Reich

Almost two decades ago, inequality of income, wealth, and opportunity in the United States began to widen, and today the gap is greater than at any time in living memory. All the rungs on the economic ladder are farther apart than they were a generation ago, and the space between them continues to spread. Perhaps the most dramatic change is that the real hourly earnings of young males with 12 or fewer years of schooling have dropped more than 20 percent in the past 20 years. Within the past 2 years, incomes have become somewhat less unequal, partly because the economic expansion that began in 1992 has resulted in more people employed and working longer hours and because elderly retirees are doing better. But earnings inequality among full-time adult wage earners has continued to widen. This is not a statistical fluke; it has nothing to do with how changes are measured in productivity or in prices.

Inequality's twin is the growing insecurity about jobs and wages. The omnipresent possibility of job loss haunts America's workplaces. Even the current tight labor market is failing to generate higher wages and benefits for most hourly workers, largely because they know how easily they can be replaced, which keeps them from seeking wage increases and continuing to accept cuts in benefits. Further, an increasing percentage of the workforce is employed intermittently—putting in extra hours when the demand is there, occasionally working two or more jobs, or doing odd jobs in addition to a full-time job, free-lancing, or subcontracting.

The most paradoxical aspect of these trends is not their cause, which, even if not understood in every detail, is at least broadly evident. Technological advances, coupled with global trade and investment, have created shortages of people with the right skills and surpluses of those with the wrong skills or without any skills. Two other forces are also at work—the shrinkage of the unionized segment of the workforce (also related, in part, to technological advances and to globalization) and the decline in the real value of the minimum wage. The first force has disproportionately affected lower wage men, while the second has impacted lower wage women. Factor in the uncertainties and insecurities of employment in an economy subject to rapid and continuous change and the larger picture is revealed.

The real paradox is why, at this fragile juncture in history, the social compact that America fashioned during most of this century to help ensure that prosperity was widely shared—and that no one should disproportionately suffer the risks and burdens of economic change—should now be coming undone. In the world's preeminent democratic, capitalist society, one might have expected just the opposite: As the economy grew through technological progress and global integration, but as wages and benefits dropped for part of the population and employment became less stable and predictable, "winners" would compensate "losers" and still come out far ahead. Rather than being weakened, the social compact would be strengthened.

AMERICA'S MID-20TH CENTURY SOCIAL COMPACT

Every society and culture possesses a social compact, sometimes implicit, sometimes spelled out in detail (usually a mix of both), that sets out the obligations of members of that society toward each other. Indeed, a society or a culture is defined by its social compact. America's mid-20th century compact had three major provisions.

The first pertained to the private sector. As companies did better, their workers should as well. Wages should rise, as well as employer-provided health and pension benefits, and jobs should be reasonably secure. This provision was reinforced by labor unions, to which about 35 percent of the private sector workforce belonged by the mid-1950s. But it was enforced in the first instance by public expectations. Everyone was in it together, and as a result they grew together. It would be unseemly for a company whose profits were increasing to fail to share its prosperity with its employees.

The second provision of the social compact was social insurance through which Americans pooled their resources against the risk that any one person, through illness or bad luck, might become impoverished. Hence, Americans instituted unemployment insurance, Social Security for the elderly and disabled, Aid to Families with Dependent Children, Medicare, and Medicaid.

The third provision was the promise of a good education. In the 1950s, America's collective conscience, embodied in the Supreme Court, finally led the country to resolve that all children, regardless of race, must have the same, not separate, educational opportunities. An ever larger portion of the population was also offered schooling beyond the 12th grade. The GI Bill made college a reality for millions of returning veterans. Others gained access to advanced education through a vast expansion of state-subsidized public universities and community colleges.

It is important to understand what this social compact was and what it was not. It defined Americans' sense of fair play, but it did not depend on redistributing wealth; there would still be the rich and the poor. The compact merely proclaimed that, at some fundamental level, as a society each individual depended on one another. The economy could not prosper unless vast numbers of employees had more money in their pockets, no one could be economically secure without pooled risks, and a better educated workforce was in everyone's interest.

THE UNRAVELING OF THE SOCIAL COMPACT

In recent years, all three provisions have been unraveling—and when they are most needed. Profitable companies now routinely downsize. As the U.S. Bureau of Labor Statistics has shown, layoffs in the current expansion are occurring at an even higher rate than they did in the expansion of the 1980s. The corollary to downsizing and down-waging might be termed "down-benefiting." Employer-provided health benefits are declining, while copayments, deductibles, and premiums are rising. Defined-benefit pension plans are giving way to 401(k)s without employer contributions or to no pension at all.

The widening wage gap is reflected in a widening benefits gap. Top executives and their families receive more generous health benefits than their employees, and executives' pension benefits have been soaring in the form of compensation deferred until retirement. Although today's top executives have no greater job security than others, when they lose their jobs it is not uncommon for them to receive "golden parachutes" studded with diamonds.

The second provision, social insurance, is also breaking down. This is evident in who is being asked to bear the largest burden in balancing the federal budget—disproportionately the poor and the near poor, whose programs have borne the largest cuts. President Clinton says he is intent on rectifying this imbalance, particularly the aspects of the new welfare legislation that reduce food stamps for the working poor and eliminate benefits for legal immigrants. But given the current makeup of Congress, it is somewhat doubtful that he will be able to prevail.

There is other evidence of the dissolution of social insurance. Unemployment insurance today covers a smaller proportion of workers than it did 20 years ago—only about 35 percent of the unemployed at any given time. This is due, in part, to competition among the states to reduce the premiums they charge businesses, and thus to draw eligibility rules ever more tightly.

In fact, the entire idea of a common risk pool is now under assault. Proposals are being floated for wealthier and healthier citizens to opt out. Whether in the form of private "medical savings accounts" to replace Medicare or private "personal security accounts" to replace Social Security, the ultimate effect will be much the same: The wealthier and healthier will no longer share the risk with those who have a much higher probability of being poorer or sicker.

The third part of the social compact, access to a good education, is also being severely strained. The administration has expanded opportunities at the federal level—more Pell grants and low interest direct loans for college, school-to-work apprenticeships, and proposed tax breaks for education and training. But there are powerful undertows in the opposite direction. As Americans increasingly segregate by level of income into different townships, local tax bases in poorer areas simply cannot support the quality of schooling available to the wealthier. De facto racial segregation has become the norm in large metropolitan areas. Across America, state-subsidized higher education is waning under severe budget constraints, and its cost has risen three times faster than median family income. Young people from families with incomes in the top 25 percent are three times more likely to go to college than young people from the bottom 25 percent.

Why is the social compact coming undone—and especially at a time that it is most needed? The reasons relate to the same basic forces that have divided the workforce. Technological advances, primarily in information and communication, and global trade and investment have rendered a substantial portion of the tax base footloose. Capital can move at the speed of an electronic impulse. Well-educated professionals are also relatively mobile. As a result, governments are forced to impose taxes disproportionately on labor—typically, lower wage labor, which is the most rooted. As technology continues to advance and global markets continue to integrate, this "mobility gap" will continue to widen, resulting in wider disparities in tax burdens.

Stated another way: Capital markets quickly and ferociously penalize any chief executive who pays more than is necessary to get a job done, and they penalize with equal severity any governor, president, or prime minister who is inclined to impose high taxes. The market for highly skilled people is not nearly as instantaneous or cutthroat as the market for capital, but its effects run in the same direction. Professionals move out of cities into remote suburbs where their property taxes do not have to pay for the costs of educating those in the inner city. They work from home offices or office complexes in the country. If necessary, they can emigrate from poorer countries with higher taxes to richer ones with lower taxes. As a result of the mobility of capital and of the highly skilled, average working people find themselves bearing an increasingly large portion of the cost of social programs, including those directed to the poor and near poor. Yet the incomes of most working people have not risen along with the growth of the economy; indeed, many of them are concerned with simply keeping their jobs. Such an environment is not conducive to a strong social compact.

Yet this does not entirely explain the paradox. Today's wealthy investors and skilled professionals are not merely winners in a growing economy; they are also citizens in a splitting society. They could, in principle, fully compensate the less well off and still come out ahead. Wealthier and more fortunate members of society have long engaged in efforts to improve their community or nation—spearheading not just charitable activities but also progressive reforms. Why would they now allow the social compact to unravel? Are other forces at work that are weakening the bonds of affiliation and empathy on which a social compact is premised?

I do not have a clear answer, but I do have several hypotheses. The first is that Americans no longer face the common perils of economic depression, hot war, or cold war that were defining experiences of the generations that reached adulthood between the 1930s and the 1960s. Each of these events posed a threat to American society and culture. Each was experienced directly and indirectly by virtually all Americans. Under those circumstances, it was not difficult to sense mutual dependence and to conceive of a set of responsibilities shared by all members that exacted certain sacrifices for the common good.

Second, in the new global economy, those who are more skilled, more talented, or richer are not as economically dependent on their local or regional economy as they once were and thus have less selfish interest in ensuring that the inhabitants of their community or region are as productive as possible. Alexis de Tocqueville noted that better-off Americans invested in their local communities because they knew they would reap some of the gains from the resulting economic growth (in contrast to Europe's traditions of honor, duty, and "noblesse oblige"). But today, where an individual lives is of less consequence; it is now possible to be linked directly to the great commercial centers of the world from almost anywhere.

Third, any social compact is premised on "It could happen to me"-type thinking. Social insurance assumes that certain risks are commonly shared. However, today's wealthy and poor are likely to have markedly different life experiences. Disparities are so large that even though some of the rich will become poor and some of the poor will grow rich, the chances of either occurring are less than they were several decades ago. The wealthy are no longer under a "veil of ignorance" about their likely futures, to borrow the philosopher John Rawl's felicitous phrase, and they know that a social compact is likely to require that they subsidize the poor rather than improve their well-being.

A THREAT TO THE NATION'S STABILITY AND GROWTH

Perhaps all of these hypotheses are at work to some degree. But there should be no doubt that, unchecked, the disintegration of the social compact threatens the stability and moral authority of the nation. It also threatens continued economic growth. Those who believe that they bear a disproportionate share of the burdens and risks of growth but enjoy few, if any, of its benefits will not passively accept their fates. Unless they feel some stake in economic growth, they are likely to withdraw their tacit support for free trade, capital mobility, liberal immigration policies, deregulation, and similar aspects of open economies that generate growth but that also impose losses and insecurities on them. Some element of this can already be observed in the resistance shown by both Democrats and Republicans to renewal of fast track legislation that would enable the President to move trade treaties quickly through Congress. Public opinion polls over the past decade have shown a distinct decline in support of free trade and immigration. The brief presidential candidacy of Pat Buchanan during 1996 revealed several of these themes. The anti-immigrant aspects of the recent welfare legislation revealed them as well. Note, too, the "communitarian" movement's increasing resistance to capital mobility. Social conservatives have recently decried the openings of Kmarts and Wal-Marts in various communities, charging that they undermine community values.

Similar voices are rising across Europe and for similar reasons. In late 1995, strikes paralyzed France, creating the worst social crisis since 1968. Jean-Marie Le Pen, leader of the far-right nationalist party, continues to gain adherents. Italy's neofascist National Alliance propounds a similar mixture of xenophobia and nationalism. The German federal government has been engaged in a bitter fight with unions over proposed cuts in pension benefits. In eastern Europe and Russia, former communists have gained ground on nationalist planks by rejecting open markets and calling for more government constraints.

The current situation—widening inequality coupled, paradoxically, with a weakening social compact—is simply not sustainable. Those who are losing ground will not allow it to continue unabated. One of two things will occur. Either a new and more virulent form of statism will emerge that achieves stability at the cost of economic growth. Or Americans can participate in the creation of a new social compact that permits dynamism and growth but that also compensates economic "losers," giving them a chance to become "winners." It is in the interest of all Americans to seek the latter.

Chapter 2

Trends in Income Inequality

◆

by Janet L. Yellen

THE U.S. ECONOMY has made great strides over the past four years. Recently, the unemployment rate has been less than 5 percent, more than 13 million new jobs have been created, inflation has been low and stable, and the deficit has been cut by more than 75 percent. But the nation still faces a number of challenges and troubling economic trends. For example, productivity has grown more slowly over the past quarter century than it did in the previous quarter century. Also, even though enormous progress has been made in reducing the deficit during the past four years—it is now less than 1 percent of gross domestic product (GDP), the lowest it has been since 1974—it will still be a challenge to keep the budget in balance as the aging population strains major entitlement programs.

Even though the relentless increase in income inequality has been stemmed in the past few years, this increase is the most challenging trend the nation faces. Ultimately, economic growth matters only to the extent that its fruits are shared by all Americans; balancing the budget would not be a worthwhile achievement if it came at the expense of unbalancing the distribution of income. The increase in income inequality is worrisome for another reason: No one fully understands why it has occurred. Although there are very good explanations for some of the rise in inequality, much of it is still puzzling.

This article is presented in three parts. First, the measurement of inequality at a point in time will be discussed. This is an important topic—discussions of income inequality frequently omit the definition of income. Second, the dimensions and causes of the rise of inequality over the past two decades, as well as the experience of the past two years, will be outlined. Finally, the proper policy responses to the rise of inequality from my point of view will be highlighted.

MEASURING INEQUALITY

"Pre-government Income" Versus "Post-government Income"

Most discussions of inequality focus on income, in particular, money income as measured by the U.S. Bureau of the Census. However, money income is a concept that is somewhere between "pre-government income" and "post-government income." At one extreme, there might be interest in measuring income generated by the market, pre-government income, which includes income from labor earnings, interest, dividends, and other private payments. Labor earnings alone represent 80 percent of money income, on average, and 100 percent of money income for many Americans. Money income also includes cash payments from the government in the form of Social Security, Supplemental Security Income, veterans benefits, and other transfers. But money income does not fully represent post-government income because it does not include the effect of government taxes (including the Earned Income Tax Credit, EITC) and noncash transfers such as food stamps. As a result, the featured measures of money income capture only some of the post-government income distribution.

Because taxes and transfers are themselves functions of income, the scope defined for money income has a substantial impact on the measurement of income inequality, as well as on the assessment of the efficacy of government policy. Economists sometimes measure inequality with a statistic known as the Gini coefficient. Based on this measure, taxes lower inequality in pre-government income by roughly 6 percent. Transfer payments—both cash and noncash payments—are even more important and lower this measure of inequality by another 18 percent.

The scope of this definitional issue can be illustrated by looking at another measure of inequality—the proportion of people living below the poverty line. In 1996, the before-tax and transfers poverty rate was 21.6 percent. If the effect of all taxes, the EITC, and government transfers had been included, the poverty rate would have been 10.2 percent. (This figure includes the imputed effect of realized capital gains; the effect is small, however.) About 30 million people—more than half of all those who are defined as being poor on a before-tax and transfers basis—escaped poverty with the help of government policies. Some of these policies, such as Social Security, are incorporated into the official poverty rate of 13.7 percent. Other policies, such as the EITC, are not.

Income Inequality Versus Consumption Inequality

Beyond definitional issues of what is included in income is the question of whether income is really the correct variable to focus on in the first place. From an economic perspective, it is consumption, not income, that is the ultimate determinant of well-being. Beyond this theoretical justification, there are important substantive justifications for focusing on consumption rather than income. Income undergoes both high and low frequency fluctuations that are smoothed out, to some degree, in consumption. For example, some portion of inequality is just between people at different stages of the life cycle—for instance, between students earning little or no income and middle-aged working people—whose consumption expenditures are probably closer than their income expenditures.

CHART 1

GROWTH IN REAL HOUSEHOLD INCOME
BY QUINTILE, 1967-79

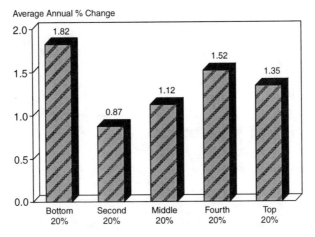

Source: Bureau of the Census, U.S. Department of Commerce, published and unpublished data.

As intuition suggests, consumption is distributed more equally than income. Also, although Gini coefficients for consumption and income tend to move together, they diverged from about 1989 through 1993 when consumption inequality flattened out and even declined somewhat while income inequality continued to rise.

TRENDS IN INEQUALITY

By almost any measure, economic inequality is greater today than it was 20 years ago. More than 30 years ago, President John F. Kennedy commented that "a rising tide lifts all boats." Indeed, the events of both the decade preceding his presidency and the decade following it supported this statement (see Chart 1 for the years 1967-79). Tremendous economic growth brought increasing incomes for all families, including the poor, and income inequality fell dramatically. However, evidence since the late 1970s suggests that not all boats are necessarily lifted by a rising tide. Chart 2 shows how dramatically the situation changed: During the 1980s and early 1990s, more than one-half of households saw their real incomes fall. If the Consumer Price Index (CPI) were biased upward, there would not be as many losers in absolute terms as these figures imply. However, the relative picture would not change—the richer the group, the greater the gains. Another metric for measuring

CHART 2

**GROWTH IN REAL HOUSEHOLD INCOME
BY QUINTILE, 1979-93**

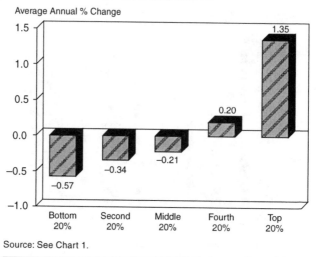

Average Annual % Change

Source: See Chart 1.

increasing inequality is the Gini coefficient, which has risen steadily since 1968 (see Chart 3).

What has caused this growing dispersion in household incomes? About one-half of increased inequality comes from rising labor earnings inequality. Ratios of annual earnings between the 90th and 50th percentiles and the 50th and 10th percentiles for male full-time, full-year workers are shown in Chart 4. Note the increased earnings power of higher paid workers since 1979. The top workers are better paid relative to the middle, and the bottom workers are worse off relative to the middle.

Much of the trend in earnings inequality is the result of rising premiums earned by some classes of workers, especially the well-educated and highly skilled. The returns to education grew tremendously during the 1980s and early 1990s, as shown in Chart 5. In 1980, a male college graduate earned one-third more than a male with only a high school education. In 1993, the college premium grew to more than 70 percent.

There are a number of explanations for this dramatic increase in the return to college. The most promising explanations center around increases in the demand for skilled workers. As new technologies have been integrated into the production process, firms have increased their demand for workers capable of using the technology. Evidence indicates, for instance, that workers who use a computer on the job earn significantly more than those who do not.

CHART 3

GINI COEFFICIENT FOR HOUSEHOLD INCOME, 1967-95

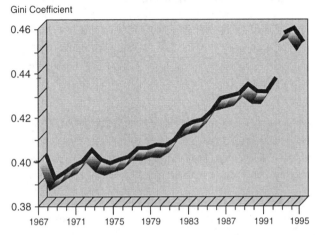

Gini Coefficient

Note: Data after 1992 are not strictly comparable to earlier data because of Current Population Survey redesign in 1994.

Source: Bureau of the Census, U.S. Department of Commerce, 1997.

CHART 4

EARNINGS RATIOS FOR MALE FULL-TIME, YEAR-ROUND WORKERS, 1967-95

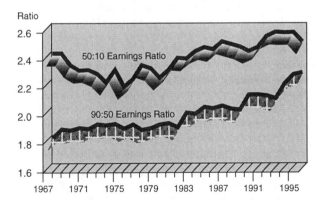

Ratio

Source: Council of Economic Advisers' calculations based on March Current Population Survey.

CHART 5

**COLLEGE/HIGH SCHOOL MEDIAN EARNINGS RATIO
FOR MALE FULL-TIME, YEAR-ROUND WORKERS, 1967-95**

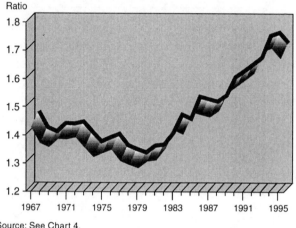

Source: See Chart 4.

Skill-biased technological change can certainly account for the rise in earnings inequality between different groups, at least in part. It is interesting that even more of the overall increase in earnings inequality is the result of greater inequality within groups that share the same education, experience, and demographic traits. Within-group inequality is on the rise and in fact accounts for about two-thirds of the total increase in earnings inequality. Although a number of creative theories have been advanced to explain this fact, none of them is very convincing.

The increase in earnings inequality, as noted, accounts for only about one-half of the overall increase in household income inequality. Much of the other half is due to changes in the composition of households. Divorces, out-of-wedlock births, and later marriages have all exacerbated income differentials between households. The share of family households headed by women has risen rapidly, from just over 11 percent in 1970 to about 18 percent in 1996. These households are more likely to have lower incomes because they lack a second wage earner, because women earn less, on average, than men, and because some of these women do not work at all. In addition to the changing composition of households, evidence suggests that nonlabor income also contributed to the increase in overall income inequality during the 1980s.

From the early 1970s through 1993, the trend of increasing income inequality was clear and pervasive. Since 1993, however, this seemingly relentless trend has apparently stalled. The poverty rate fell from 15.1

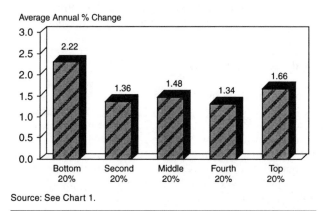

CHART 6

**GROWTH IN REAL HOUSEHOLD INCOME
BY QUINTILE, 1993-95**

Average Annual % Change

Source: See Chart 1.

percent in 1993 to 13.7 percent in 1996. This decline is based on the official poverty rate, which is before taxes. If the effects of the EITC are included, the reduction in the poverty rate has been even larger.

Incomes at all points of the distribution have increased since 1993, and the gains have been largest for low income households (see Chart 6). This probably represents a genuine change and not just accidental movements in the data. But these reversals, though important, do not undo 20 years of increasing inequality. It would be rash to declare an end to a 20-year trend based on a few years of data. This is especially true for a complex phenomenon such as inequality whose causes are not fully understood. Still, the best information suggests that these developments are significant.

POLICIES TO AFFECT THE DISTRIBUTION OF INCOME

Regardless of the interpretation of the past few years, a question remains: What role does government policy play in reducing income inequality?

Mitigating the Inequality Produced by the Market

Government policies play an important role in mitigating the inequality produced by the market. As has already been discussed, through its taxes and, more important, its transfers, government has a large effect on the consumption possibilities of individual households. Taxes and transfers eliminate about one-fifth of pre-government inequality, as measured by the Gini coefficient, and more than one-half of pre-govern-ment poverty. The programs for the aged—Social Security, Medicare, and parts of Medicaid—have been so successful that poverty rates for the elderly (10.8 percent in 1996) are near record lows and are less than one-half the level that predominated in the 1960s. Ensuring that these programs continue to provide the same level of income security is an important challenge for policymakers.

Enhancing the Returns to Work

Mitigating inequality, however, is only one step. A second step is enhancing the returns to work. The EITC and the minimum wage are important aspects of this step. The EITC is a refundable tax credit of up to 40 percent of earnings. It was expanded in 1990 and 1993. During that period, the number of families receiving the EITC rose by almost 50 percent to 18 million, and the average credit more than doubled. In 1996, over 4 million people were lifted out of poverty by the EITC, more than twice as many as only a few years before.

At the same time, the minimum wage plays an important role in reducing inequality. Between 1981 and 1990, the national minimum wage remained constant at $3.35 an hour even as inflation eroded its value by 44 percent. The 1990 increase did not restore the minimum wage to its real 1981 level. The Clinton administration worked hard to persuade Congress to increase the minimum wage to $5.15. Despite concerns that this wage increase would cost jobs, since the first stage of the increase was enacted in October 1996, no noticeable declines have occurred in employment growth in industry-occupation groups whose employment is disproportionately composed of minimum wage work-ers. However, although wages have accelerated in these industry-occu-pation groups, the effect on overall wage or price acceleration has been relatively muted.

The expansion of the EITC combined with the rise in the minimum wage have increased the return to work for low wage workers to the point that, after the next scheduled increase in the minimum wage, a full-time, year-round minimum wage worker with two children will make about $14,000 a year, well above the 1981 level in real terms.

Creating Opportunity

Although mitigating inequality and enhancing the returns to work are important elements of the strategy to address inequality, the Clinton administration's most important emphasis is on creating opportunity. One of the most significant contributions any administration can make to the nation's economy is to help ensure that every American seeking work will find it. The decline in the unemployment rate from more than 7 percent in 1992 to 4.9 percent in September 1997 represents a major step forward not only for growth, but also for opportunity.

In the long run, a strategy to expand opportunity will work to reduce inequality only if it changes both access to skills and the distribution of rewards to skills. For example, the government can improve access to education and training programs that help create a more uniformly high skilled workforce. Between fiscal years 1993 and 1997, the government increased spending on education and training by 19 percent. There have been large increases in funding for programs targeted at every stage of a person's life, ranging from Head Start (up 43 percent) to training and employment programs (up 19 percent). The new balanced budget agreement approved by the President and Congress includes large increases for education and training programs such as Head Start, the Technology Literacy Challenge, Pell grants, the America Reads Challenge, the Hope scholarship, and the Job Corps.

In an era of budget stringency, the expansion of these programs—both past and planned—represents a remarkable achievement. However, there is not a simple production function that translates money spent on education and training into more productive workers and a more equal economy. In the private sector, competition ensures that, subject to some caveats, returns are equalized across different investments. No similar force to automatically ensure the productivity of government programs exists, although there is a large and high quality body of research by labor economists and others to draw on in designing these programs. This research shows the following:

- *Prenatal care and care for ages 0-3.* Medical care, both prenatal and during the first few years after birth, is very important to a child's subsequent development. Often, very small investments such as immunization for polio or home-based smoking cessation programs yield large benefits. But this is not just a public health issue: Family income is an important contributor to children's well-being. Children in low income families, for example, are 1.2 to 2.2 times more likely than the average child to have low birth weight. Children who were low birth-weight babies are more likely to have learning disabilities, to have attention deficit disorder, to repeat grades, and to be enrolled in special education programs. These factors can translate into lower earnings and increased inequality later in life. It is not expensive to ensure that a baby is born healthy, nor is it difficult to target expenditures on social programs to those very young children who have the greatest needs.

- *Early education.* Early education programs lead to significant improvements in educational attainment, behavior, and health status (although it is interesting that they show no persistent effects on IQ). Particularly suggestive evidence has been obtained from the Perry Preschool Study, in which children living in a predominantly black neighborhood in Ypsilanti, Michigan, were randomly assigned to one of two groups, the first of which attended preschool and the second of which did not. Researchers estimated that every dollar spent on Perry Preschool returned up to $8.75 in benefits, with these benefits including lower future expenditures on special education and public assistance and lower rates of criminal activity in later life. However, financial constraints mean that children from poor families are half as likely to attend preschool as children from more affluent families. Programs such as Head Start attempt to help ensure that children from poor families can also enjoy the benefits of preschool.

• *Education.* One of the clearest results in the research literature on education is that an additional year of schooling adds about 10 percent to future earnings. Programs like Pell grants that enable more people from low income families to get more education will clearly help reduce inequality while boosting productivity. For this reason, Congress has agreed to the largest increase in the maximum Pell grant award in more than two decades. The budget agreement will also provide resources to extend the program to more students.

• *Training.* The payoff from government training programs can be substantial, although their success is not universal. For example, a study of a government-sponsored Job Training Partnership Act for out-of-school youth in 1987-89 found no increase in earnings; the best results were obtained by adults assigned to receive on-the-job training. Another difficulty involves targeting training programs so as to ensure that they increase skills at the margin rather than merely subsidizing training that would have taken place anyway. These concerns suggest that school-to-work strategies for youth and programs that combine vocational with conventional classroom education may have the highest payoffs. Also important are programs that ease the adjustment process for dislocated workers by helping them improve their skills and find new jobs.

None of these programs can change the income distribution (or productivity) instantly. The purely economic benefits of Head Start, for example, take at least 15 years to ripen—the time it takes for a Head Start child to grow up and join the labor force. Over the long term, however, properly designed programs that target high reward areas (such as ages 0 to 3), that change incentives and opportunities at the margin rather than just subsidizing training, and that promote opportunity instead of dependence should not only improve the skills of the workforce but also alter the distribution of rewards to skill. As the supply of college (or high school) graduates relative to high school graduates (or high school dropouts) increases, the earnings premium discussed earlier should start to narrow, reducing an important source of income inequality.

CONCLUSIONS

The data and a growing body of research point to three conclusions. First, economic inequality is much greater today than it was 20 years ago. Second, decades of social policies have not been futile, and these policies do not need to be completely overturned. Social Security, Medicare, the EITC, and support for education continue to play an important role in reducing inequality. Third, the most important policies for reducing inequality are policies that enhance opportunity. This means sound macroeconomic policy in the short term and programs for education, training, and work opportunity in the long term. These policies need to emphasize program design, building on successes and learning from failures.

The trend toward rising inequality is indeed troubling. But long-term trends can be broken. I am hopeful—I might say almost confident—that America is on the road to addressing this challenge in a meaningful way.

PART II
THE DIMENSIONS OF THE PROBLEM

Introduction

◆

by James P. Harris
Senior Vice President, Exxon Chemical Company

THE TITLE "GROWTH OF INCOME DISPARITY" was chosen with care, to take some of the emotion out of the subject. The phrase income inequality is often used instead as a sound bite, helping to polarize the debate. The focus should be on the real problem—the plight of the lowest 10 or 20 percent of families in America. This is where the attention is really deserved. After all, income differences are natural and expected in a complex economy like the United States. Perhaps only in countries with a stronger safety net could a more equal distribution occur. However, the downside of this is demonstrated by the current problems in continental Europe, which is experiencing unprecedented unemployment and stagnating economies.

The first part of this study will focus on the dimensions of the issue. How should income disparity be measured? How has it grown in recent years? Is it the result of changes in the economic system or of changes in a variety of factors, demographic and social?

The possible causes can be grouped into four categories—technological advancement, market forces, structural changes, and social factors. Much has been made of the increasing educational demands of a high technology society. This is obvious in my work in the oil, gas, and petrochemical industry, as it is in other industries such as communications and entertainment where, for example, starting salaries in digital animation are as much as $90,000 a year. This example also points to the effects of market forces—demand far exceeds supply.

Structural changes embody the impact of laws, regulations, and judicial interpretations. For instance, deregulation in the telecommunications industry has led to lower consumer prices for its products and more competitive companies. But it has also resulted in displaced workers and a greater reliance on outsourcing.

Social factors can be quite complex in that they include some of the troubling issues of today, such as the increase in single parent households and limited access to quality education for certain groups in society. The effects are hardest felt in the inner cities. However, social factors also include positive trends such as the rise of two-income households among the more educated.

It is important that we first understand the dimensions and the scope of the problem before we examine policy responses to the rise in income inequality.

Chapter 3

The Facts About Rising Economic Disparity

◆

by Richard B. Freeman

SINCE THE 1980-81 RECESSION, the U.S. economy has performed well in many ways. Gross domestic product (GDP) increased by $2.3 trillion from 1980 to 1996, while per capita income rose by 29 percent.[1] Currently, the rate of inflation is modest, and manufacturing productivity is increasing at a healthy clip. The ratio of the federal budget deficit to GDP is lower than in most other advanced countries. Although the United States still has a large trade deficit, American business has reestablished its competitiveness with the Japanese in high technology industries.[2]

American performance in employment and unemployment has been particularly impressive. In the mid- to late 1990s, the employment-to-population rate has risen to new heights, and unemployment has fallen below orthodox estimates of the "natural rate" (unemployment consistent with nonaccelerating inflation) without setting off inflation. The contrast with western Europe is stark. In 1974, the United States and western Europe had similar employment-to-population rates—64.8 percent. In 1995, the employment-to-population rate was 73.5 percent in the United States and 60.1 percent in the European countries that are members of the Organization for Economic Cooperation and Development (OECD-Europe). For the first time in decades, the United States has a lower unemployment rate than other advanced countries. In the 1990s, unemployment has been roughly 3 percentage points lower than in OECD-Europe, including Sweden (which many once trumpeted as an alternative model of advanced capitalism) and Germany (the archetype European economy). In the United States, just 10 percent of the unemployed are long-term unemployed (unemployed for more than one year), compared with 40-50 percent long-term unemployed in the United Kingdom, France, and Germany and 60 percent in Italy.[3]

If the U.S. economy has an Achilles' heel it is the distribution of economic output. The U.S. record in distributing the gains of economic growth to average workers and their families through wage or benefit increases has been abysmal. Most of the GDP gains of the 1980s and 1990s have gone to the upper 5 percent of families; from 1979 to 1994 (periods of roughly similar rates of unemployment), the share of gains going to the upper 5 percent was a staggering 99 percent (see Table 1).[4] Whether wages and salaries or total compensation rose or fell depends on which earnings series (household or establishment based; inclusive

TABLE 1

**DISTRIBUTION OF THE GAINS
OF ECONOMIC GROWTH, 1979-94**

Mean gain in family income	$ 4,419
Mean gain of upper 5 percent	$87,295
Gain to upper 5 percent vs. all families	$ 4,365
Percentage gain to upper 5 percent	99%

Source: Author's calculations based on Table 1.9 in Lawrence Mishel, Aaron Bernstein, and John Schmidt, *The State of Working America 1996-1997* (Armonk, NY: M.E. Sharpe for Economic Policy Institute, 1996). Other tabulations may yield somewhat different fractions of gain accruing to the top, but they will still show the same pattern of concentration.

of all workers or production workers only), which average measure of earnings (median or mean), and which price deflator (the Consumer Price Index [CPI] or some adjustment thereof for unmeasured improvements in the quality of goods) is used. Regardless, the gains, if any, have been minuscule, and low paid workers have suffered economic losses. A low paid, full-time, year-round male worker, for example, earned about 20 percent less in 1996 than in 1973 using the CPI deflator. That the United States has distributed the gains from economic growth more unevenly than any other advanced country should make every American uneasy about the nation's economic performance. Is an economy based on huge income disparities healthy or—dare an economist say— morally justifiable? How well can a democracy function when the well-to-do have so much more than average citizens?

The facts about America's rising income disparity are beyond dispute. However, there is no consensus about the causes of this growing inequality. Most analysts reject the notion that there is a single cause, although some see trade with less developed countries as the root of the problem, while others assign most of the blame to technology, particularly to computerization of the workplace. The general view, to which I subscribe, is that many factors have been working in the same direction to increase inequality: technology and trade, to be sure, but also changes in wage-setting institutions, notably the fall in union density in the private sector, and changes in labor supply conditions—a deceleration in the rate of increase in the number of college graduates and an immigration-induced slower decline in the number of less skilled workers.

There is also no consensus about the social significance of rising earnings disparity. Some believe that increased inequality is not worth getting overly excited about. Perhaps increased disparity reflects increased mobility. Perhaps the market will cure the problem relatively quickly. Perhaps inequality is the price America must pay for its good employment record. Chapter 12 (by this author) presents the argument that Americans should be deeply concerned about this economic problem and should seek policies to reduce extant disparities.

The argument does not end there, however. Agreeing that economic disparity has risen to such a level that reducing it should be a national goal does not mean that any particular policy or program should be supported. Virtually any policy or program has costs, and those costs may exceed their benefits. Perhaps the nation's toolkit has no cost-effective strategies to fight economic disparity. Perhaps Congress cannot enact programs that meet a benefits-cost test. In either case, the new inequality may prove to be inescapable—driven by overwhelming market or political realities that cannot be controlled. This chapter makes no attempt to analyze the social significance of the new disparity or to assess policies that might reduce it.[5] The goal is more modest—to point out the facts about rising disparity on which all Americans can agree, regardless of their views of the consequences of disparity and the need to reduce it.

FACTS ABOUT RISING DISPARITY

From the 1980s, if not earlier, through the mid-1990s, U.S. earnings and employment changed in ways that sharply broke with the preceding half-century or so. The distribution of earnings grew more unequal. The job market for low skilled and medium skilled workers deteriorated. No one expected these changes, and no one is certain how long they will persist. But among labor market experts there is no debate over what happened.

Table 2 presents a 10-point summary of the basic facts about disparity. The message is clear: U.S. economic success is marred by one great failure—the maldistribution of the fruits of that success. Consider briefly each of these facts.

1. Rising Differentials by Skill

Historically, differences in earnings among U.S. workers with different levels of education or experience or between those working in more and less skilled occupations fell as the workforce acquired more skills. For example, in the 1970s, the returns to attending college declined when a large proportion of the huge baby boom generation entered the job market with college degrees. The 1980s and 1990s broke with this pattern, as differences in pay by education group rose massively (see Table 3). The change in earnings by education group brought the premium to schooling to an all-time post-World War II high. Similarly, there was a rise in earnings by age, with older workers gaining relative to younger workers. This occurred despite a drop in the number of young workers, which should have increased the relative pay of the young but did not.

TABLE 2

10 FACTS ABOUT DIVERGING INCOMES

1. Highly skilled and educated groups have obtained greater pay increases than less skilled and less educated groups. Women (still paid less than men) are the only low paid group to advance in the earnings distribution.

2. Inequality in hourly pay among male and female workers has increased significantly.

3. Earnings divergence has increased within virtually all skill groups.

4. Divergence in the provision of fringe benefits has increased; fewer low paid men and women receive pensions or employer-paid health insurance.

5. Real hourly pay has stagnated for a large proportion of the workforce.

6. Americans work more hours than Europeans and roughly as many hours as the Japanese, so that America's higher level of GDP per capita exaggerates the U.S. advantage in living standards.

7. Real hourly pay has fallen sharply for those on the bottom rungs of the earnings distribution.

8. The living standards of low paid American workers are far below those of low paid workers in Europe and Japan.

9. There is rising disparity in hours worked, with the high paid working more hours and the low paid working fewer hours, producing even greater disparity in annual earnings than in hourly pay.

10. Rising disparity of earnings translates into disparity in family incomes, so that low income American children are absolutely poorer and high income American children are absolutely wealthier than comparable children in other advanced countries.

2. Rising Overall Disparity in Hourly Pay

One summary statistic of income disparity is the ratio of the earnings of people in the top percentiles of the distribution—for instance, the upper 10 percent—to the earnings of those in the lower percentiles—for instance, the median (50th percentile) or the bottom (10th percentile). When the ratio of earnings in the top percentiles rises relative to that in the lower percentiles, the distribution of earnings widens. From 1979 to 1995, the pay of top quintile male workers increased by about 18 percentage points more than the pay of low quintile male workers; the pay of top quintile women increased by 29 percentage points more than that of bottom quintile women (see Table 4).

Most, though not all, other advanced countries have also experienced increases in the ratio of the earnings of highly paid workers to low paid workers. However, in those countries the rise in inequality has been modest, and in a few, including Germany, inequality has decreased. This

TABLE 3

**EDUCATIONAL LOG WAGE DIFFERENTIALS
FOR U.S. NATIVES, 1960-95**

	(1) College / HS	(2) College+ / HS	(3) HS+ / Dropout
1960	.319	.317	.280
1970	.362	.374	.312
1980	.279	.304	.301
1990	.412	.458	.374
1995	.420	.495	.410

Column (1) reports the log wage differential between those with exactly 16 years of schooling and those with exactly 12 years of schooling. Column (2) reports the gap between those with 16 or more years of schooling (a fixed weighted average of the dummy variable coefficients for 16 years of schooling and 18 or more using 1990 PUMS employment shares) and those with exactly 12 years. Column (3) presents the difference in the fixed weighted average of the coefficients for those with 12 or more years of schooling and those with less than 12 years using 1990 employment shares by education group.

Notes: Educational log wage differentials are from regressions of log hourly earnings on 5 education dummies (0-8, 9-11, 13-15, 16, and 18 or more years of schooling, a quartic in age, female and nonwhite dummies, and three regional dummies for full-time U.S. native wage and salaried workers, age 18-64 years. The 1960-90 estimates are from the 1 percent Census PUMS samples and refer to 1959, 1969, 1979, and 1989; the regressions are weighted by annual hours worked. The 1995 estimates are the sum of the estimated 1990-95 change from the February 1990 Current Population Survey (CPS) and 1995 CPS MORG samples to the 1990 (1989) Census PUMS estimate. The 1990-95 changes were estimated for all full-time workers (natives and immigrants) and then adjusted for the difference in the estimated educational wage differentials for natives and all workers in the 1995 CPS MORG and 1990 Census PUMS.

Source: George Borjas, Richard B. Freeman, and Lawrence Katz, "How Much Do Immigration and Trade Affect Labor Market Outcomes?" *Brookings Papers on Economic Activity*, Vol. 1 (1997).

is shown in Chart 1, which compares the ratio of the weekly earnings of men in the top 10th percentile of the earnings distribution to that of men in the bottom 10th percentile among OECD countries in 1979 and in 1995. Because the United States started with a high level of income disparity and has experienced a sizable increase in disparity, it has been by far the "lead" advanced country in income disparity in the 1990s.

TABLE 4

**PERCENTAGE CHANGES IN EARNINGS
BY SKILL GROUP, 1979-95**

	Men	Women
Top quintile workers	1%	21%
Bottom quintile workers	−17	− 8
College graduates	1	20
HS graduates	−17	− 4
Less than HS graduates	−27	−11
Professionals	6	18
Administrative support (clericals)	−14	2
Machine operators	−16	− 9
Laborers	−21	na
Starting HS grads	−27	−19
Experienced HS grads	−21	− 4
Starting college grads	−11	3
Experienced college grads	− 3	21

Note: Starting workers have 1-5 years of experience; experienced workers have 16-22 years of experience.

Source: Calculated from Mishel, Bernstein, and Schmidt, *The State of Working America,* Tables 3.5, 3.7, 3.8, 3.19, 3.20, and 3.22.

3. Rising Disparity in Pay Within Skill Groups

The earnings distribution has widened not only among skill groups but within groups as well. Among workers in the same occupation or with the same years of schooling and age in an occupation, earnings of the higher paid have increased more than those of the lower paid. For example, in 1979, the ratio of the earnings of the top decile of college graduates to those of the lowest decile of college graduates was 3.46, whereas in 1995 the ratio was 4.22—a 22 percent increase.[6] In examining the earnings distribution in separate occupations, I have found that inequality has risen in the vast majority, even among workers of the same age and with the same education. Across all occupations there is a greater gap in pay between the highly paid and the low paid now than in the past. Moreover, because much of the difference among employees

CHART 1

LEVELS AND CHANGES IN EARNINGS INEQUALITY AMONG ADVANCED OECD COUNTRIES MEASURED BY THE RATIO OF 90TH TO 10TH DECILE, MALE WEEKLY EARNINGS, 1979 and 1995

1979 or Other Early Year

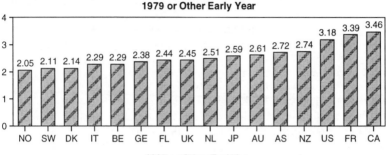

1995 or Other End Year

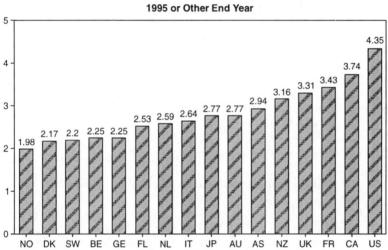

Source: Calculated from OECD, *Employment Outlook, July 1996*, Table 3.1. The 1994 ("Other End Year") figure for Austria was calculated from changes in the 80:50 decile statistic reported in the table, assuming the 90:80 decile earnings ratio was the same in 1994 as in 1989. The figures for Belgium were adjusted for a change in reporting between 1988 and 1989. The numbers for New Zealand are suspect. The New Zealand Department of Labour reported no rise in inequality in hourly pay, so that the rise in inequality in weekly pay appears due solely to changes in hours worked (David Maree, personal communication, Aukland, New Zealand).

occurs within measured groups, even if the differences among groups— such as the level of education or age premium—were to fall to their 1979 level, overall pay inequality would still be much higher than it was in earlier years.

4. Rising Disparity in Fringe Benefits

In the 1990s, less skilled and lower paid workers have been less likely than in the past to receive fringe benefits relative to skilled and higher paid workers.[7] In 1979, 57 percent of male high school graduates and 39 percent of male high school dropouts had employer-provided pensions; in 1993, these figures had dropped to 45 percent and 21 percent, respectively. In 1979, 78 percent of male high school graduates and 58 percent of men with less than a high school education were covered by employer-provided health insurance; in 1993, the proportions had fallen to 62 percent and 35 percent, respectively. The proportion of workers whose employers paid all of the premiums also dropped sharply. Among women, the probability that a less educated woman had an employer-funded pension or health insurance plan was lower in 1993 than in 1979, while the probability that a female college graduate had these benefits barely changed.

In 1993, the U.S. Department of Labor reported huge disparities in employer coverage by hourly earnings. Although 36 percent of workers earning less than $5.00 per hour worked for employers that offered health insurance plans, only 14 percent were covered; 62 percent of workers earning $5.00 to $7.49 per hour worked for employers that offered plans, but only 35 percent were covered. At the high end of the earnings distribution, 92 percent of employers of workers earning $15.00 or more per hour offered employer health care plans, and 83 percent of those workers were covered.[8]

In short, taking fringe benefits into account raises inequality in the earnings distribution and the extent to which inequality has increased.

5. Stagnant Real Earnings for Average Workers

Consider the following situation. A's income rises by 100 percent, from $1,000 per week to $2,000 per week; and B's income rises by 20 percent, from $500 per week to $600 per week. The earnings of both workers have increased substantially. Because A's gain is much larger than B's gain, earnings disparity rose, but both A and B are better off. If the rising inequality of the 1980s and 1990s were one of economic gain for all, with highly paid workers obtaining exceptional increases in pay while low paid workers had smaller gains, no one would be ringing alarm bells about the distribution of earnings. But the story of rising income disparity is different. It is a story of stagnant real wages for the average worker and falling real wages for the low paid.

The trend growth rate of various real wage series from about 1973 to the mid-1990s has been stagnant, a sharp fall in the historical pattern of rising earnings for all American workers. Table 5 shows the growth rates for several earnings series. The most widely used statistical measures of real pay—hourly earnings reported by workers in the Current Population Survey of households or hourly earnings reported by employers in

TABLE 5

PERCENTAGE CHANGES IN REAL EARNINGS IN THE UNITED STATES, 1973-95

(1) Mean, average hourly earnings for production workers, in all private industry		−12%
(2) Median weekly earnings of full-time workers	Male	−13
	Female	7
(3) Average annual compensation of all workers in manufacturing		4.6
(4) Mean compensation per hour, business sector		10
(5) Mean compensation per hour, all workers in economy (through 1994)		16

Sources:
Line 1, *Economic Report of the President, 1996,* Table B-43.
Line 2, Bureau of Labor Statistics, Employment and Earnings Bulletin 2307, monthly January issues, and unpublished data; "International Comparisons of Manufacturing Productivity and Unit Labor Cost Trends," July 17, 1996.
Line 3, For 1990-94, *Statistical Abstract of the United States, 1996,* Table 1355; for 1973-90, *Statistical Abstract of the United States, 1992,* Table 1394.
Line 4, *Economic Report of the President, 1996,* Table B-45.
Line 5, Mishel, Bernstein, and Schmidt, *The State of Working America,* Table 3.2, where the deflator is the personal consumption deflator from the national income and product accounts.

the national employer survey, divided by the CPI—have trended downward since 1973. The big losers are men. Between 1973 and 1995, the real median earnings of full-time wage and salaried men fell by 13 percent, while those of women rose by 7 percent. Over the shorter period 1987 to 1995, the employment cost index of the Bureau of Labor Statistics (BLS), which includes the cost of fringe benefits, showed a drop for all workers of 7.8 percent. Still, not all earnings series showed declines in real earnings. The hourly compensation figures for the business sector reported by the Council of Economic Advisers recorded a 10 percent rise from 1973 to 1995; total compensation from the national income and product accounts (NIPA) increased by 16 percent. According to the BLS, the real earnings of all workers in manufacturing rose by 3.2 percent from 1980 to 1994.[9] Even these gains, however, are a marked slowdown from the historical trend. The NIPA increase of 0.7 percent per year, for example, is just one-fourth the trend increase of 2.8 percent per year in earlier decades.[10]

6. Americans Have Less Leisure Time than Workers in Other Advanced Countries

Americans work considerably more hours than Europeans—200-400 more hours per year or 5 to 10 full weeks—and, given the decline in hours worked in Japan, are now working roughly as many hours as Japanese workers. According to the OECD, in 1995, Americans worked 1,743 hours compared with 1,534 hours for German employees, 1,542 hours for French (1992), and 1,409 hours for Dutch. In 1996, the OECD changed its method of estimating U.S. hours worked and reported that Americans averaged 1,945 hours per year, producing an even larger U.S.-Europe gap in hours and higher reported hours for Americans than Japanese.[11] The major reason Americans work so much is that they take just 2 weeks or so a year of vacation compared with the 4 to 5 weeks common in Europe. In addition, 6 percent of Americans hold a second job; 18 percent do job-related work at home; overtime hours have risen substantially; and fewer Americans work part time than Europeans.

It was not always this way. In years past, the United States led the world in reducing work time. The United States was among the first countries to establish the 40-hour workweek and to give paid vacations to average workers. As recently as 1970, Americans worked fewer hours than, for example, Germans. It is only in the past 20 years, as inequality has risen, that Americans have chosen work over leisure. That working Americans have such short vacations and work so many hours implies that comparisons of national product per employee overstate the U.S. lead in productivity per employee and that comparisons of GDP per capita, which do not take into account time worked, overstate the U.S. advantage in living standards compared with living standards in Europe.[12] Americans have more material possessions but less free time in which to enjoy them.

7. Falling Real Earnings for the Low Paid

The real earnings of low paid workers have fallen. When average pay stagnates and the distribution of pay widens greatly, workers at the bottom necessarily suffer drops in real earnings. As shown in Table 4, in the 1980s and 1990s, the real earnings of high school graduates fell by about one-fifth; those of male high school dropouts in the same age bracket fell even more. The real hourly earnings of men throughout the lower rungs of the earnings distribution dropped sharply, and the real earnings of women in the lower rungs, who constitute the lowest paid workers in society, also fell sharply.

8. Low Paid Americans Are Poorer than Low Paid European and Japanese Workers

Declining real earnings of low paid Americans and rising real earnings of low paid workers in other advanced countries have produced the anomalous situation that low paid workers in the United States—the most productive economy in the world—have markedly lower living standards than low paid workers in other advanced economies (see Chart 2). OECD estimates of hourly U.S. pay show that a male worker in the bottom decile of the earnings distribution earns 38 percent of the median in the United States compared with 68 percent of the median in western Europe and 63 percent of the median in Japan.[13] Using purchasing power parity prices that measure the cost of the same consumption bundle across countries to transform foreign earnings into U.S. dollars, the greater inequality in the United States translates into lower pay for 10th decile Americans than for 10th decile workers elsewhere. German low paid workers earn roughly twice as much per hour as low paid Americans. Even in the United Kingdom, which has just two-thirds of U.S. GDP per capita, low paid workers earn more than Americans.[14]

It is not just the bottom decile of American workers that trails workers in other advanced countries. Approximately one-third of American

CHART 2

EARNINGS OF LOWEST DECILE WORKERS IN GERMANY, ADVANCED EUROPE, AND THE UNITED KINGDOM, RELATIVE TO THOSE IN THE U.S. IN PURCHASING POWER PARITY, 1991

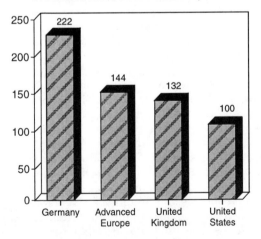

Source: Richard B. Freeman, "The Limits of Wage Flexibility to Curing Unemployment," *Oxford Review of Economic Policy,* Vol. 11, No. 1 (Spring 1995), p. 13, based on hourly earnings figure in OECD, *Employment Outlook, July 1993.* As noted in the text, OECD, *Employment Outlook, July 1996,* shows that in terms of weekly earnings, the U.S.-Europe gap is smaller.

workers are paid less in purchasing power units than comparable workers overseas. Not until the 30th-40th decile of earnings do Americans do
better than Europeans. That so many American workers fare poorly
compared with their peers in other countries shows that the problem of
low pay is not "simply" a matter related to low skilled immigrants or
poorly educated inner city minority youth. It is a problem of the entire
distribution of income.

9. Disparity in Hours Worked

If falling wages for the low skilled had created a job boom for those
workers, it might be argued that increased inequality has been, on net,
positive even for them. But the employment of low skilled workers has
not increased absolutely or relative to that of high skilled workers as
inequality has risen in the United States. Rather, the trend has been that
work has decreased for the low skilled groups whose earnings have
fallen. The most striking evidence that the American jobs miracle has
bypassed the low paid is found in statistics on the annual hours worked
by adult men according to their position in the wage distribution.[15] From
the 1970s through 1990, annual hours worked of men in the bottom
deciles of the earnings distribution fell, while hours worked of those in
the upper deciles were stable or rising (see Chart 3). Inequality in hours
worked has increased along with inequality in hourly pay, producing an
even greater increase in annual earnings inequality.

10. Rising Disparity in Family Incomes

From 1979 to 1996, GDP per family increased substantially, so that
there has been much more output to distribute to the American people
than in the previous two decades. But, as noted at the outset, the gain
has gone to those with high incomes. Median family incomes have
remained roughly constant, while the incomes of those in the lower two
quintiles of the distribution have fallen. The incomes in the middle
quintile have barely changed. The top 20 percent of families have obtained essentially all of the gain in income, and within that group the
vast bulk of the gain has gone to the upper 5 percent. Again, as shown
in Table 1, the gain in mean family income from 1979 to 1994 was $4,419,
but 99 percent of that gain went to families in the upper 5 percent of the
family income distribution.[16] Looking over a longer period, in 1993, U.S.
median household income was roughly the same as in 1974, but the
percent of people living in poor families rose from 11.2 percent in 1974
to 15.1 percent in 1993 because the distribution had widened.[17]

One reason that gains in family incomes have been so concentrated
is that increased employment, increased hours worked, and increased
earnings of women have been concentrated among high income families. In years past, women from low income families tended to work
more and contribute more to family income than women from high

CHART 3

**PERCENTAGE CHANGE IN ANNUAL HOURS WORKED
BY WAGE DECILE, MALE WORKERS, 1970-90**

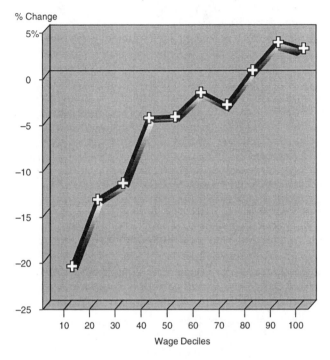

Source: Tabulated from U.S. Census of Population public use data files, 1970
and 1990. The number of observations for the 1970 samples is 121,078; the
number for the 1990 samples is 135,434.

income families, reducing inequality in family incomes. But in the 1970s
and 1980s, the employment rate and earnings of women with husbands
in the upper percentiles of the wage distribution rose relative to those
of women with husbands in the lower percentiles of the wage distribution.[18] Today, two-earner families are at the top of the family income
distribution, while single-earner families, particularly those headed by
female single parents, are near the bottom of the distribution.

In sum, the claim that the distribution of individual earnings and
family income has diverged, with the rich getting richer and the poor
getting poorer, is not the rhetoric of politicians running for office. Although different analysts summarize the data differently,[19] what has
happened to the U.S. economy in the past 20 years or so is that earnings
and other economic outcomes have diverged massively. The 10 facts in

Table 2 are the labor market reality that the country must address as it approaches the 21st century. Income inequality exists, but should the United States be concerned? Chapter 12 (by this author) will answer this question in the affirmative, but even those who disagree and say we have no reason to worry must accept the facts about rising disparity that this chapter has presented.

NOTES

1. Council of Economic Advisers, *Economic Report of the President, 1997* (Washington: U.S. Government Printing Office [GPO], 1997), Tables B-90 and B-29.

2. To be sure, the U.S. economy has some weak spots—large deficits in the balance of trade despite a huge devaluation of the dollar and improved labor cost competitiveness. The national health system remains a sore spot in financing and coverage, but most other advanced countries would gladly trade their problems for America's.

3. International comparisons of unemployment rates are subject to statistical problems, even when they are based on similar survey questions. Unemployment varies across countries for idiosyncratic reasons: Someone who is jobless for a long time in the United States might leave the labor force, while someone in Europe would not leave because he or she would lose social benefits. In Japan, unemployment is low partly because many unemployed women report that they are no longer participating in the workforce. Some European countries do not count people in government training programs as unemployed. In the 1980s, the British government redefined unemployment many times in ways that reduced the reported level.

4. The 1979 to 1994 pattern is particularly stark—chosen in part for its shock value—but there is no gainsaying that the vast bulk of economic gains have gone to the well-to-do.

5. For such efforts, see Richard B. Freeman, "Toward an Apartheid Economy?" *Harvard Business Review* (September-October 1996); and Freeman, *When Earnings Diverge: Causes, Consequences, and Cures for the New Inequality in the U.S.* (Washington: National Policy Association, 1997).

6. Calculated from Lawrence Mishel, Aaron Bernstein, and John Schmidt, *The State of Working America 1996-1997* (Armonk, NY: M.E. Sharpe for Economic Policy Institute, 1996), Table 3.23.

7. Susan Houseman, "Job Growth and the Quality of Jobs in the U.S. Economy," Upjohn Institute Working Papers 95-99 (August 1995), Tables 9 and 10.

8. U.S. Department of Labor, *Report on the American Workforce* (Washington: GPO, 1996).

9. U.S. Bureau of the Census, *Statistical Abstract of the United States, 1995* (Washington: GPO, 1996), Table 1355.

10. There are various reasons for the differences among series. The surveys cover different groups of workers and different measures of earnings, ranging from annual earnings to usual weekly earnings. Some series include fringe benefits, while others do not. The series may differentially miss a sizable number of low wage young men in inner cities and/or the earnings of workers in the underground economy. These problems do not mean that any particular survey gets the facts wrong, but that one should examine all of them to obtain a balanced picture. See Katherine Abraham, James Spletzer, and Jay Stewart, *Divergent Trends in Alternative Real Wage Series* (Washington: Bureau of Labor Statistics, October 19, 1995).

11. The differential reported in 1996 is about 400 hours versus Europe. This is larger than my best estimate, based on Current Population Survey reports on hours worked, that U.S. workers put in about 300 more hours than Europeans. But to err on the side of caution, I used the more conservative 1995 OECD numbers in the text. The Japanese hours reported by the OECD do not include employees at small Japanese firms and thus may understate Japanese hours worked. OECD, *Employment Outlook, July 1995* (Paris: OECD, 1995); and OECD, *Employment Outlook, July 1996* (Paris: OECD, 1996).

12. Linda Bell and Richard B. Freeman, "Working Hard," paper presented at the SERF/Upjohn Institute Conference on Working Hours, Ottawa, Canada, June 13-16, 1996.

13. When I first discovered that low paid Americans were so much poorer than low paid workers in other advanced countries, I found it hard to accept, though anyone who has compared U.S. and European "slums" knows that America's poor are indeed relatively badly off. Still, I checked the consistency of this result with other economic statistics, such as GDP per capita figures, which show that the United States indeed has a considerably higher production per person than Europe or Japan. My conclusion is that the finding is not some aberration due to comparisons of particular earnings series (which give ranges of estimated real earnings) but follows from the diminished gap between the United States and other advanced countries in GDP per hours worked and the much wider distribution of earnings in the United States. See Freeman, *When Earnings Diverge.*

14. OECD statistics on the lowest decile of weekly earnings show low paid Americans closer to the median (48 percent) than do OECD statistics on hourly earnings presumably because Americans work more hours per week. But these data still show that the United States is far out of line with other countries, with low paid Americans having markedly lower earnings than low paid workers in advanced European countries and Japan. OECD, *Employment Outlook, July 1996,* Table 3.1.

15. Chinhui Juhn, Kevin M. Murphy, and Robert Topel, "Why Has the Natural Rate of Unemployment Increased Over Time?" *Brookings Papers on Economic Activity,* Issue 2 (1991), pp. 75-142; and Richard B. Freeman, "The Limits of Wage Flexibility to Curing Unemployment," *Oxford Review of Economic Policy,* Vol. 11, No. 1 (Spring 1995).

16. These are my calculations based on Table 1.9 in Mishel, Bernstein, and Schmidt, *The State of Working America.* The table shows that the average family income of the top 5 percent increased by $87,295. This is equivalent to $4,365 per family. Other tabulations may yield somewhat different fractions of gain accruing to the top, but they will still show the same pattern of concentration.

17. In 1974, median household income was $31,175 in 1993 dollars; it was $31,241 in 1993, using the CPI-U-X1 deflator.

18. Chinhui Juhn and Kevin M. Murphy, "Wage Inequality and Family Labor Supply," NBER Working Paper 5459 (February 1996).

19. Richard V. Burkhauser gives a more favorable reading of some of the trends in household incomes than most analysts. He argues that changes in the number of earners and in family size mitigate some of the impact of falling real earnings for workers on the real incomes of households. See Burkhauser, "Income Mobility and the Middle Class," paper presented at the American Enterprise Institute Seminar on Understanding Income Inequality, Washington, D.C., April 15, 1996.

Chapter 4

Collective Bargaining Bridges
the Income Gap

◆

by Morton Bahr

T HE GROWING INCOME DISPARITY in the United States is a problem that poses a serious challenge for the nation and one that organized labor has been concerned about for more than a decade.

On the surface, the U.S. economy looks enormously successful, with millions of new jobs created, low unemployment, moderate inflation, high productivity, competitive U.S. companies, and a stock market that achieved record gains. But looks can be deceiving. There were more layoff announcements in 1996 than in 1995, and 1995 was a banner year for layoffs.[1] Working families are more anxious than ever. They are working longer and harder without any real improvement in their standard of living.

The rise in wage inequity is now the largest since the Great Depression. Even more troubling is that the United States has the highest rate of child poverty among industrialized nations. It is encouraging that labor market experts no longer debate what has happened to wages in the United States. They finally acknowledge the growing wage inequality that plagues the economy and the dangers it presents.

Now that everyone has agreed on the problem, there must be a focus on ways to solve it. In this regard, collective bargaining as an economic theory has significant potential to narrow the growing disparity in wages.

UNIONIZATION AND INCOME DISTRIBUTION

A correlation exists between rates of unionization and income distribution. Parallel lines can be drawn between the drop in the number of workers represented by unions and the lower or stagnant standard of living that most American families now have. At the same time, the gap between the top and bottom in household income has widened as the middle class is being squeezed.

The Organization for Economic Cooperation and Development (OECD) recently completed a study of collective bargaining and earnings inequality.[2] The OECD measured income distribution and the percentage of workers represented by unions in 12 industrialized nations—the United States, Japan, Canada, Australia, and 8 European nations. Its findings are predictable. The United States, which has the lowest rates of unionization, has a higher income gap than ever before; in fact, it tops the list of industrialized nations in the study (see Chart 1). In every category of the OECD's findings, the higher the rate of unionization, the lower the measures of wage inequality. Statistical evidence thus indicates a direct relationship in each of the industrialized nations studied by the OECD.

In the United States, collective bargaining has had a positive impact on women's wages. Wages of women historically have been lower than those of men. Heidi Hartman, Director of the Institute for Women's Policy Research, analyzed the impact of collective bargaining on women's wages. She found that unionized women's wages were $2.50 more per hour than nonunionized women's wages, and after controlling for variables such as education, industry, and firm size, she concluded that collective bargaining adds 12 percent to women's pay.

Collective bargaining had a similar impact in the competitive long distance telecommunications industry, which is supposed to be the nation's job engine of the future. It is estimated that since 1984, when the Bell system was divested and real competition began, 115,000 jobs have been added at new long distance companies compared with the 124,000 jobs that AT&T has shed.[3] The new jobs are mainly nonunion and pay significantly less than the union jobs that were eliminated, resulting in a decline in average wages in the long distance sector. For

CHART 1

COLLECTIVE BARGAINING COVERAGE AND EARNINGS INEQUALITY, INDUSTRIALIZED COUNTRIES, EARLY 1990s

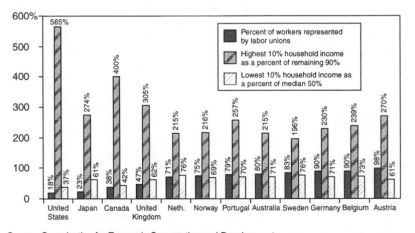

Source: Organization for Economic Cooperation and Development.

example, a nonunion service representative at Sprint Long Distance earns two-thirds what a union service representative at AT&T earns, and a Sprint technician earns 85 percent what his or her union counterpart at AT&T earns. Similar disparities exist at MCI.

UNIONIZATION AND BENEFITS

The wage gap is not the whole story. Nonunion workers in the new jobs receive fewer benefits, pay more for their health care, and can look forward to smaller retirement checks, if they get any. When workers employed by the new long distance competitors attempt to exercise their right to form a union to improve their wages and working conditions and to create employment security, the new market players fight hard and tough, and even illegally. In 1987, for example, 500 MCI workers in Detroit attempted to organize a union. Just a week before the scheduled National Labor Relations Board (NLRB) vote, MCI fired the workers, shut down the facility, and moved the work out of state. The message was clear from then on: MCI management would eliminate hundreds of jobs rather than deal with organized workers.

Sprint Long Distance adopted similar tactics in 1994 when 175 employees at a Sprint-owned telemarketing center, La Connexion Familiar (LCF), in San Francisco tried to organize a union. The workers complained of low wages and terrible working conditions. The predominantly female and Hispanic workforce earned about $7.00 an hour, compared with an average hourly wage of about $15.83 for telephone service workers in 1994.[4] Working conditions were reprehensible. Among other things, company policy discouraged workers from drinking water to cut down on the need for bathroom breaks, even though the job required workers to talk on the phone all day.   '

To gain a voice in decisions about wages and working conditions, the LCF-Sprint workers filed a petition for union recognition with the support of 70 percent of the workforce. Less than a week before the election was scheduled, Sprint fired the LCF workers, shut down the office, and transferred the work to another location. Following an investigation, the NLRB filed a complaint against Sprint, charging the company with more than 50 labor law violations. Sprint admitted to many of the charges, and a Sprint vice president was fired for fabricating evidence submitted to the NLRB. An administrative law judge found the company guilty of most of the charges. The main charge, that Sprint illegally shut down the LCF office to thwart the union organizing campaign, was appealed.

In December 1996, two and one-half years after the fact, the NLRB found Sprint guilty of that final charge and ordered the company to rehire the workers and to provide full back pay. The employer's ability to operate with impunity during that time had a chilling effect on the efforts of other Sprint workers to organize and sent a message that telecommunications employers would do anything—including break the law—to keep workers from organizing.

In response to competitive pressures and in spite of its 50-year bargaining history with the Communications Workers of America (CWA), AT&T has also used tactics that have cut labor costs rather than enhance employment. In particular, AT&T has begun replacing bargaining unit jobs with temporary, part-time, and agency workers and contracting out work that historically has been performed by company employees and bargaining unit members. The company thereby evades its obligation to pay the wages and provide the health benefits, pensions, sick time, vacations, and holidays that were negotiated in the union labor agreement.

AT&T demonstrated its labor-cutting tactics at American Transtech, its telemarketing center subsidiary in Jacksonville, Florida. In 1995, about 5,000 people worked at Transtech's Jacksonville operation. Of those workers, 1,200 were management employees, 800 were "regular" Transtech employees performing telemarketing and customer service functions, and 3,000 were temporary workers under contract to an employment agency who also performed telemarketing and customer service functions. CWA organizers discovered that most of the temporary workers in Jacksonville had been working 40 hours a week at Transtech for three to five years.

Although much of the Transtech work had previously been performed by CWA members in AT&T bargaining units throughout the country, hourly wages paid to Transtech workers ranged from roughly $6.00 for telemarketers to about $12.00 for the most complex service jobs—a fraction of the union-negotiated rates for the same jobs.

By using a separate subsidiary, AT&T can avoid paying union-negotiated wage rates. By using a temporary agency, the subsidiary, Transtech, can avoid paying wages and benefits earned by its regular employees. These management strategies effectively undermine workers' efforts to improve their living standard.

When Transtech workers attempted to organize a union, management waged an all-out assault. Transtech management defied with impunity a corporate policy to maintain a respectful relationship with the union and to remain neutral in union organizing drives. Instead, the company ordered workers to attend meetings at which the workers were pressured to oppose the union. Transtech also required managers to distribute antiunion materials and to speak out against the union.

By using a very damaging and highly illegal tactic, the company implemented, for the first time in years, a 4 percent wage increase; it awarded bonuses totaling thousands of dollars; and it budgeted long-awaited monies for training and employee development. All of these were key employee issues identified during the organizing drive. The NLRB considers such management tactics unfair labor practices because they could be considered inducements to vote against the union and could thwart the democratic voting process.

TAKING WAGES OUT OF COMPETITION

A significant issue facing workers involves the strategic business decisions that are made in response to global competition. Will businesses pursue a high road strategy of good-paying, high skilled jobs that requires investing in the quality of their permanent workforce? Or will employers take the low road of cheap-wage jobs and a "just-in-time" workforce of temporary, contracted-out, and part-time employees?

CWA's goal as a union is to take wages out of competition in telecommunications. We and our employers know that there is always someone who is willing to cut the price a little more to win market share. Our objective is to develop a marketplace in which competition is based on quality customer service, technological innovation, and creative products that can best meet the customer's need.

CWA is committed to improved productivity and quality, and we are working successfully with some employers toward these goals. CWA has been involved in developing new processes for worker participation and quality improvement for many years. Our employers and our members have benefited.

OPENING NEW OPPORTUNITIES

Long ago, our collective bargaining strategy shifted from trying to guarantee job security to our members to opening new opportunities to ensure their employment security. Through collective bargaining, we have created new worker training and education programs, engaged in strategic planning with management, and launched new employee involvement processes that provide frontline workers with greater control over their work. In each area, CWA members improve existing skills and learn new skills that we hope will make them more productive for employers and more employable in the economy if they lose their jobs.

In the area of worker training and education, we can document the benefits to both workers and employers. CWA has negotiated outstanding education and training programs with its major employers in the telecommunications industry. Three of the best programs are the Alliance for Employee Growth and Development for union workers at AT&T and Lucent Technologies, Pathways at US WEST, and the Nynex/Bell Atlantic-CWA Next Step program. All of these programs have been nationally recognized for their innovation and success. A recent study by Pathways found both a high degree of participation by workers and a clear benefit to the company in higher productivity and quality service.[5]

Next Step is one of the most unusual programs. In the Next Step program, systems technicians work four days a week and go to school one day a week. On graduation, they receive an associate degree in applied science, with a focus on telecommunications technology. Remedial training to qualify for the program is provided to those who need it.

These college benefits are also one of the best affirmative action programs we have. Many operators, mainly female, whose jobs are at risk can enroll in Next Step and qualify for high skilled technical jobs for which they would never have had the opportunity to apply in the past.

Nynex/Bell Atlantic recognizes the competitive edge it derives from its partnership with CWA. According to the company, "The Next Step program represents the work force development partnership of the future and brings with it the opportunity to cultivate creativity, trust and cooperation into a powerful alliance."[6] The Nynex/Bell Atlantic contract exemplifies what American industry can do to further the job security and job skills of workers.

Because of the credibility the union brings to these efforts, CWA's employers in the telecommunications industry are beginning to realize the competitive edge that the union workforce can bring to their companies. In lines of business in which true partnerships exist, our companies are winning in the marketplace.

In response, employers recognize the union's need to grow with them. For example, Nynex/Bell Atlantic, SBC (Southwestern Bell), and Pacific Telesis have signed unprecedented agreements with CWA in which the companies will grant union recognition for their new subsidiaries or lines of business based on a card check. The companies have agreed to strong contract language that bars their managers from interfering in union organizing campaigns. The key language from the SBC agreement is an example:

> Neutrality means that management shall not within the course and scope of their employment by the company express any opinion for or against union representation of any existing or proposed new bargaining unit, or for or against the union or any officer, member or representative thereof in their capacity as such.
>
> Furthermore, management shall not make any statements or representations as to the potential effects or results of union representation on the company or any employee or group of employees.

Our experiences totally debunk the myths that union companies cannot compete in the global economy and that collective bargaining is an adverse economic force. "CWA has been very helpful in making Ameritech competitive. We are beating the nonunion shops and winning in the marketplace. The union and management have created flexible situations that have significantly helped to improve Ameritech's profitability," says Ameritech Chief Executive Officer (CEO) Richard Notebart.[7]

ADDRESSING THE CHALLENGE OF WAGE DISPARITY THROUGH COLLECTIVE BARGAINING

In looking for cures for wage disparity, collective bargaining is a proven economic theory that works well. It is a process that functions within the philosophy and traditions of the free market system. Through free and independent unions, workers sit together as equals with their employers to reach bargaining agreements over wages, benefits, other conditions of employment, and joint processes for improving the business.

As the nation moves from an industrial-based to a knowledge-based economy, the new relationships that CWA is building with our employers reflect global economic realities. The collective bargaining process is an invaluable resource for both the union and its employers to meet the demands of the global economy, as demonstrated by the many successful labor-management agreements in industries such as the automobile industry. At AT&T, where CWA has an innovative process called Workplace of the Future (WPOF), we are working toward a living contract that permits mid-term amendments to meet rapidly changing market conditions. WPOF involves the union as a strategic partner with management in making decisions that affect the future of the business. In the workplace, WPOF labor-management teams engage in a participative process to improve quality, production, and customer service. In AT&T's lines of business in which WPOF is fully implemented, layoffs have been minimized and worker satisfaction is high.

In a recent AT&T annual employee survey, employees who participated in WPOF scored higher in every category than those who did not. This finding is a powerful argument for employers to engage in meaningful worker participation processes through their union representatives. Indeed, union participation in worker empowerment processes is vital to their success. The union provides an organized voice by which workers can express their concerns and prioritize their issues. The union serves as a vital communications link that helps workers overcome their natural distrust of management. The union can also help overcome employee resistance to new work processes and the introduction of new technologies.

To the union, WPOF is a natural extension of the democratic principles that serve as the foundation of the collective bargaining process. Despite the everyday tumble of labor relations, participative processes such as WPOF allow management and union to work together for the overall health of the business. At the same time, the union protects and asserts its union values as a part of the company's corporate culture.

Clearly, some of AT&T's top management see a competitive advantage in their strategic partnership with CWA, a significant value-added component of their corporate strategy. We certainly agree with AT&T.

Other businesses and competitors of AT&T are beginning to recognize the value of empowering their workers. Indeed, CWA has been approached by GTE about embarking on a similar process. WPOF and employee empowerment processes like it are becoming more and more widespread throughout U.S. industry.

Much of what CWA learns and has achieved can be applied to its smaller employers and employers in the public sector. CWA is the largest union representing state workers in New Jersey. It is planning to work with the state to develop new forms of worker participation and involvement.

Worker empowerment also has become a major focus of the entire labor movement. I serve as chairman of the AFL-CIO's Committee on Workplace Democracy. The purpose of this committee is to encourage unions and their members to work with employers to give workers more decisionmaking power on the job. In February 1997, the AFL-CIO Executive Council adopted a set of policies and definitions to guide us in this work.

But until collective bargaining is recognized and supported as an effective economic policy, workers will face many roadblocks to developing their full potential. Wage inequality could very well remain a permanent feature of the knowledge-based economy. Serious repercussions could result if the inevitability of wage inequality in the new economy becomes an accepted fact of life.

CEO pay is the most visible sign of growing income disparity in today's workplaces. When company proxies are sent out, my members dig through them and read about the astronomical salaries, bonuses, and stock options their CEOs are receiving. These sums are staggering—Michael Eisner at Disney received $770 million in compensation in 1996 and in November 1997 exercised stock options worth more than half a billion dollars, while a Disney subsidiary, ABC, is seeking givebacks at the bargaining table. At Frontier Communications, the CEO was receiving $1.5 million in pay and $20.8 million in option grants while demanding a wage freeze and discontinuance of the defined benefits pension plan. This level of corporate greed weakens the fabric of democratic society.

Without collective bargaining, individual employees cannot strike a fair bargain for their wages and benefits. Even with collective bargaining, reaching a fair settlement requires struggle. Unless collective bargaining rights are extended, most Americans will not have a way to insist on their fair share.

Large numbers of young people are already convinced that no matter what, they will not do as well as their parents. Why then should adults be shocked to hear frustration, anger, alienation, and violence in their music and videos?

On top of these pressures is layered the impact of the new welfare reform bill. The nation must absorb millions of welfare recipients into the workforce who will compete for the very jobs that are shrinking in a knowledge-based economy. Some states want to go so far as to deny welfare workers their rights under federal labor laws when they enter the workforce. Organized labor strenuously opposes this policy because we are convinced that it will only exacerbate wage inequality. The Clinton administration took appropriate action in this area.

When Robert Reich was Secretary of Labor, he pushed hard for school-to-work programs. He correctly saw a need for public policy to address the concerns of young people for decent jobs, to give them hope for the future, and to help keep them from dropping out and continuing the cycle of welfare. With assistance from a Department of Labor school-to-work grant, CWA developed a systems technician apprenticeship program with US WEST to provide job opportunities for young people in the company's 14-state region. We also are talking with Pacific Bell, Ameritech, the Bell Atlantic subsidiary BACCSI, and Lucent Technologies to establish similar programs.

CWA is excited about answering a real need for skills training that can lead to good-paying union jobs for young people. We want to expand this program throughout the industry. We are, however, concerned about our future progress. Just as these programs are beginning to get through the pipeline, national priorities are shifting. School-to-work has been shoved to the sidelines because of the demands of the welfare reform bill. America must continue to make these programs a priority despite the pressures of welfare reform, and the collective bargaining process can respond to this serious need.

The Collective Bargaining Forum, the brainchild of Malcolm R. Lovell, Jr., National Policy Association President and CEO, brings together national labor and business leaders to work toward common goals. The Forum has issued two reports on the importance of collective bargaining and the cooperative labor-management relationship.[8] Unfortunately, in my opinion, the work of the Forum has not received the attention that it deserves. A greater effort must be made to get this information into the mainstream of economic and political thinking. These reports offer powerful tools for encouraging the spread of collective bargaining.

Finally, America could do nothing and hope that the free market corrects the wage inequality problem. I do not think that will happen. The widening income gap between the rich, the middle class, and the working poor is an economic cancer that could have very unhealthy consequences for America's future.

Any discussion of cures for wage inequality cannot ignore the influence of unionization and the role of collective bargaining as an economic theory for addressing this challenge. Collective bargaining offers workers the tools to take control of their own destinies and to better share in the fruits of their labor. Worker education and training, worker participation processes, union involvement in strategic business decisionmaking, and many other innovations that improve workers' employability and their standard of living have been pioneered through collective bargaining, in which unions can convince management to take the high road of job creation.

Unfortunately, employer resistance to unions appears to be growing, and the number of workers who participate in collective bargaining is declining. Workers' fears are the well-documented obstacles to successful union organizing: fear of job loss, fear of strikes, fear of management retaliation. Unorganized workers are well aware that management opposition creates real and potential risks when they try to form a union. The powerful negative impact of fear and conflict in union organizing is revealed in a recent study by CWA Director of Organizing Larry Cohen and Cornell University Professor Richard Hurd.[9]

But organized labor today is committing enormous resources to help workers form their own unions so that they, too, can engage in collective bargaining to improve their lives. Despite weak labor laws and enormous employer resistance, we will persevere. A strong labor movement is absolutely essential for the health of the nation.

NOTES

1. "1996 Job Cuts Up 8.5 Percent," Associated Press, January 1997.

2. Organization for Economic Cooperation and Development (OECD), *Collective Bargaining Coverage and Earnings Inequality, Early 1990's* (Paris: OECD, 1996).

3. Communications Workers of America (CWA), "Prospects for Employment in Competitive Local Telephone Markets," mimeo, February 1997.

4. Bureau of Labor Statistics, *Employment and Earnings* (Washington: U.S. Department of Labor, September 1994).

5. Pathways to the Future, *Summary of Research Findings 1997* (Denver: Pathways to the Future, 1997).

6. Nynex/Bell Atlantic-CWA-IBEW, *Next Step Strategic Plan* (1996).

7. Minutes, Collective Bargaining Forum meeting, Washington, March 7, 1997.

8. Collective Bargaining Forum, *New Directions for Labor and Management* (Washington: U.S. Department of Labor, 1988); and Collective Bargaining Forum, *Labor-Management Commitment: A Compact for Change* (Washington: U.S. Department of Labor, 1991).

9. Larry Cohen and Richard Hurd, *Fear, Conflict and Union Organizing* (Washington: CWA, 1996).

Chapter 5

Perspectives on Income Disparity

◆

by Gail Fosler and Lynn Franco

THE FIRST STEP in assessing income disparity is to assess economic progress. Some analysts assert that inequality is growing because the "rich are getting richer and the poor are getting poorer." Others maintain that most groups in society are making progress, with some advancing at a much faster pace than the rest. The comments that follow are organized around key questions:

1. What is the evidence on economic progress? Are Americans better or worse off than they were 25 or 30 years ago?

2. How large is the income gap, and is it growing? Is everyone's welfare improving at the same rate?

3. Is income disparity the result of changes in the economic system or the result of changes in a variety of factors, demographic and social?

ASSESSING ECONOMIC PROGRESS

On the question of economic progress, the evidence is indisputable. Real per capita income has shown substantial progress since 1970 (see Chart 1). Although per capita income has clearly stagnated during recessions, it has advanced significantly during expansions and has risen about 55 percent during the past 25 years or so. This progress is even more striking in light of the turbulence of the past two decades, which included massive oil price hikes, high real interest rates, enormous budget deficits, a war, and dramatic and ongoing restructuring throughout the American business community.

The increase in real per capita income during this period translates into a 1.8 percent a year advance. Although this is not nearly as rapid as the recent growth in some emerging markets, it approximates the rate of U.S. economic progress in the mid-1800s—the golden age of U.S. economic development. Thus, despite some major challenges in recent years, Americans' standards of living are rising almost as rapidly as ever.

Income Versus Earnings

Although these general measures of income suggest significant economic progress, the earnings of the average worker have fallen. Why?

CHART 1

PER CAPITA INCOME, 1970-95
(Based on 1996 $)

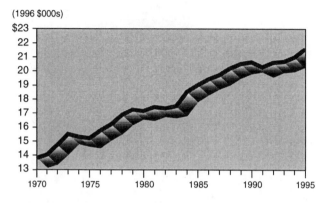

(1996 $000s)

Sources: U.S. Bureau of the Census; and The Conference Board.

One explanation can be found in the changing mix of personal income. Real wage and salary income as a share of personal income has declined, while interest and dividend income and transfer payments have increased. In 1970, for example, wages and salaries accounted for 64 percent of personal income, whereas in 1997, they accounted for only 54 percent. Dividend and interest income and transfer payments accounted for about 20 percent of personal income in 1970, but account for about 31 percent of income today. (See Chart 2 for income breakdown for 1997.)

Further, over the past two and one-half decades, average hourly earnings have declined by almost 15 percent. Some of this decline can be explained by the increasing share of benefits in workers' total compensation. Since 1970, benefits have grown from 20 percent of total compensation to 28 percent, while workers' wages have declined relatively. Clearly, most of the increase in workers' compensation in recent years has come in the form of benefits.

However, real compensation trends, which take benefits into account, do not tell an entirely positive story. Real hourly compensation increased only about 15 percent between 1970 and 1997, with most of the increase occurring in the 1970s. In fact, real compensation has improved very little since the early 1980s.

A second explanation for the deceleration in wage growth is the slowdown in productivity that began in the 1970s. On average, productivity grew at a 3.1 percent annual rate in the 1960s; since then it has slowed sharply to an average annual rate of only 1.1 percent in the 1990s.

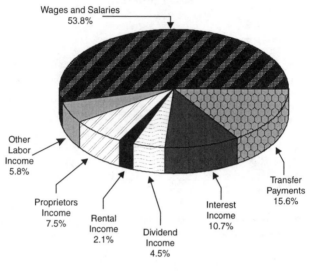

CHART 2

INCOME BREAKDOWN, 1997

Wages and Salaries
53.8%

Other
Labor
Income
5.8%

Proprietors
Income
7.5%

Rental
Income
2.1%

Dividend
Income
4.5%

Interest
Income
10.7%

Transfer
Payments
15.6%

Source: See Chart 1.

Slower productivity growth translates into slower wage growth (see Chart 3). Moreover, this simple comparison between productivity growth and real hourly compensation growth does not capture the full impact of the productivity slowdown because of the differences between output prices and consumer prices.

The Role of Prices

The divergence between real hourly compensation deflated by the Consumer Price Index (CPI) and real output per hour deflated by the nonfarm business output deflator has been widening sharply since the mid-1970s. This increasing disparity in price measures provides important insight into why real earnings, however measured, have diverged from aggregate output measures.

The nonfarm business output deflator includes not only prices of consumer goods, but also prices of investment goods, government goods and services, and net exports. Hourly compensation, on the other hand, is adjusted using the CPI. The CPI is derived from an entirely different survey source and methodology and attempts to measure changes in the prices that consumers actually pay for consumer goods.

CHART 3

PRODUCTIVITY AND REAL WAGES, 1960-97

Index, 1960 = 1.0

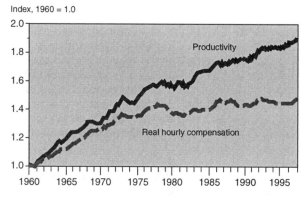

Source: See Chart 1.

Despite the shift to the new chain-weighted price deflator, the gap between the two measures is substantial and can be attributed primarily to the relative importance of investment goods (increasingly dominated by computers and information technology) and imports in the calculation of output prices. Computer prices are declining almost 20 percent per year, and import prices are falling about 3 percent annually, thus dragging down the output deflator relative to the CPI.

Bosworth and Perry show that the differences between the two indices account for virtually all of the decline in real compensation and earnings.[1] More important, the contrast between these two measures of inflation shows the shift in the terms of trade between the prices of the output that workers produce relative to the prices that they pay for the goods and services they consume. From 1973 to 1983, labor's terms of trade improved by 3 percent, resulting in real wage gains that exceeded productivity growth. Subsequently, however, workers have experienced a 6 percent decline in relative wages.

More recent findings by the Commission on the Consumer Price Index, commonly called the Boskin Commission after its chair, Michael Boskin, raise questions about how well the CPI measures the prices that consumers actually pay.[2] This report highlights several biases in the consumer price data that tend to exaggerate the rate of increase in consumer prices, with particular attention to the introduction of new products and the adjustment for quality improvements across consumer purchases, especially in services. For example, if the CPI were overstated by 0.5 percent in the 1980s and by 1.0 percent in the 1990s (both assumptions below the 1.1 percent bias in the Boskin Commission's report), all measures of economic progress, including per capita income, household and family income, and real compensation earnings, would rise significantly over time, and the gap between real income and output would be much narrower.

THE INCOME GAP

In spite of the substantial evidence of economic progress, every measure of income inequality shows that the relative distribution of this progress has become more unequal. Standing out in almost every analysis is the substantial improvement in the relative position of the top 5 percent of all Americans. In other words, while most people are, on average, better off, those in the very highest ranks have progressed at a much faster pace.

There are several ways to gauge income disparity. One is to look at the median income of each quintile. The median income in the bottom three-fifths of the population declined relative to the top one-fifth from 1970 to 1995. Using an adjusted CPI shows that even though there have been gains across all income groups, the largest gains have been concentrated in the top 20 percent—and especially in the top 5 percent.

A second way to gauge income inequality is by the share of household income in each quintile. This approach tracks more closely the relative gains among the various income groups irrespective of whether income is rising or falling. The share of household income earned by the top 20 percent grew from 43.3 percent in 1970 to 48.7 percent in 1995. The share of the bottom 20 percent declined over this time span, from 4.1 percent to 3.7 percent—not a very dramatic change, but a decline nonetheless (see Chart 4). The results are the same when examining the distribution of family income.[3] Again, the bottom quintile's share of income has decreased over the past two and one-half decades, from 7.9 percent to 6.4 percent. Meanwhile, the top quintile's share has grown from 37.6 percent to 41.6 percent (see Chart 5).

A final measure of income disparity is the Gini coefficient, the ratio of income of the highest 20 percent of individuals or households to the lowest 20 percent. The ratios for households and families further support the argument that income disparities are widening (see Chart 6). The 90:10 ratio that compares the highest and lowest percentiles has risen at an even faster pace than the 80:20 ratio since 1970.

Thus, even though most groups have made substantial economic progress, virtually every measure of income inequality shows a growing divergence between the highest income groups and the rest of the American population. This holds true even when allowing for the distortion caused by the use of different deflators. The simple fact is that over the past several decades, the income gap among Americans has widened. The question is whether the disparity in income is the result of changes in the economic system or is the result of a variety of factors, both demographic and social, that have reshaped and redistributed economic fortunes.

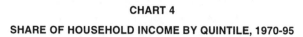

CHART 4

SHARE OF HOUSEHOLD INCOME BY QUINTILE, 1970-95

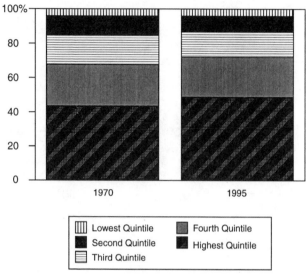

Source: See Chart 1.

THE DEMOGRAPHICS OF INCOME INEQUALITY

Since 1970, median household income has grown only about 6 percent, while median family income has increased by almost 12 percent. (See Chart 7 for the changes in the dollar amounts of median income from 1970 to 1995.) These measures are driven as much by changes in household structure and size as by changes in the underlying distribution of income. For example, because of the rapid growth in recent years of single-person, single-parent, and other nontraditional households, the number of households in the United States has been growing considerably faster than the growth rate of the population as a whole. Hence, over time, the growth in income is spread among more and more households. Further, median income growth for these important consumer units has not kept up with per capita income growth. Thus, important distributional issues are also at work.

The progression of the baby boomer population has been a primary, though largely silent, contributor in creating large income differentials among Americans. In the 1950s and 1960s, average household income was roughly the same for all age groups. Today, average household income in the 35-54 age group is $56,000, almost twice that of the

CHART 5

SHARE OF FAMILY INCOME BY QUINTILE, 1970-95

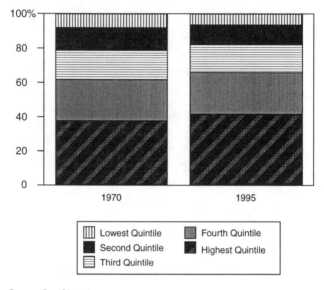

Source: See Chart 1.

CHART 6

GINI COEFFICIENT: HOUSEHOLDS AND FAMILIES, 1970-95
(Based on 1996 $)

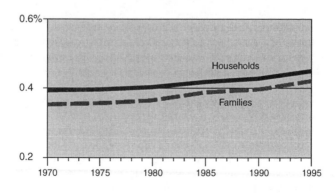

Source: See Chart 1.

CHART 7

MEDIAN INCOME: HOUSEHOLDS AND FAMILIES, 1970-95
(Based on 1996 $)

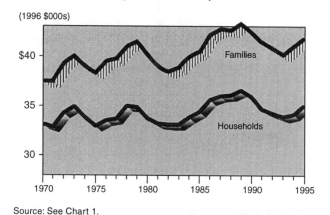

Source: See Chart 1.

under-25 age group. The demographics of the baby boom population and the corresponding changes in values and household structure over the past 25 years have played an important role in widening the income gap.

Over the past two and one-half decades, the U.S. population has grown from about 205 million to more than 265 million, an increase of approximately 30 percent. During this time, the population aged 35-49, the most income-productive years, has expanded from 35 million to more than 62 million, an increase of more than 75 percent.

The baby boom generation has been a constant and powerful force in reshaping American society over the past 50 years, and it will continue to be a dominant force for decades to come. Between 1970 and 1995, for example, the total number of households in the United States increased from about 63 million to about 100 million, a growth of more than 55 percent. During this period, the number of households headed by people aged 35-49 grew from approximately 18 million to almost 33 million, an increase of more than 80 percent. Today, one-third of all households are "boomer" households.

The structure of the American household has undergone extensive and radical changes during the past several decades. Most of the growth has been in nontraditional households, while the once traditional households, married couples with children, have been growing at a much slower rate (see Chart 8). In 1970, of the 63 million total households, almost 70 percent were husband-wife families. Today, there are approximately 100 million households, but fewer than 55 percent are married

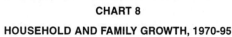

CHART 8

HOUSEHOLD AND FAMILY GROWTH, 1970-95

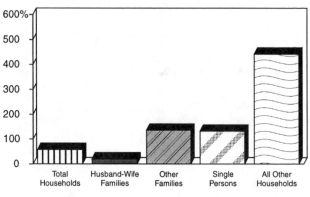

Source: See Chart 1.

couple homes. During this time, the number of single and other households has exploded. The number of one-person households has more than doubled—from about 11 million to about 25 million households. Single-person households are composed primarily of young adults and the elderly, traditionally groups with lower incomes than the rest of the population. Other families, the overwhelming majority of whom are single-parent households, have also grown at an above average rate. These once not-so-typical households accounted for less than 7 million households in 1970, but have ballooned to more than 16 million today, accounting for 16 percent of all households.

These vast changes in such a short period have had a profound effect on the distribution of income in the United States. The surge in single-person households, single-parent households, and all other households has helped to hold down incomes at the lower end of the income range. The decline in the poverty rate among the elderly, who make up a significant proportion of single-person households, has helped keep the gap between the low and the high end from widening even further. At the same time, married couple households, especially those with two earners, have expanded the top end of the income scale.

The trends in household structure are expected to continue well into the next century. Although single-person and single-parent households will grow at a slower pace than in the past, by the year 2005 they will account for approximately 47 percent of the household population. Married couple households will continue to be the slowest growing sector. This trend in household formation is likely to continue to polarize the income gap.

Although the changing composition of households helps explain the widening income gap, especially at the lower end, both demographic and social changes help explain the movement of households from middle income status into the more affluent income brackets. Not only has the composition of the household changed profoundly as the baby boom generation has come of age, but so has its economic profile. The dramatic changes in the composition of the labor force and in education standards have enabled a significant segment of the population to rapidly advance economically.

The baby boomers were the first generation that chose to pursue a college education rather than to marry after leaving high school. Chart 9 shows the number of degrees conferred on men and women over the past four and one-half decades. In 1950, less than 25 percent of all women obtained a college degree. As the boomers reached college age, that figure began to rise, and today almost 55 percent of all college degrees are given to women. This profound change in educational achievement has affected income distribution, as higher educational achievement leads to higher income and increased lifetime earning potential.

The increase in women's educational attainment has helped shape the biggest and most visible change over the past several decades—the emergence of the working woman. Between 1970 and 1995, women entered the labor force at a rate never before experienced. Education and the postponement of marriage and childbearing not only have led to a decrease in the size of families, but also have been instrumental in allowing women to enter and reenter the labor force—the latter not an option

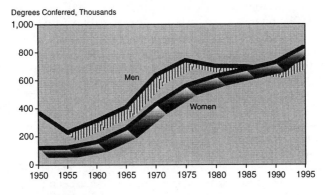

CHART 9

INCREASE IN THE DEGREES CONFERRED ON MEN AND WOMEN IN THE UNITED STATES, 1950-95

Degrees Conferred, Thousands

Source: See Chart 1.

readily available to prior generations. During the past two and one-half decades, the number of women in the labor force has skyrocketed, increasing from about 30 million to more than 60 million. Female labor force participation rates have risen from 40 percent to almost 60 percent.

The increase in working women has allowed many families not only to enter the ranks of the middle class, but also to climb the ladder further to the land of affluence. Indeed, an important source of the large difference in baby boomers' household income relative to other groups has been the increase in dual-earner families coupled with the narrowing income gap between men and women. This is a clear example of how closing one income gap can create another. These trends in educational achievement and participation rates of women are projected to continue, albeit much less dramatically, during the next decade.

Between 1995 and 2005, aggregate household income in the United States is projected to increase from more than $4 trillion to more than $5 trillion, a growth rate in excess of 25 percent. Currently, boomers account for more than 30 percent of total household earnings, or approximately $1.5 trillion. By the year 2005, they are projected to account for more than 45 percent of all dollars flowing into American households. In fact, of the total growth in income projected to occur over the next decade, boomers will account for almost 80 percent. Thus, the purchasing power of baby boomers will continue to increase over the next decade. This, coupled with the increase in smaller families and the proliferation of dual-earner households, may well widen the income gap further.

EARNINGS INEQUALITY

The increasing disparity in earnings between skilled and unskilled workers, as well as among workers in the same education/skill class, provides another perspective on income inequality. Two trends are apparent. First is the increasing returns to education. A number of researchers have pointed to the growing earnings difference between high school graduates and college graduates. Obviously, as with all analyses based on means, there is a wide disparity within a given range. Also, some of the growing income disparity between high school and college graduates may be due to selection bias because an increasing share of the workforce has some post-high school education. Nonetheless, the notion that better educated workers earn more than their less educated counterparts is borne out both by the growing earnings gap between skilled and unskilled workers and, in recent years, by the dramatic shift in employment opportunities to higher paying and presumably higher skill jobs.

Moreover, ongoing Bureau of Labor Statistics research shows that almost two-thirds of the jobs created since 1989 have been in high paying occupations.[4] The second fastest growing sector has been the low paying occupations (see Chart 10). Middle paying jobs have declined as a percent of the total workforce, but even within this group, technical,

CHART 10

HIGH AND LOW EARNINGS GROWTH, 1989-95

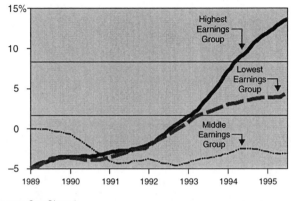

Source: See Chart 1.

administrative, and service jobs are more in demand, while the demand for the traditional skilled manufacturing occupations has been declining. These shifts underscore the role of computer and information technology in substituting for labor and in creating new combinations of high and low paying jobs that eliminate the need for intermediate and semiskilled workers.

REGIONAL SOURCES OF INCOME DISPARITY

A final perspective on income disparity focuses on the gap among various U.S. regions. From the 1960s to the 1980s, the differences in per capita income among the regions narrowed. In 1960, median per capita income in the highest income region (Pacific) was 51 percent higher than in the lowest region (East South Central). By 1980, that difference had narrowed considerably to 37 percent. (Table 1 shows per capita income by region from 1960 to 1996.)

Beginning in 1980, however, the gap began to widen. Obviously, geographic definitions of a region are somewhat arbitrary, and the implication here is not causal. Rather, during the 1980s, certain regions (principally on the East and West Coasts) had rapid increases in highway jobs, positive demographic patterns, and overall growth rates that were more rapid than the rest of the country. By 1990, the income disparity between the highest income region (now New England) and the lowest (still East South Central) reached 40 percent. Other regions, particularly the Midwest and the South, were hit hard by a severe, prolonged recession in important sectors such as agriculture and oil that

TABLE 1

PER CAPITA INCOME BY REGION, 1960-96

	Per Capita Income					Index (Total U.S. = 100)					
	1960	1970	1980	1990	1996	1960	1970	1980	1990	1996
Total U.S.	$2,276	$4,077	$10,062	$19,191	$24,426	100	100	100	100	100
New England	2,498	4,480	10,705	22,783	28,989	110	110	106	119	119
Middle Atlantic	2,614	4,613	10,864	22,344	28,250	115	113	108	116	116
East North Central	2,442	4,175	10,219	18,750	24,575	107	102	102	98	101
West North Central	2,124	3,814	9,512	17,830	23,414	93	94	95	93	96
South Atlantic	1,896	3,720	9,304	18,652	23,825	83	91	92	97	98
East South Central	1,538	3,016	7,822	15,128	20,219	68	74	78	79	83
West South Central	1,865	3,441	9,437	16,430	21,300	82	84	94	86	87
Mountain	2,140	3,757	9,559	16,897	22,139	94	92	95	88	91
Pacific	2,706	4,647	11,539	20,903	25,141	119	114	115	109	103
Standard Deviation						17	14	11	14	12

Source: Bureau of Economic Analysis; and The Conference Board.

depressed the economy and incomes. Then, during the first half of the 1990s, the faster growing regions on the East and West Coasts stagnated, while the Midwest and the South boomed. By 1996, median per capita income in the highest income region was just 36 percent above the lowest.

HOW DO CONSUMERS EVALUATE THEIR WELFARE?

Milton Friedman observed that the ultimate test of an economic theory is whether it works in practice. One way to examine the seriousness of the income disparity issue is to examine Americans' attitudes. The long-term trend in The Conference Board's *Consumer Confidence Survey* (primarily a cyclical indicator) suggests consumer unease with the pace and distribution of economic progress. Although consumer confidence rises and falls in sync with the business cycle, the long-term trend in the index has been somewhat downward since its inception in 1969.

During 1997, however, consumer confidence set new records, with consumers' evaluation of the economy at its highest level since 1969. This optimism may suggest that while income disparities are no narrower than they were several years ago, many consumers appear to sense opportunities to advance their welfare.

In fact, in a special survey conducted in 1997 for The Conference Board by NFO Research, Inc., of Greenwich, CT, when consumers were asked to compare their standard of living today versus the beginning of the decade, more than 45 percent of the respondents claimed to be better off. In a similar Conference Board survey conducted by NFO just two years ago, only about one-third of the respondents thought that their families' economic conditions had improved.

CONCLUSION

Income disparity is a complex issue. As this analysis has shown, the composition of personal income is changing in favor of capital income, on the one hand, and transfer payments, on the other. Given the growth in retirement accounts and individual equity holdings, capital income is likely to continue to grow in importance. The increasing role of transfer payments means that a smaller share of income comes from workers' compensation. The use of price deflators, whether the CPI or the output deflator, has only created more distortion in the income picture.

Technological advances and growth of the service industries have further accentuated the income disparity trend by creating huge numbers of jobs in high paying occupations while encouraging, through computer and information technology, rapid job growth at the other end of the spectrum.

Further, individuals with a higher level of education have a greater probability of earning higher incomes than those with lesser education. The baby boomers have helped to widen income disparities because they tend to be better educated than their predecessors, they are in their peak earning years, and they have participated fully in a radically changed family and household structure that has given rise to two-earner families.

Thus, despite the complexity of the issue, it is clear that the income gap among Americans has widened over the past several decades. The severity of the disparity depends on which particular measure is analyzed and which deflator is used to adjust the data. When all the factors are considered, the widening income gap is due as much to the dramatic demographic and social changes America has experienced in a rather short time frame as it is to the forces of the economic system.

NOTES

The authors would like to thank Tom Higgins and Daniel Vasquez for their valuable assistance.

1. Barry Bosworth and George L. Perry, "Productivity and Real Wages: Is There a Puzzle?" *Brookings Papers on Economic Activity*, Vol. I (1994), pp. 317-335.

2. Michael J. Boskin, "Toward a More Accurate Measure of the Cost of Living: Findings and Recommendations of the CPI Commission [the Boskin Commission]," testimony before the Senate Budget Committee, January 30, 1997.

3. Households consist of both related and unrelated persons, while families consist of only related or married couples.

4. Randy E. Ilg, "The Nature of Employment Growth: 1989-95," *Monthly Labor Review* (June 1996).

PART III
CONTRIBUTING CAUSES AND CONSEQUENCES

Introduction

◆

by Barbara J. Easterling
Secretary-Treasurer, Communications Workers of America

THE RISE IN INCOME DISPARITY has been significant, and many factors have been pointed to as the causes of this trend. The factors range from shifts in technology, globalization, the changing workplace, the breakdown of the family, immigration, the decline in unionization, and changes in public policies such as tax and social welfare policies.

The authors in this section explore the contributing causes and consequences of the growth of income disparity. Chapters examine technological change and international trade and their impact on the growing income gap, family income mobility, the influences of immigration policies on income disparity and unionism, and the effects of income disparity in the inner city.

In terms of the role of declining unionization rates in income inequality, the statistical evidence shows that, all other things being equal, higher unionization rates are associated with lower levels of income disparity. Unions have not only won wage and employee benefits for their members, but have also helped those in society who are in the lowest quintiles of the income distribution. Unionization has also strongly bolstered democratic forces in the U.S. economy and in other countries. Recent declines in unionization have hurt the middle class and those on the lower rungs of the economic ladder. There has been increased downward mobility in recent years as many social policies have shifted. Meanwhile, the rise of contingent workers has further contributed to growing income disparity.

By itself, economic growth has been unable to reduce the rise of disparity. Because the growth of income inequality is the result of many economic, social, and political factors, dealing with this issue will require efforts on many different fronts.

Chapter 6

Technological Change and International Trade: How Well Do They Explain the Rise in U.S. Income Inequality?

◆

by Gary Burtless

AMERICANS' INCOMES have become strikingly less equal since 1979. The incomes of poor Americans have shrunk, while the incomes of the affluent have continued to grow. This increased income inequality has not been confined to the United States; nations throughout the industrialized world have seen disparities in personal income rise since the early 1980s. In many western European countries, growing unemployment, especially among the young and least skilled, has contributed to the trend toward greater income inequality.

The recent growth in earnings inequality has stimulated a vast amount of research by labor economists who have examined a variety of explanations for this trend.[1] Among the leading explanations are the increased level and changing character of immigration into the United States, the shrinking size and bargaining power of unions, declines in the minimum wage, and technological change.

Another alternative explanation favored by many noneconomists focuses on the growing importance of international trade for industrialized economies, especially trade with the developing world. According to this view, liberalized trade with low wage countries has disproportionately affected and threatens to impoverish low skilled and middle class workers in the advanced industrialized countries. This argument was forcefully advocated by opponents of the North American Free Trade Agreement (NAFTA), who warned that freer trade with Mexico and other poor countries would eliminate industrial jobs and reduce the wages of unskilled and semiskilled U.S. workers.

Most economists who study the influence of international trade are skeptical of these claims, finding little evidence that global trade is the main reason for growing wage disparities in the United States. Nonetheless, economists who support free trade must face an uncomfortable fact. A classic doctrine of modern trade theory, the factor price equalization theorem, predicts that under plausible assumptions, the elimination of trade barriers between a high wage country and a low wage country can lead to reductions in real wages in the high wage country. Consistent with this theory, the increase in manufactured exports from the developing world to industrialized countries has been accompanied by loss of manufacturing employment in the industrialized countries and serious erosion in the relative wages and job prospects of unskilled and semiskilled workers.

Of course, even though the assumptions behind the factor price equalization theorem seem plausible, they are not necessarily true. The trends in manufacturing employment and wage disparities could be due to factors completely unrelated to trade. Even if the theorem's assumptions are approximately true and the trends in manufacturing employment and relative wages are partly due to liberalized trade, it is important to establish whether trade has been a major contributor to the trend in inequality or has played only a bit part.

Many American economists believe that the most persuasive explanation for widening wage disparities is the shift in employers' demand for labor that is linked to the introduction of new production techniques. Technological change has occurred in industries in which trade is not very important as well as in those in which trade is significant. Technological innovation has put pressure on employers to change their production methods in ways that require a more able and skilled workforce. Employers have persisted in this strategy despite sharply rising wage premiums for the highly skilled, which make it more expensive to hire a skilled workforce today than in the 1960s or 1970s.

This chapter makes three main points about the role of technological change and international trade in the trend toward greater income inequality in the United States.

First, neither technological change nor international trade can provide a direct explanation for most of the rise in U.S. income inequality. The reason is straightforward. Even if all of the growth in inequality of wages were attributable to these two factors, much less than one-half of the recent rise in family income inequality would be explained. Although the increase in earned income inequality is an important source of growing family income inequality, it directly explains less than one-third of the recent rise in overall inequality. Most of the increase is due to other factors—principally demographic trends, changing work patterns among partners in married-couple families, and growing inequality in the distribution of income from nonlabor sources. The disintegration of traditional family organization and changing gender roles have produced an increasingly affluent population of dual-working-spouse families and childless persons as well as a growing and relatively impoverished population of single-parent families.

Second, international trade has almost certainly played a less important role than technological change in pushing up wage disparities in the United States. As discussed in the next section, research by several economists suggests that liberalized trade and rising imports are unlikely to explain most of the growth in inequality of labor earnings. The trend toward greater earnings inequality is nearly universal in the United States. While the gap between the wages of skilled and unskilled workers has widened in trade-affected industries, it has widened to an equal degree in industries not directly affected by trade. Trade-affected industries have shed massive numbers of unskilled and semiskilled workers in an effort to remain competitive. But employers who are not involved in trade have similarly reduced their use of unskilled and semiskilled workers.

This does not mean that the role of international trade in determining income inequality is unimportant or unworthy of careful examination. It simply means that the globalization of the U.S economy is unlikely to explain more than one-fifth of the huge rise in either wage or income inequality since 1969.

Third, even though technological change is most economists' favorite reason for the growth in wage disparities, it is not a very satisfying or helpful explanation. One reason is that, as noted above, the direct evidence to support it is not strong. Analysts do not directly observe the skill requirements of new jobs or technologies. Instead, they observe some easy-to-measure characteristics of workers who hold different kinds of jobs, the pattern of wages paid to workers in different skill classes, and trends in the number of workers in different skill groups. When they conclude that the trend in absolute or relative wages is "explained" by technological change, they typically mean that the pattern of wage change is not accounted for by other changes in the environment, such as increased international trade or immigration. Technological change is usually the reason that is left after all other plausible explanations have been accounted for.

Another reason is that "technological change" does not have the narrow interpretation that most noneconomists assume. It is important for noneconomists to understand the wide variety of changes included under the broad umbrella of technological change. This explanation for wider pay disparities is so broad that it is not very helpful as a guide to solutions to the social and economic problems arising out of greater inequality. In one important sense, then, technological change may not be much of an explanation at all.

GROWING INEQUALITY

Most Americans recognize that income disparities have grown over the past quarter century. Few may realize the extent of the rise, however. Chart 1 shows trends in the growth of cash incomes at different points in the income distribution. The tabulations are based on annual incomes reported to the U.S. Bureau of the Census on the Current Population Surveys (CPS) in March 1970, March 1980, and March 1994. Incomes are measured for every individual in the population using the concept of "adjusted personal income." Since this concept differs significantly from the income concept used to measure inequality in Census Bureau reports, it is worth explaining the concept in some detail.

Most census measures of inequality are based on tabulations of the unadjusted cash incomes received by households or families. This in-

CHART 1

**ANNUAL RATE OF INCOME CHANGE BY DECILE,
1969-79 AND 1979-93**

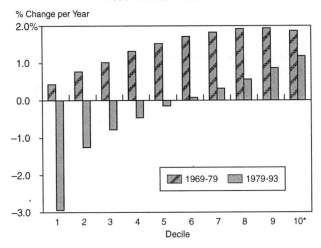

*10th decile extends only through the 97th percentile.

Source: Author's tabulations of 1970, 1980, and 1994 Current Population Survey (CPS) files.

come concept makes no allowance for differences in household or family size. Twenty thousand dollars received by a two-person family is treated as equivalent to $20,000 received by an eight-person family. The adjusted income concept used in this chapter relies on a family-size correction to reflect economies of scale in consumption enjoyed by people who live in larger family units. People who are members of the same nuclear family are each treated as receiving an identical income. Inequality is measured by ranking all persons (rather than families or households) represented in the CPS file according to their adjusted income.

The amount of adjusted (or "equivalent") money income per person in each family unit is calculated by making a correction for the number of people who live together and are presumed to share income and consumption.[2] The adjustment for family size is chosen so that it corresponds roughly with the adjustment that is implicit in the official poverty thresholds. As in the official U.S. poverty index, for example, a quadrupling of family size yields a doubling of income needed to sustain an equivalent consumption level.[3] Unlike many Census Bureau statistics on inequality, the estimates here reflect the experiences of unrelated individuals as well as members of families.

After calculating the adjusted personal income of each individual on the CPS files, I ranked individuals by adjusted income and calculated the average adjusted income in each decile of the income distribution. The patterned bars in Chart 1 show the annual rates of change of adjusted income in each decile between 1969 and 1979. The gray bars show rates of change between 1979 and 1993. The chart shows that income inequality grew in both periods, though it increased much faster in the more recent period than in the earlier one. Between 1969 and 1979, adjusted income increased 1.9 percent a year in the top two income deciles, but less than 0.5 percent a year in the bottom decile. Income grew more slowly in every decile after 1979. In fact, it fell in the bottom five deciles. While adjusted income rose 1.2 percent a year between 1979 and 1993 in the top decile, it fell almost 3 percent a year in the bottom decile. In 1969, a person at the 95th percentile of the adjusted income distribution received 11.7 times as much income as a person at the 5th percentile. By 1993, the ratio of adjusted incomes at the 95th and 5th percentiles was more than 25:1.

The Census Bureau and academic researchers often measure overall income inequality using a statistic known as the Gini coefficient. The Gini coefficient ranges in value from 0 (indicating perfect equality) up to 1 (indicating that all income is received by a single person or household). The trend in family income inequality since 1967, measured using the Gini coefficient, is shown by the line in Chart 2. The official Census Bureau series shows a pattern of generally declining inequality through the late 1960s, moderately growing inequality in the 1970s, and sharply increased inequality after 1980. Family income inequality rose sharply in the early 1990s and reached a new postwar high in 1993.

I also calculated the Gini coefficient using the concept of adjusted personal income. The ovals in Chart 2 represent estimates of the Gini coefficient of adjusted income for five years: 1969, 1973, 1979, 1989, and 1993. The first four years were years of economic expansion that ended periods of sustained economic growth. The last year, 1993, was a year of robust economic expansion following two years of slow and relatively intermittent recovery from the 1990 recession. It was also the year of peak postwar inequality.[4] Note that my alternative estimates of the Gini coefficient are similar to the official estimates published by the Census Bureau. The official census series shows that income inequality among all U.S. families climbed 15 percent from 1969 through 1989. The alternative series implies that inequality of adjusted income among all non-institutionalized people rose 14 percent over the same period. The official series shows a jump in inequality of 23 percent over the full period from 1969 to 1993, whereas the alternative series implies that inequality rose almost 19 percent.

Earnings inequality among adult men and adult women also rose sharply over this period. Chart 3 shows trends in American wages over the recent past. Changes in real earnings are calculated using information from the March 1970, 1980, and 1994 CPS files. These surveys obtained information about earnings received in 1969, 1979, and 1993,

CHART 2

**GINI COEFFICIENT OF INCOME INEQUALITY:
OFFICIAL CENSUS AND ALTERNATIVE SERIES, 1967-95**

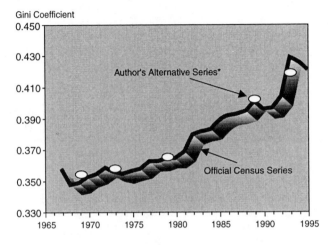

*Author's estimates of the Gini coefficient of adjusted personal income for five years: 1969, 1973, 1979, 1989, and 1993.

Sources: U.S. Bureau of the Census, Series P-60 Reports, and author's tabulations.

respectively. Men and women who were between 25 and 64 and were working on full-time, year-round schedules are separately ranked by their annual earnings and then divided into five equally sized groups. The chart shows the annual rate of growth in inflation-adjusted wages within each of these five groups between 1969 and 1979 (the patterned bars) and 1979 and 1993 (the gray bars).

The long-term trend in male wage growth is particularly striking (see top panel in Chart 3). For the entire 1969-93 period, annual earnings fell in the bottom 40 percent of the earnings distribution, remained unchanged in the middle quintile, and rose only moderately at the top. For workers in all five quintiles, trends were much more adverse in the second half of the period than they were in the first. Wages grew more slowly (or fell more rapidly) between 1979 and 1993 than between 1969 and 1979. In both periods, wage disparities widened. The fall in earnings in the bottom one-fifth of the male distribution is sizable. Over the entire period from 1969 through 1993, wages dropped 15 percent. In contrast, average wages in the top fifth of the distribution rose 17 percent over the 24-year period.

CHART 3

**ANNUAL RATE OF CHANGE IN FULL-TIME,
YEAR-ROUND EARNINGS BY QUINTILE, 1969-93**

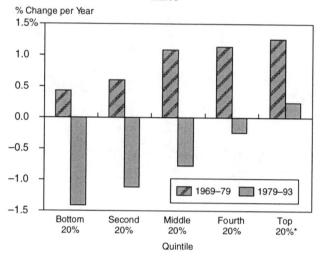

Males

% Change per Year

*Top quintile extends through the 95.9th percentile.

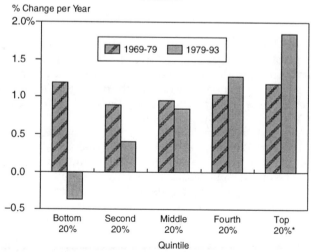

Females

% Change per Year

*Top quintile extends through the 99.3rd percentile.

Source: Author's tabulations of March 1970, 1980, and 1994 CPS files.

Labor market conditions have been much more favorable for American women. The bottom panel in Chart 3 shows what happened to the real earnings of women who worked at least 35 hours a week on a year-round basis. Earnings rose everywhere in the distribution between 1969 and 1979. But in the more recent period, the trend in wage inequality was the same among women as it was among men. After 1979, women at the top of the wage distribution saw their earnings rise more than 25 percent. At the bottom, women's annual earnings fell 4 percent. Between 1979 and 1993, the percentage increase in women's earnings was more than six times larger in the top quintile than at the bottom.

SOURCES OF CHANGE IN INCOME INEQUALITY

The similarity of the trends in overall income inequality and in earnings disparities has led many observers to conclude, erroneously, that the trend in wages largely accounts for the trend in overall inequality. This view would imply that if the trend in wages could be explained, so would the trend in overall income inequality. Research suggests, however, that rising earnings inequality is only one of several important sources of the jump in income inequality. In percentage terms, it is a less important part of the increase that occurred after 1979.[5]

Changes in the individual earnings distribution do not necessarily produce equivalent changes in the distribution of family or personal income. One reason is that families receive income from other sources besides labor earnings. Nonlabor income has risen faster than labor income over most of the period since 1969. Unearned income may have become more or less equally distributed over time, reinforcing or offsetting the trends in earned income. In addition, the structure of U.S. households has changed enormously. A growing percentage of Americans live in families with only a single adult head, where they are more likely to be poor than they would be in families where two adult heads are present. The impact of wage inequality on family incomes cannot be understood apart from this important change in the composition of U.S. households. Finally, the employment rates of American women increased dramatically during the past quarter century. The rise in their labor income could reduce overall inequality if women's earnings growth was concentrated among families that would otherwise have received low incomes; it could boost inequality if women's earnings gains were concentrated among families that would have been well off even without a woman's earnings.

Before the sources of change in overall inequality since 1969 are discussed, it is useful to show how income from different sources has changed over time. Table 1 shows changes in adjusted income by income source since 1969 among people represented on the CPS. The top row of the table shows adjusted male-head labor earnings in 1969, 1979, and 1993. In 1969, these earnings averaged $13,600 per person (1993 dollars).[6] (The average includes zeroes for people in families where the male head

TABLE 1

CHANGES IN ADJUSTED INCOME BY SOURCE OF INCOME
AMONG PERSONS AND FAMILY COMPOSITION, 1969 TO 1993

	1969	1979	1993
1. Average income by source (1993 $)			
Male-head earnings	$13,600	$13,951	$13,072
Female-head earnings	3,288	4,617	6,678
Other earnings	846	1,078	545
Nonlabor income	2,200	3,793	4,647
Capital income	773	1,210	1,367
Means-tested transfers	159	233	273
Other government transfers	178	303	323
Public retirement	614	1,140	1,367
Employer-sponsored pensions	337	628	895
Other income	139	279	422
Total Income	**$19,933**	**$23,439**	**$24,943**
2. Share of income (%)			
Male-head earnings	68	60	52
Female-head earnings	17	20	27
Other earnings	4	5	2
Nonlabor income	11	16	19
3. % of persons who have income			
Male-head earnings	79	70	63
Female-head earnings	46	53	57
Other earnings	25	23	15
Nonlabor income	57	83	80
4. Gini coefficient among persons who have income			
Male-head earnings	0.328	0.344	0.393
Female-head earnings	0.521	0.491	0.483
Other earnings	0.586	0.547	0.585
Nonlabor income	0.668	0.699	0.696
5. Gini correlation			
Male-head earnings	0.81	0.79	0.78
Female-head earnings	0.53	0.50	0.61
Other earnings	0.41	0.43	0.37
Nonlabor income	0.16	0.19	0.31
6. Persons in families with head present (% of all people)			
Male head present	86	81	77
Female head present	95	91	88
7. Number of family units (unweighted)	50,828	73,632	68,341

Source: Author's tabulations of March 1970, 1980, and 1994 CPS files.

did not work and for people in families with no male head.) The average person thus lived in a family unit in which $13,600 of adjusted income was derived from the labor earnings of the male head. Total adjusted income in 1969 averaged $19,933, implying that 68 percent of average income was derived from the earnings of the male head (see No. 2 in Table 1).

Labor earnings rose rapidly in the 1970s and 1980s among female heads of families. (Female heads of families include wives in two-parent families as well as unmarried women who head families or live alone.) For the population as a whole, female-head earnings rose 3 percent a year. The income derived from the earnings of a male head of family actually fell slightly over the period. From 1969 to 1993, income derived from male-head earnings declined from 68 percent to 52 percent of total adjusted personal income. In contrast, the fraction of adjusted income derived from female-head earnings rose from 17 percent to 27 percent. Income from unearned income sources, especially from capital assets, public retirement benefits, and employer-sponsored pension programs, also grew substantially over the period.

Part of the decline in income from male-head earnings was due to a slowdown in real wage growth among men who worked, but part was due to a decline in the share of men holding jobs and to a drop in the proportion of families where a male head was present. If an adult male is absent from a family, the contribution of male earnings to family income is zero, bringing down the average contribution of male earnings to family income and greatly increasing the chances a family will be poor. In 1969, 14 percent of Americans lived in families where there was no male head present (see No. 6 in Table 1). By 1993, the proportion of Americans in families without a male head had climbed to 23 percent, depriving many low income children of a potential male breadwinner. It is doubtful whether either technological change or the globalization of the U.S. economy played a huge role in the trend toward single-head families. The trend was already well under way in the 1960s and early 1970s before earnings inequality began to grow.

There was also a sharp decline in the fraction of Americans living in families with a working adult male. This fraction fell from 79 percent to 63 percent. In contrast, there was a big increase in the proportion living in families with a working adult woman; the fraction rose from 46 percent in 1969 to 57 percent in 1993. As would be expected, growing inequality in male earnings tended to push up the Gini coefficient of male earnings among people deriving some of their income from a male head's earnings (see No. 4 in Table 1). In spite of the growth in earnings inequality among adult women on a full-time, year-round work sched-ule, the Gini coefficient of female-head earnings dropped among people who received some income from a female head's earnings. The inequal-ity of nonlabor income rose moderately over the 1970s.

The statistics at the top and in the middle of Table 1 highlight the contribution of different income sources to the trend in overall income growth. Those near the bottom offer some evidence of the changing correlation among income sources over time (see No. 5 in Table 1). This kind of correlation can be important, as a simple illustration will show. Capital income is received more frequently by people with a high position in the income distribution than by people further down the distribution. If capital income grew faster than other sources of income, it would be reasonable to expect incomes in the top tail of the distribution to grow faster than incomes lower down in the distribution. However, if the correlation between capital income and all other sources of income increased, income inequality would also rise, even if capital income grew no faster than other types of income. Thus, the change in the correlation among different income sources can be an important determinant of inequality.

I measure income correlation using the concept of "Gini correlation." This is defined as the covariance between a particular income source (say, nonlabor income) and the rank of people's total income, divided by the covariance between that income source and the rank of people's income from that source. Like the correlation coefficient, the Gini correlation ranges between –1 and 1. By the logic of this definition, some sources of income—such as welfare benefits and food stamps—should have a negative Gini correlation. People who receive large amounts of income from these sources will usually have a low position in the income distribution. Other sources of income—such as capital income and male earnings—have a large positive Gini correlation. People with large amounts of income from these sources usually have a high rank in the overall income distribution. Estimates of the Gini correlation for 1969, 1979, and 1993 suggest that the correlations between female-head earnings and total income and between nonlabor income and total income have risen strongly, especially in the period after 1979 (shown in No. 5 in Table 1).

The two most important sources of family income are the earnings of the male and female heads (see the top two rows of Table 1). The changing correlation between these two income sources has had a major influence on the distribution of income over time. As has been seen, the percentage of people in families with a working female head rose between 1969 and 1993. The increase in the percentage of women at work was matched by a growing correlation between the labor supply of male and female heads. In 1969, the correlation between male- and female-head earnings among working-age families was significantly negative. A person in a working-age family with a working male head was less likely than average to receive labor earnings from a working female head. By 1993, the correlation between male- and female-head earnings in working-age families had become significantly positive. People who lived in a family with a well-paid male earner were more likely than average to receive income from a well-paid female earner, too. It is doubtful whether this trend can be traced to the effects of technological change or globalization. Women in higher income families were disproportionately drawn to enter the workforce and work longer hours even though their husbands enjoyed comfortable gains or suffered comparatively small losses as a result of structural changes in U.S. labor markets (see Chart 3). The trend in labor force participation among higher income women is more easily explained by changing social attitudes toward work among women than it is by technology or globalization.

To determine how changes in the distribution of individual earnings and demography have affected the distribution of U.S. income across people, I used an analytical technique proposed by Lerman and Yitzhaki.[7] The Lerman-Yitzhaki method decomposes changes in the distribution of income into separate components that help identify the separate contributions of earned income changes, changes in household structure, and trends in the correlation of different sources of income. The decomposition is presented in full in the appendix to this chapter. The appendix contains an extension of my earlier research with Lynn Karoly, in which we analyzed income trends between 1959 and 1989 among families with a working-age family head.[8] The appendix analyzes the rise in income inequality among people in all families between 1969 and 1993.

The analysis in the appendix confirms the importance of rising wage disparities. This trend contributed to growing earned income inequality among men who work, which in turn contributed to an increase in family income inequality. The trend toward increased earnings inequality among people at work does not account for most of the increase in overall income inequality, however. People in the bottom part of the income distribution derived smaller incomes from male earnings for reasons besides the shrinking hourly and weekly earnings paid to low income men. First, as already noted, a growing percentage of families contained no male head. By definition, these families did not receive any income from male-head earnings. Second, even the families with an adult male were less likely to receive income from his employment, since a dwindling percentage of adult men held jobs.

The change in the amount of earnings inequality among men who work accounts for less than 30 percent of the rise in overall inequality since 1969. The rising percentage of adult women who had earnings reduced the overall Gini coefficient over the entire period after 1969, but this had a small impact on overall inequality. However, a key influence of women's earnings on overall inequality came through its correlation with total family income. During the 1970s, this correlation fell moderately, tending to reduce overall inequality. The correlation soared after 1979, when women's earnings gains were concentrated among women in high income families. This factor explains more than a quarter of the total rise in inequality since 1969. Strikingly, it accounted for more than 40 percent of the jump in overall inequality after 1979. Rising unearned incomes and a growing correlation between unearned income and other income sources, especially since 1979, have also produced significant increases in income inequality.

It seems doubtful that the trends in unearned income, family composition, and the correlation of husband and wife earnings are directly attributable to the influence of trade or technology. The trends in family dissolution and out-of-wedlock births were already well established even before wages began to grow less equal after the mid-1970s. Increased labor force participation among women is also a trend that began long before wages started to grow less equal. Contrary to a common assertion about changing work patterns among women, a disproportionate share of the gains in employment, annual hours of work, and earnings since the late 1970s have been concentrated among women in relatively affluent households. This is hardly a pattern to be expected if women had been pushed into the labor force mainly as a result of rising inequality among men or shrinking wages among husbands.

In sum, increased earnings inequality among people who work is an important reason for increased U.S. income inequality, but it does not account for even one-third of the growth in overall income inequality. Changes in family composition, declining male labor force participation, increases in unearned income, and a sharp rise in the correlation of married partners' earnings account for more than two-thirds of the growth in U.S. income inequality since 1969. Even if all of the increase in earnings inequality among working Americans was due to technological change and global trade, less than a third of increased income inequality could be explained by these factors.

INTERNATIONAL TRADE AND EARNINGS INEQUALITY

A popular explanation for rising inequality is that increased global trade has disproportionately affected workers who are paid low wages. Because very poorly paid unskilled workers are abundant overseas, especially in newly industrializing countries, unskilled workers in the United States, western Europe, and Japan have suffered relative earnings or employment losses in the new trade regime. Of course, the trade and technology explanations are not mutually exclusive. Industries in the traded goods sector may adopt technologies that require advanced skills precisely because they face growing competition from countries where less skilled labor is abundant and cheap.

Noneconomists seem more inclined than economists to accept the view that global trade has hurt unskilled workers. Nonetheless, the number of economists who have attempted to assess the effects of trade on labor earnings is growing.[9] Researchers have used a variety of theoretical approaches and statistical methods to investigate the issue. On balance, it would be fair to say that most empirical studies of the influence of trade have found effects that are comparatively small, probably accounting for less than one-fifth of the decline of relative earnings of low paid or low skilled workers.

Economic Theory Linking Trade and Wages

The most useful theory to explain the link between trade and wages is the Heckscher-Ohlin model of international trade. Two aspects of the model deal explicitly with the effect of trade on wages and other factor prices. The factor price equalization theorem asserts that under the assumptions of the Heckscher-Ohlin model and a regime of unrestricted free trade, prices of the factors of production will be equalized among trading partners. In other words, if the model's assumptions are true, free trade between the United States and Mexico will equalize U.S. and Mexican wages for equivalent labor, even if labor cannot move across the U.S.-Mexican border.[10]

If these assumptions are correct, a free trade agreement between the United States and Mexico is good news for most Mexican workers and bad news for American workers whose skills are similar to those of average workers in Mexico. Because a typical Mexican worker's skills are equivalent to those of a less skilled American, factor price equalization will require that less skilled American workers accept a reduction in their real wage when the free trade agreement is fully implemented.

Another theorem based on the Heckscher-Ohlin model predicts that a reduction in the domestic price of a product, brought about by a lower tariff or reduced protection, will lower the real price of the productive factor that is used relatively intensively in producing that product.[11] If shoes are produced using labor intensively and land sparingly, then a reduction in tariff protection for shoes will reduce the real wages received by laborers. If the theorem's assumptions are correct, a reduction in protection of apparel and footwear, which use less skilled labor relatively intensively, will tend to reduce the real wages of less skilled workers in the rich industrialized countries, as long as those countries continue to produce apparel and footwear.

Although trade economists are confident of the implications of the Heckscher-Ohlin model, assuming its assumptions are true, they are not very confident that its assumptions are valid. For example, many are skeptical of the assumption that the same technology is available in rich and poor countries. If some of the crucial assumptions of the theory are untrue, the implications of the model may be untrue as well.

The claim that global trade is the main reason for the declining fortunes of unskilled and semiskilled workers would be more convincing if it could be shown that the demand for less skilled workers in rich countries has fallen dramatically in trade-affected industries but has remained strong in industries that are comparatively unaffected by trade. However, economists have not found this to be true.[12]

Economists typically find that the relative wages of unskilled workers have fallen in both traded goods industries and in industries unaffected by trade. This pattern of wage change, by itself, provides no evidence about the source of change in wage inequality; it simply demonstrates that relative wages move in the same way across a variety of labor markets and industries. If labor markets are efficient and relatively fluid, as they are in the United States, this result is not surprising. An economic shock that affects relative wages in part of the labor market, such as the market for workers in traded goods industries, is quickly reflected in relative wages in other parts of the labor market as well. This shock could have occurred as a result of a development in international trade or a change in technology.

However, there is no reason to expect that the intensity of use of less skilled labor outside the trade-affected sector will decrease if the shock that caused relative wages to change occurred as a result of a trade development. Firms that do not produce internationally traded goods and services should take advantage of the declining wage of unskilled workers by hiring more of them. But if they instead adopt techniques that use unskilled labor less intensively, technological change or another development has likely reduced their demand for less skilled workers. Pressures originating from international trade cannot explain a reduced demand for unskilled workers in industries not involved in international trade.

To determine whether trade can provide a plausible explanation for the trend in relative demand for less skilled labor, I calculated wage movements and employment changes across broad classes of U.S. industries, using data from March CPS files for 1970, 1974, 1980, 1990, and 1994, which cover annual earnings received in calendar years 1969, 1973, 1979, 1989, and 1993, respectively. These years were selected because, except for 1993, they represent equivalent points in the U.S. business cycle (1993 was the most recent year for which data were available when the analysis was performed). The industries are classified into three broad groups, defined to reflect the probable impact of trade.[13] It is interesting to compare industries that participate in international trade with those that are comparatively uninvolved in trade.

Chart 4 shows trends in the inequality of earnings among full-time wage and salary workers. Inequality is calculated as the ratio of annual earnings at the 90th percentile of the earnings distribution to earnings at the 10th percentile. The chart compares the trends in inequality, as measured by the 90:10 earnings ratio, among male and female workers employed in the most trade-affected and in the least trade-affected industries. Although inequality is lower in every period in trade-affected industries, the pattern of growing inequality among men is indistinguishable in the two kinds of industries—inequality climbed 47 percent in both types of industries between 1969 and 1993 (top panel of Chart 4). There is little evidence that pressure from international trade caused wage disparities to climb faster in trade-affected than in unaffected industries. However, job loss in trade-affected industries would tend to push up earnings inequality slightly because it would force workers to move from low inequality industries to high inequality industries. But the effect of declining traded goods employment on overall earnings inequality is not large. Earnings inequality has grown

CHART 4

RATIO OF WAGES AT 90TH PERCENTILE TO WAGES AT 10TH PERCENTILE IN TRADE-AFFECTED AND NONTRADE-AFFECTED INDUSTRIES

Males

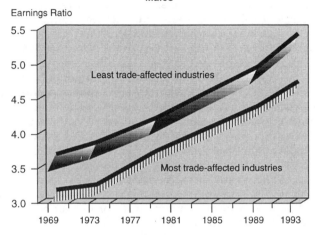

Females

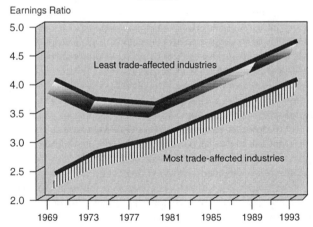

Source: Author's tabulations of March 1970, 1974, 1980, 1990, and 1994 CPS files.

in the United States mainly because inequality has jumped within many industries, not because workers have shifted from industries in which inequality is low to industries in which inequality is high.

The lower panel of Chart 4 shows the trends in inequality among women. These are somewhat more consistent with the claim that international trade affects the earnings distribution. As was the case among men, women employed in trade-affected industries experienced less earnings inequality than women in industries least influenced by trade. However, women in trade-affected industries have seen a larger and more sustained increase in inequality since 1969. Between 1969 and 1993, the gap between earnings at the 90th and 10th percentiles climbed 67 percent in the most trade-affected industries, but only 17 percent in the least trade-affected industries. However, the timing of the rise in inequality does not seem consistent with the international trade explanation. Compared with inequality in the least trade-affected industries, inequality in the trade sector rose fastest during the decade after 1969. Since 1979, inequality has grown faster in nontrade industries. This is surprising in view of the fact that U.S. trade problems and manufactured imports were concentrated in the period after 1979.

If the earnings distributions of men and women are combined and the overall pattern of inequality within major industries is examined, the increase in inequality in the most trade-affected industries does not seem especially large. The 90:10 earnings ratio rose 29 percent between 1969 and 1993, exactly the same percentage as the rise in inequality across all industries.

The same pattern of relative earnings changes is apparent when trends among workers with different schooling levels are compared. Chart 5 shows trends in the educational pay differential in industries most affected by trade and in all industries for full-time wage and salary workers (male and female) in two broad educational categories—those who have not completed high school and those with one to three years of college education.[14] The median earnings were first calculated and then the ratio of median earnings of workers with less than a high school diploma to median earnings of workers in the same industry with one to three years of college.

Educational pay differentials rose in every industry and for both sexes. However, the differentials did not rise faster in industries most affected by trade than in other industries. For working men as a group, the differential for post-college education rose 36 percent between 1969 and 1993; for men in trade-affected industries, the post-college pay premium rose 33 percent. At the other end of the educational scale, the gap in pay between high school dropouts and men with some college rose exactly as fast among men in trade-affected industries as it did among men as a whole (top panel of Chart 5). Women in the trade-affected industries experienced a somewhat greater increase in educational pay differentials than women in other industries, but the difference was not large (bottom panel of Chart 5).

CHART 5

MEDIAN PAY RECEIVED BY FULL-TIME WORKERS WITH LESS THAN HIGH SCHOOL DIPLOMA AS PERCENT OF PAY RECEIVED BY WORKERS WITH 1 TO 3 YEARS OF COLLEGE IN TRADE-AFFECTED AND ALL INDUSTRIES

Males

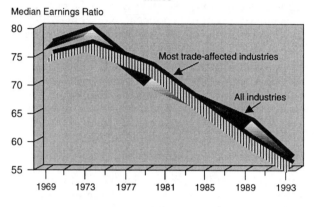

Females

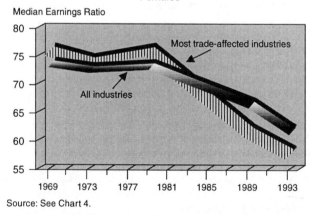

Source: See Chart 4.

If the U.S. labor market is competitive and efficient, pay differentials should rise and fall across industries in a parallel fashion. The fact that wage inequality and educational pay differentials have moved similarly across different industries offers little evidence about the relative influence of trade and technology on the earnings distribution. But if trade from newly industrializing countries is putting special pressure on employers in trade-affected industries, those industries should shed low wage workers faster than industries in which competitive pressure comes exclusively from other domestic firms. To determine whether the data support this hypothesis, I estimated the labor input in broad skill classes. After dividing U.S. workers into five broad educational categories, I measured the number of full-time equivalent employees who contribute to production in each of the major industrial groups. According to these calculations, 38 percent of male full-time equivalent employees in 1969 had less than a high school diploma; 32 percent had graduated from secondary school; 16 percent had some college; and the remaining 14 percent had either completed college or had obtained additional schooling after graduating from college.

U.S. workers in the industries most affected by trade have somewhat less schooling than other workers. In 1969, for example, 42 percent of male full-time equivalent workers in trade-affected industries and 45 percent of female full-time equivalent workers in those industries had not completed high school. Over the next 24 years, trade-affected industries slashed the number of less educated workers on their payrolls. By 1993, only 18 percent of male workers and 17 percent of female workers in those industries lacked a high school diploma. Although the reduction in the use of less skilled workers was large, it was no larger than reductions that occurred in other industries. For example, the percentage of male workers without a high school diploma in least trade-affected industries fell from 35 percent to 13 percent in the same period, a drop of almost two-thirds.

Chart 6 shows trends in the use of full-time equivalent workers with less than a high school diploma. The top panel shows the percentage of the full-time equivalent workforce with less than a high school degree in industries that are most affected and least affected by trade. Again, the trends in the two kinds of industries are similar. The lower panel shows the trend in the use of workers with less than a high school education when the utilization rate in 1969 was normalized at 100. This panel suggests that by 1993 the use of less skilled workers fell 59 percent in industries most affected by trade; it fell 67 percent in the industries least affected by trade.

Chart 6 offers little evidence that less skilled workers were displaced faster in trade-affected than in nontrade-affected industries. (The same conclusion is reached if educational attainment is divided into narrower classes.) If anything, the percentage decline in the use of low skilled workers has been slightly greater in industries unaffected by trade than it has been in trade-affected industries. This pattern of labor utilization is hard to square with the claim that earnings inequality has been driven mainly by pressures originating from foreign trade. Unless their hiring decisions were affected by some other set of factors (including changes in the technology of production), employers who do not produce internationally traded products should have no reason to reduce the intensity of their use of unskilled and semiskilled labor. The shrinking relative wage of less skilled workers offers employers in those industries an

CHART 6

UTILIZATION OF WORKERS WITH LESS THAN HIGH SCHOOL DIPLOMA IN TRADE-AFFECTED AND NONTRADE-AFFECTED INDUSTRIES

Percent of workforce with less than high school diploma

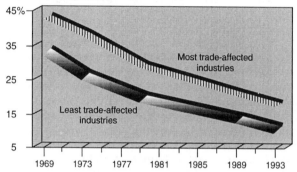

% of Full-Time Equivalents

Proportion of workforce with less than high school diploma (1969 = 100)

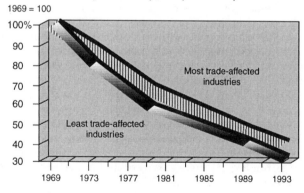

1969 = 100

Source: See Chart 4.

incentive to substitute unskilled for skilled labor with existing production methods, as well as a powerful inducement to seek out new production technologies that take advantage of the increasingly cheap factor of production. Employers in nontrade industries have instead chosen to reduce their use of less skilled workers. It would be difficult to find an explanation for this decision based on international trade theory.

On the other hand, technological change does provide a straightforward explanation for the parallel trends inside and outside traded goods industries. Changes in technology that have enabled employers in nontrade industries to shed less skilled labor may be operating in trade-affected industries as well. In that case, the proportion of inequality that is attributable to liberalized trade or rising imports from developing countries must be modest.

TECHNOLOGICAL CHANGE AND EARNINGS INEQUALITY

Among economists who have examined the issue, the leading explanation for rising earned income inequality is that changes in technology have favored workers with advanced skills and have reduced the demand for workers with below-average skills.[15] This view suggests that developments in the technology of production have pushed employers to demand greater numbers of workers with advanced skills. Although the proportion of very highly trained and educated workers is comparatively small, these workers have obtained a disproportionate share of all earnings gains since 1979. Innovations such as the personal computer may have given an edge to highly educated and technically adept workers. According to this theory, the introduction of new machines and new production processes has given a significant advantage to workers possessing the skills and the background needed to exploit them.

Direct evidence about the effects of technological change on wage inequality is hard to find. The Census Bureau and the U.S. Department of Labor do not routinely survey employers to determine whether and how much their skill requirements have changed. Analysts must draw conclusions about shifts in technology using evidence about changes in the relative price of different kinds of labor and the relative supply of those kinds of workers. Thus, the shift in the industrial composition of demand can explain only a small share of the change in the structure of wages. Further, most economists who have carefully studied the question find that supply-side changes also account for only a small percentage of the growth in inequality. This has led many economists to conclude that technological change must be an important part of the explanation of greater earnings inequality.

Some readers might assume that it is inevitable that technological change will boost employers' demand for advanced skills. But even if this were true, it would not necessarily lead to wider pay differentials between skilled and unskilled workers. Relative wage changes also depend on trends in the relative abundance of skills. If the increasing supply of skilled workers is keeping pace with the increasing demand, pay differentials might remain unchanged or fall, as they did during the 1960s. The huge rise in the proportion of the workforce that has obtained a high school diploma or education beyond high school has helped keep down the pay premium received by highly educated workers. The size of the pay premium is affected by the race between technology-driven demand for a more skilled workforce and public policies and private actions that produce an increase in the supply of highly trained workers.

It is also important to recognize that technological progress may not always increase the demand for advanced skills. For example, it is widely believed that technological progress sometimes results in a "dumbed-down" production process. Many factory assembly lines require constant repetition of very simple tasks. Before the introduction of the assembly line, many workers performed a much wider variety of tasks that required considerable effort and ability to learn. Retail clerks were once obliged to use simple arithmetic to calculate bills and make change. Now many push buttons on electronic machines that are illustrated with pictures of the items for sale. Taxes and change are computed by cash registers rather than clerks, who may have only a hazy knowledge of arithmetic. If technological advance helps to create dumbed-down jobs, it is hard to see why skill differentials would widen; rather, they should narrow. Assuming that skilled workers continue to disdain these kinds of jobs, the relative wages of unskilled workers will almost certainly rise.

Some simple types of evidence suggest that recent technological change has favored the more skilled over the less skilled. For example, the pay premium offered to highly educated workers soared after 1979. In addition, pay increases have been greater in high skilled than in low skilled occupations. The fast-growing occupations within most industries are those requiring high levels of education and skill. This is confirmed by Labor Department projections that the most rapid employment gains have been and will continue to be in occupations requiring advanced skills. Economists have also found evidence of a positive association between simple measures of technological progress and the rate of change within industries in pay premiums for advanced education. Faster technological change, as indicated by, for example, research and development spending or high technology capital, is associated with increasing pay differentials between highly educated and less educated workers.[16]

One economist, Alan Krueger, has also found that workers who used computers on the job enjoyed faster wage increases in the 1980s than workers who did not use or know how to use them.[17] Although the number of computer-literate workers was comparatively small, they received a disproportionate share of all wage gains in the middle and late 1980s. Computer use is particularly common among well-educated workers in skilled occupations, but it is becoming increasingly common among all types of workers. Krueger's research suggests that the introduction of microcomputers has conferred a significant advantage on workers who have the skills and background necessary to learn how to use them. Unskilled workers, by definition, do not fit this description.

Although this kind of evidence indicates that technological progress has favored the more skilled, especially since 1979, it is unclear how large a percentage of the growth in overall wage inequality the evidence can explain. About two-thirds of the jump in earnings inequality among male workers has occurred because of widening earnings differences among workers who have the same amount of education and previous work experience.[18] Only one-third of the increase has occurred because of larger pay disparities among groups with different levels of schooling or work experience.

Several researchers have suggested that the sharp increase in inequality within groups of workers defined by their age, education, occupation, industry, and work experience signals larger wage premiums for unmeasured job skills. Analysts who examine wage developments can directly observe only the dimensions of skill that are measured on census surveys, such as education, occupation, and work experience. If researchers could measure other dimensions of skill or ability such as specific job training or general aptitude, they might be able to obtain a clearer picture of the ultimate sources of growing wage inequality. Most economists believe that if these dimensions could be measured accurately, the measurements would show that inequality across skill categories has risen in recent years. The increases in skill premiums reflect the fact that employers' demand for highly skilled workers has outpaced the supply. To explain the surge in wage inequality that has occurred since the early 1980s, some economists hypothesize that the trend toward increased demand for highly skilled workers that has been driven by changes in technology has accelerated. So far, however, the evidence is suggestive rather than conclusive.

By and large, then, it is inconclusive whether technological change is behind recent inequality trends because, as noted at the outset, economists cannot directly observe the skill requirements embodied in specific technological advances. In fact, economists have little evidence about the skill requirements embodied in most production processes. What they observe instead is the skill distributions of workers employed in different plants or industries and the absolute levels of pay of workers in different skill classes. The changing pattern of use of workers in different skill classes and the changing pattern of their pay are easy to "explain" by saying that production technology has changed in a way that makes production more intensive in its requirement for skill. But this statement simply means that other explanations of changing pay patterns (such as increasing international trade or weaker labor unions) cannot satisfactorily account for a large percentage of the trend in the relative wage structure or the relative intensity of use of workers at different skill levels. The explanation is analogous to "explaining" the slowdown in productivity growth after 1973 by saying that there has been a slowdown in technological advance. In both cases, the explanation would be more useful and convincing if it were based on specific evidence about technological change that would tend to support the explanation.

Readers should also bear in mind that technology is a very broad economic concept. One standard economic textbook defines it as the "state of knowledge about the various methods that might be used to transform inputs into outputs."[19] The personal computer is one technological advance with which most people are familiar. The dramatic decline in the cost of stand-alone computers has influenced the way goods and services are produced in a wide variety of industries and occupations. Arguably, this change has put a premium on the ability of workers to acquire the skills needed to operate computers. Workers who possess this ability might be favored; workers who lack it might suffer.

But this is only one in a broad class of workplace changes that fits economists' definition of technological change. The introduction of the assembly line in automobile production during the early 20th century also represented technological change. The assembly line technique was driven mainly not by the development of a new piece of machinery, but by a different and more efficient concept of how workers and materials could be organized to produce an automobile.

Sometimes neither machinery nor scientific advance is involved in a technological change. The evolution of corporate governance also represents a kind of technological change. As recently as the early 1970s, many observers believed that stockholders were too numerous and poorly organized to exert effective control over company management. As a consequence, lax, foolish, or unprofitable company managers were able to survive for as long as they could keep their companies out of bankruptcy. By the middle of the 1980s, it was plain that this view was seriously incomplete. Innovations such as leveraged buyouts made it possible for a small number of well-organized stockholders and lenders to take over a company's management and fundamentally change the direction of the corporation—for example, by modifying historical pay patterns in the company, selling off unprofitable operations, or outsourcing the production of important company inputs.

This kind of innovation can clearly influence pay disparities both within and between companies. Conservative managers may be reluctant to change traditional pay patterns in their companies. If maintenance staff have historically received the same pay as workers on the assembly line, orthodox managers may be reluctant to tamper with the historical pay ratio as long as the company remains out of bankruptcy. However, this pattern cannot survive long when managers realize they can be removed by organized stockholders determined to minimize costs. If maintenance workers can be hired at a lower wage than that paid to assembly line workers, these options will be chosen over the traditional pay pattern by managers who are zealous to minimize costs. Leveraged buyouts and other new corporate takeover techniques can lead to the removal of senior company managers reluctant to take cost-minimizing steps. Obviously, these kinds of steps can also lead to wider pay disparities. New techniques in corporate governance such as leveraged buyouts are not the type of innovation most people have in mind when discussing technological change as the main source of growing inequality.

Because measurable changes in the economy and in the structure of supply and demand for labor cannot account for most of the trend in wage disparities, economists then consider changes in the environment that are less easy to quantify. Technological change is undoubtedly one of the hardest to quantify, and it is equally hard to refute. The problem is that almost any observed pattern of change in relative factor proportions and factor prices can be explained by a shift in technology. Perhaps more troubling is the fact that skill-biased technological change is such a broad explanation for changes in the wage structure that it is not easy for economists and policymakers to devise concrete policies for significantly narrowing the wage gap. In that sense, technological change is not a particularly illuminating explanation for the recent growth in earnings inequality.

* * *

Over the past 25 years, the United States has seen a dramatic shift in the pattern of demand for workers with different levels of skill. Job opportunities for the less skilled have disappeared, and relative wages for the unskilled and semiskilled have plunged. These trends have not been confined to the traded goods industries, however. They are also evident in industries such as construction and retail trade where international trade plays only a small role. This suggests that trade cannot be the most important factor pushing down wages of the less skilled and pushing up overall inequality. Other factors must play a larger role.

Economists' leading alternative explanation for increased wage inequality is biased technological change. Changes in the technology of production, such as the invention of the personal computer and the introduction of new forms of business organization, have favored workers with greater skills and reduced the value of unskilled labor. However, economic deregulation, new patterns of immigration into the United States, the declining minimum wage, and the dwindling influence of labor unions have also contributed to the job woes of unskilled and semiskilled workers. Liberal trade with newly industrializing countries has undoubtedly hurt unskilled workers to some degree. But it is hard to believe that introducing new forms of trade protection will provide unskilled workers much relief. Too many other forces are combining to push their wages down.

Appendix

This appendix extends an earlier analysis that examined the sources of change in income inequality among all people between 1969 and 1993.[20] This extension focuses on changes in income inequality that can be attributed to changes in the level and distribution of different components of income. If total income is the sum of K different kinds of income, the Gini coefficient can be decomposed as

$$G = \sum_{k=1}^{K} S_k R_k G_k$$

where S_k is the share of total income from the kth component, R_k is a measure of the "Gini correlation" of the component, and G_k is the Gini coefficient of the kth income component. The Gini correlation, R_k, is calculated as the covariance between income source k and the rank of total income, divided by the covariance between income source k and the rank of source k. By definition, it ranges between -1 and 1. The share of overall inequality due to any source of income is calculated as

$$I_k = \frac{S_k R_k G_k}{G}$$

where the I_k's sum to 1. A source of income that reduces inequality (for example, means-tested transfers) will have a negative Gini correlation, R_k, and thus make a negative contribution to overall inequality.

One way to summarize the effect of a change in any of the income components is to decompose the change in the Gini coefficient between two time periods. The change in the Gini coefficient between years 0 and 1 can be written as

$$\Delta G = G_1 - G_0$$

$$= \sum_{1}^{K} (S_{k1} - S_{k0})\, G_{k1} R_{k1} + \sum_{1}^{K} S_{k1}\, (G_{k1} - G_{k0})\, R_{k1} + \sum_{1}^{K} S_{k1} G_{k1}\, (R_{k1} - R_{k0}) + \epsilon$$

where ϵ is a residual not accounted for in the decomposition. The total change in inequality can thus be decomposed along two dimensions: the contribution of each income source due to changes in the *share* of income from that source, changes in the Gini correlation of income from that source, and changes in the inequality or Gini coefficient of income from that source, or alternatively, as the contribution of changes in S_k, R_k, and G_k across income sources. The decomposition assumes that it is possible to hold all components in the decomposition constant but one, and to measure the impact of a change in that element on the level of inequality. To the extent that the different components are correlated with one another (for example, a change in family composition may occur as a result of a change in the wage distribution), the accounting can be misleading. In spite of this limitation, the decomposition is a worthwhile approximation for assessing the relative importance of changes in each income component under the assumption of independence.

Table A-1 shows the decomposition for the two subperiods covered by the data, 1969-79 and 1979-93. The table displays the decomposition based on four principal income sources—the earnings of male family heads, the earnings of female family heads, the combined earnings of other family members, and unearned cash income. The total change in the Gini coefficient to be explained is reported in the last column of the table. Between 1969 and 1979, for example, the Gini coefficient increased from 0.354 to 0.365, yielding an overall change of 0.011, or about 3 percent. The column immediately to the left shows the size of the unexplained residual. The residual is small in absolute value though large as a percentage of the change in the Gini in 1969-79; it is very small for the period 1979-93 both in absolute level and as a percentage of the actual change. The fourth column shows the total change "explained" by the Lerman-Yitzhaki decomposition. (This is simply the sum of the three entries in the columns immediately to the left.) Further to the left in the same row is the difference between the actual Gini coefficient in the second year and the Gini coefficient that would have occurred if all income shares, all Gini correlations, or all Gini coefficients were held constant at their levels in the initial year (and all other components changed to their new level). Thus, a negative term implies that the factor tended to reduce inequality over the period; a positive term implies that it increased inequality over the period.

The biggest jump in inequality occurred between 1979 and 1993, when the Gini coefficient rose 0.053, or about 15 percent. This period is the focus here. The Lerman-Yitzhaki decomposition implies that holding all income *shares* constant at their initial 1979 level would have yielded a Gini coefficient that was higher by 0.006 in 1993. In other words, the combined changes in the shares of income derived from the four income sources tended to slightly depress U.S. income inequality over the period compared with what inequality would have been if the income shares had remained unchanged. (Note the estimate of 0.006 in the bottom row of Table A-1.) This effect was due primarily to the shrinking share of male-head earnings in total family income, an income source that accounted for 60 percent of all income and 69 percent of all inequality among people in 1979. The shrinking share of male earnings was of course offset by the rising share of other income sources, principally female-head earnings. Increases in these shares tended to boost overall inequality. But the combined effect on inequality of the changed income shares from all four sources was slightly negative.

TABLE A-1

DECOMPOSITION OF CHANGE IN GINI COEFFICIENT BY INCOME SOURCE, 1969 TO 1993

Change Due to Income Source	Change Due to Factor			Total Change	Residual	Δ Gini
	S	R	G			
1969–79						
Male-head earnings	−0.037	−0.006	0.034	−0.009		
Due to no male head			*0.016*			
Due to no earnings of head			*0.012*			
Due to Gini among nonzeros			*0.005*			
Female-head earnings	0.012	−0.005	−0.005	0.002		
Due to no female head			*0.002*			
Due to no earnings of head			*−0.005*			
Due to Gini among nonzeros			*−0.002*			
Other earnings	0.001	0.001	0.000	0.002		
Nonlabor income	0.007	0.005	−0.002	0.010		
Total	**−0.017**	**−0.005**	**0.027**	**0.006**	**0.006**	**0.011**
1979–93						
Male-head earnings	−0.034	−0.002	0.031	−0.005		
Due to no male head			*0.010*			
Due to no earnings of head			*0.007*			
Due to Gini among nonzeros			*0.013*			
Female-head earnings	0.031	0.022	−0.004	0.049		
Due to no female head			*0.003*			
Due to no earnings of head			*−0.006*			
Due to Gini among nonzeros			*−0.001*			
Other earnings	−0.008	−0.001	0.000	−0.009		
Nonlabor income	0.006	0.016	0.000	0.023		
Total	**−0.006**	**0.035**	**0.028**	**0.057**	**−0.003**	**0.053**

Notes: Sample consists of all unrelated individuals and all persons who are members of families. The factor "S" refers to the share of adjusted income that is derived from income source *k*; "R" is the Gini correlation, i.e., the covariance between income source *k* and rank of total income; and "G" is the Gini coefficient of income from source *k*.

Source: Author's tabulations of 1970, 1980, and 1994 CPS files.

There was a sharp rise in the inequality of male-head earnings, a trend that outweighed the slight shift toward lower inequality in female-head earnings. The effect of a change in the Gini coefficient of an earnings source can be decomposed into three components: the effect of the change in the fraction of families with no male or female head; the effect of the change in the fraction with no earnings from the male or female head; and the pure effect of a rise in inequality among those who actually derived earnings from a male or female head. (Each of these effects is displayed in italicized rows in Table A-1.) The first of these terms measures a family composition effect; it shows what would have happened had there been no change in the distribution of people by family type. The second term captures the effect of changing labor force participation by measuring the effect of holding the fraction of nonearners constant at the initial level. The third term measures both a labor supply effect (through the amount of time worked during the year) and a wage effect. This last term comes closest to measuring the "pure" effect of a rise in earnings inequality among men or women with earnings.[21]

The rise in inequality of male earnings in 1979-93 was the product of all three factors just mentioned. Nearly one-third of the increase in the Gini coefficient of male-head earnings (0.013/0.031) was due to changing family composition, that is, to the rise in the proportion of people in families with no male head. The rate of female headship increased more slowly after 1979 than it did in the 1970s, however, making it unlikely that this trend was the result mainly of rising male earnings inequality. About a quarter of the increase in the male-head Gini coefficient after 1979 was the result of reduced male labor force participation in families where a male head was present (0.007/0.031). The remainder—roughly 40 percent—was caused by the rise in earnings inequality among men who continued to work (0.013/0.031). This decomposition suggests that while growing earnings inequality among men was indeed an important source of increased inequality after 1979, most of this increase was caused by the declining presence of adult males in U.S. families and the movement out of market work among male heads of families. Of course, the lower employment rate of adult males after 1979 may have been caused in part by wage developments, including developments that were the product of changing technology or increased international trade. Lower wages made work less attractive for some men, driving them from the workforce. But lower male participation rates were also fueled by the trend toward earlier retirement, a trend that was already visible during the 1960s and 1970s.[22]

The effect of higher Gini correlations was somewhat more important than the growth of inequality in the individual income components (compare the entries in column 2 with those in column 3 for the period 1979-93). Female-head earnings became more highly correlated with total family income after 1979, as did nonlabor income. Of the total increase in the Gini coefficient over this period, more than 40 percent is explained by the increased correlation of female earnings with the rank of income (0.022/0.053). Increases in female-head earnings and nonlabor income over the period were disproportionately concentrated among families with high incomes from other sources. This pattern is mainly the result of the sharp rise in the correlation of male- and female-head earnings after 1979. As noted in the main text, this source of higher inequality is very unlikely to be due, directly or indirectly, to either technological change or international trade.

Falling inequality in the distribution of female-head earnings was one of the few factors operating to reduce overall inequality after 1979. Most of this effect was produced by the continued entry of women into paid employment. By itself, this factor reduces inequality because it equalizes the distribution of female-head earnings across all people—fewer people are members of families with no female earnings. However, if the entry of women into the labor force was concentrated among women in high income families, the trend would increase the correlation of women's earnings with family income and hence raise inequality. Both factors were at work after 1979, but on balance, the growing correlation of female earnings with other family income produced a much bigger effect.

In sum, growing inequality in the distribution of male labor earnings accounted for slightly more than half of the growth in overall inequality between 1979 and 1993. About 40 percent of this increase, in turn, can be traced to the rise in earnings inequality among men who worked. But an even bigger part was caused by major changes in family composition and male employment rates. Fewer households contained working male heads of family. Labor market developments among women played an equally important role in the trend toward greater overall inequality. Female employment rates and earnings rose during the entire 1969-93 period, but the growth in women's earnings after 1979 was particularly concentrated among women in high income families, contributing to the sharp rise in inequality. Trends in the distribution of unearned income also played a role in boosting inequality. Increases in income from capital assets and from public and private pensions were especially common among families with a high rank in the income distribution. Other government transfer programs had little effect in ameliorating the trend toward inequality. If anything, these programs became less effective in redistributing incomes to low income families after 1979.

NOTES

The author gratefully acknowledges the research assistance of Sheryl Zohn and J.J. Prescott.

1. Frank Levy and Richard J. Murnane, "U.S. Earnings Levels and Earnings Inequality: A Review of Recent Trends and Proposed Explanations," *Journal of Economic Literature*, Vol. 30 (September 1992), pp. 1333-1381; and Richard B. Freeman, *When Earnings Diverge: Causes, Consequences, and Cures of the New Inequality in the U.S.* (Washington: National Policy Association, 1997).

2. The definition of "adjusted income per person" is

$$Y_A = \frac{Y_u}{F^\theta}$$

where A = adjusted money income per person; Yu = unadjusted total family income; F = number of people in the nuclear family unit; and Θ = adjustment for family size. For a person in a single-person household, adjusted income under this definition will always be equal to unadjusted total income. For a person in a larger family, adjusted income will be less than unadjusted family income, depending on the assumed value of Θ. The following analysis assumes that Θ = 0.5. Nuclear families are sometimes part of larger households containing two or more families or unrelated individuals. In that case, the family-size adjustment is a bit more complicated. See Lynn A. Karoly and Gary Burtless, "Demographic Change, Rising Earnings Inequality, and the Distribution of Personal Well-Being, 1959-1989," *Demography,* Vol. 32, No. 3 (August 1995), p. 382.

3. An alternative assumption is that Θ = 1.0. Under this assumption, adjusted income is equal to average income per person in the family. The assumption is equivalent to believing that there are no economies of scale in consumption. In contrast, the Census Bureau implicitly assumes that Θ = 0 when it calculates family income inequality.

4. All tabulations were performed using the public use version of the March CPS. The public use files are top-coded to preserve the confidentiality of respondents. The top-code values are not consistent over time, whether measured in constant dollars or at a fixed point in the top part of the income distribution. To make inequality measures consistent over time, I have consistently top-coded male earnings at the 96.9th percentile of the male earnings distribution and top-coded female earnings at the 99.5th percentile of the female earnings distribution. For that reason, and because the public use files are top-coded at a lower income level than the files available to the Census Bureau, my estimates of the Gini coefficient will differ from estimates of the Census Bureau or those I would have obtained with uncensored data.

5. Karoly and Burtless, "Demographic Change, Rising Earnings Inequality, and the Distribution of Personal Well-Being, 1959-1989."

6. For a person in a single-member household, this would be the exact amount (unadjusted) of earnings received by the household. For members of larger families, the amount of male earnings actually received was equivalent to the $13,600 received by a single-member household. For a member of a four-person family, for example, the average amount received would be 2 x $13,600, or $27,200. Nominal income amounts in each year have been deflated using the Consumer Price Index (CPI)-U-X1 deflator.

7. Robert I. Lerman and Shlomo Yitzhaki, "Income Inequality Effects by Income Source: A New Approach and Applications to the United States," *The Review of Economics and Statistics,* Vol. 67 (February 1985).

8. Karoly and Burtless, "Demographic Change, Rising Earnings Inequality, and the Distribution of Personal Well-Being, 1959-1989."

9. Gary Burtless, "International Trade and the Rise in Earnings Inequality," *Journal of Economic Literature,* Vol. 33 (June 1995), pp. 800-816; and William R. Cline, *Trade and Wage Inequality* (Washington: Institute for International Economics, 1997).

10. Mexicans and Americans do migrate across the border, of course. But the possibility of cross-border migration only reinforces the pressures that would tend to equalize wages in the two countries.

11. Wolfgang Stolper and Paul A. Samuelson, "Protection and Real Wages," *Review of Economic Studies,* Vol. 9 (1941), pp. 58-73.

12. Lawrence F. Katz and Kevin M. Murphy, "Changes in Relative Wages, 1963-1987: Supply and Demand Factors," *Quarterly Journal of Economics,* Vol. 107 (February 1992), pp. 35-78; John Bound and George Johnson, "Changes in the Structure of Wages During the 1980s: An Evaluation of Alternative Explanations," *American Economic Review,* Vol. 82 (June 1992), pp.

371-392; and Eli Berman, Stephen Machin, and John Bound, "Implications of Skill-Biased Technical Change: International Evidence," Department of Economics, Boston University, December 1996, mimeo.

13. Manufacturing, mining, and agriculture, forestry, and fisheries are classified as highly trade-affected industries. Construction, retail trade, personal services, professional and related services, and public administration are classified as non-trade-affected. Transportation, wholesale trade, finance, insurance, and real estate, business and repair services, and entertainment and recreation services are classified in an intermediate category. An effect of trade on these industries cannot be ruled out, but little of their output is internationally traded.

14. Changes in pay differentials among other educational groups would show a similar pattern. There is little systematic difference between the trends in trade-affected industries and in all U.S. industries.

15. In a survey of 18 interested economists attending a 1994 conference on earnings inequality at the Federal Reserve Bank of New York, the average respondent assigned 45 percent of the responsibility for increased U.S. wage inequality to changes in technology and just 11 percent of the responsibility to changes originating in foreign trade. Responsibility for the remaining 44 percent of the rise in inequality was assigned to a variety of factors, including the decline in unionization and minimum wage and the rise in immigration. David Brauer, Federal Reserve Bank of New York, personal communication, January 4, 1995.

16. For example, see Jacob Mincer, "Human Capital, Technology, and the Wage Structure: What Do Time Series Show?" NBER Working Paper 3581 (1991); and Steven G. Allen, "Technology and the Wage Structure," North Carolina State University, February 1997, mimeo.

17. Alan B. Krueger, "How Computers Have Changed the Wage Structure: Evidence from Microdata, 1984-89," *Quarterly Journal of Economics*, Vol. 108 (February 1993), pp. 33-60.

18. Gary Burtless, "Earnings Inequality over the Business and Demographic Cycles," in *A Future of Lousy Jobs? The Changing Structure of U.S. Wages*, ed. Gary Burtless (Washington: Brookings Institution, 1990), pp. 106-109.

19. Robert S. Pindyck and Daniel L. Rubinfeld, *Microeconomics*, 2nd ed. (New York: Macmillan, 1989), p. 167.

20. Karoly and Burtless, "Demographic Change, Rising Earnings Inequality, and the Distribution of Personal Well-Being, 1959-1989."

21. The estimated effect is not strictly comparable to estimates from other studies of wage inequality because it reflects my adjustment for differences in family size as well as a weighting procedure that adjusts for the number of people dependent on each worker's earned income. In general, however, the conclusions in this appendix are not sensitive to the decision to focus on inequality among people rather than among families, nor are they sensitive to the adjustments for family size. For further details, see Karoly and Burtless, "Demographic Change, Rising Earnings Inequality, and the Distribution of Personal Well-Being, 1959-1989."

22. Chinhui Juhn, "Decline of Male Labor Market Participation: The Role of Declining Labor Market Opportunities," *Quarterly Journal of Economics*, Vol. 107 (February 1992).

Chapter 7

Family Income Mobility—
How Much Is There, and Has It Changed?

◆

by Peter Gottschalk and Sheldon Danziger

Hᴵᴳʜ ʟᴇᴠᴇʟs ᴏꜰ ᴘᴏᴠᴇʀᴛʏ and inequality and their failure to decline to the levels of the 1970s, despite the economic recoveries of the 1980s and 1990s, are an unresolved problem of the American economy. Although the mean family income level in the United States is substantially higher than that in other industrialized countries, its poverty rate is one of the highest.[1] The ratcheting up of the official poverty rate from the 11-12 percent range in the 1970s to the 13-15 percent range in the 1980s and 1990s is due, in large part, to the substantial increase in family income inequality that has occurred over the past two decades.[2] The poverty-reducing effect of growth in mean family incomes has been offset by growth in the dispersion of income.

Rising inequality has generated intense public policy debate. Although most analysts agree that inequality has increased, some argue that the high, rising level of inequality would not be cause for concern if it were accompanied by increased family income mobility. Central to the debate is the extent of mobility in any given year and changes in the rate of mobility over time.

Inequality of yearly income may overstate the low income problem if people do not remain in the same place in the income distribution in successive years. If a family's low income in one year is offset by high income in another year, then inequality based on family income averaged over several years will be lower than inequality of annual income. Further, the trend in inequality may be overstated if the growth in inequality over the past two decades has been accompanied by growing mobility. Finally, cross-national comparisons of annual measures of poverty and inequality may present an overly pessimistic view of American living standards because they ignore cross-national differences in mobility. If there is more income mobility in the United States than elsewhere, then the perception that the United States is one of the most unequal industrialized countries based on annual income may be misleading.

To address these and related issues, new descriptive tables were prepared that show the level and trend in mobility using both annual and multiple-year measures of family income. The focus is on both short- and long-term mobility, and the recent American experience is contrasted with that of other industrialized countries.

Our work builds on a methodology recently developed to primarily analyze earnings mobility.[3] This chapter applies this framework to family incomes and discusses how mobility is measured and how it has changed over the past quarter century.[4] We conclude that there is no evidence that significant family income mobility increases have occurred or that family income mobility in America is significantly higher than it is in other industrialized countries. Thus, inequality in the 1990s, whether measured over one year or over longer periods, is substantially higher than it was two decades ago.

ANALYTICAL ISSUES

Mobility and Inequality

Mobility and inequality are closely related, but distinct concepts. Inequality measures the dispersion of personal earnings or family income in any year. Mobility measures how individuals or families move within the distribution between two points in time. If family income mobility is high, then a family with low income in one year is likely to have higher income in a subsequent year. Similarly, a high income family may lose its advantaged position over time. The greater the extent of income mobility, the greater the likelihood that a family will move among various parts of the distribution over time.

Although inequality and mobility are distinct concepts, they are often confused in public policy discussions. To clarify the concepts, we present an often used analogy that distinguishes between changes in inequality and changes in mobility. Then, we provide a more formal presentation that links these concepts to well-known statistical definitions.

Analogy

Income inequality among families at a point in time is analogous to the situation of a group of people who stay in a hotel with rooms that vary widely in quality.[5] Some rooms are luxurious, while others are spartan. The hotel guests, therefore, have unequal accommodations on any night. The extent of inequality at a point in time is reflected by the variation in the quality of the rooms in which guests sleep on any night.

Economic mobility is akin to movement between rooms. If every guest must stay in the same room on every night, there is no mobility. This analogy shows that information about the extent of mobility reveals nothing about the extent of inequality, and vice versa. Inequality and mobility are conceptually distinct. Hotels with large variations in room quality may have low or high mobility.

Both mobility and inequality, however, do affect inequality measured over longer time periods. If guests are moved randomly from room to room each night, then those in the best rooms on any night may find themselves in undesirable rooms the following night. In this case, inequality in the distribution of nightly room quality is still high because the wide variation in room quality has not changed. But if inequality were instead measured over a period of many nights, it would decline because a guest's initial good room assignment would tend to be offset by less luxurious accommodations on subsequent nights. Mobility over time would indeed partially offset the effects of nightly inequality.

The implication of this analogy for analyzing growth in mean family income, changes in inequality, and mobility should be clear.[6] The absolute well-being of the hotel guests is affected by three distinct changes that can occur: upgrading the furnishings of all rooms (growth), redistributing furniture among rooms (changes in inequality), or reshuffling people among rooms (mobility). If people living in sparsely furnished rooms are considered poor, then there are three ways for them to escape poverty: adding furniture to all rooms (growth), reallocating furniture from better furnished rooms to their rooms (decreases in inequality), or moving them to better rooms (mobility).[7]

Now consider the effects of growing inequality (each night the better rooms get even better furniture, while the quality of furniture in the least desirable rooms deteriorates). Inequality measured over multiple nights will now also increase, even if the extent of mobility continues to be substantial. Mobility can offset increased inequality only if the extent of mobility also increases. It is the change in mobility, not its level, that is relevant to discussions about increased inequality. This important distinction is often neglected by those who cite the extent of mobility as a reason for not being concerned about rising income inequality.

Statistical Concepts[8]

The relationships among growth, inequality, and mobility can be specified more precisely using standard statistical concepts. The basic building block is the joint distribution of family income (Yi) measured over T periods, $f(Y_1, Y_2, \ldots Y_T)$.[9] Economic growth is reflected in differences in the means of the marginal distributions. The extent of inequality is reflected in the variance of the marginal distribution in each year. Mobility is captured by the correlation in incomes across years, which reflects covariances as well as variances.

This framework demonstrates that mobility and inequality measure conceptually different aspects of the joint distribution of income. Knowing that mobility (as reflected in the correlation between income in two adjacent periods) is high provides no information about the extent of inequality in any period (as reflected in the variance).

Both mobility and single period inequality, however, affect long-run inequality, the variance of income averaged over multiple periods. Consider the distribution of $\overline{Y}_i$, income averaged over K periods for the ith individual:

(1)
$$\overline{Y}_i = \sum_{t=1}^{K} Y_{it}$$

The variance of this multiple period income, which reflects not only the covariance of income across years, but also the yearly variances, is given by

(2)
$$var(\overline{Y}) = \left[\frac{1}{K^2}\sum_{t=1}^{K} var(Y_t) + \sum_{t=1}^{K}\sum_{s \neq t} cov(Y_t, Y_s)\right] = \frac{\overline{var}}{K} + \frac{K-1}{K}\ \overline{cov}$$

$$\text{where}\quad \overline{var} = \frac{1}{K}\sum^{k} var(Y_t)$$

$$\text{and}\quad \overline{cov} = \frac{1}{K^2-K}\sum\sum cov(Y_s Y_t) \text{(see note 10)}$$

The variance of multiple period income ($var\ \overline{Y}$) is, therefore, a function of the average variance ($\overline{var}$) and the average of the covariances ($\overline{cov}$).[11]

Equation 2 shows that increased yearly inequality, as captured by increases in $\overline{var}$, must be offset by a sufficiently large increase in mobility, as captured by the decrease in $\overline{cov}$, or $var\ (\overline{Y})$ will also increase. The extent of mobility, as captured by the level of $\overline{cov}$, is irrelevant to changes in inequality.

The discussion now turns from the conceptual distinction between the level and trends in inequality and mobility to the measurement issues that must be resolved when studying either levels or trends in mobility. These include the choice of the measure of family income and the accounting period, whether to measure mobility using a single summary measure or to display the full transition matrix, and whether to use absolute or relative thresholds in constructing transition matrices.

Income Measure

The family income measure we use includes all forms of cash income, including transfers, but does not include in-kind transfers received, such as food stamps, nor does it subtract taxes paid. Two further issues must be addressed in determining the appropriate income concept—how inclusive to make the income-sharing unit and how to adjust for differences in the number of people in the unit.

Because the family best approximates the grouping of people who share income, we focus on family income.[12] However, families are not a good unit to follow over time because family structure changes often. Children moving out to form their own households, deaths of individuals, or the splitting of families through divorce or separation all lead to composition changes that make it difficult to define a family over time. Therefore, we follow persons rather than families. Each person is positioned in the income distribution based on total family income from all sources adjusted for family size.

The need for clarity in defining an appropriate income concept is illustrated by the misinterpretation of a widely cited study by Cox and Alm.[13] They assign individual income (not family income adjusted for family size differences) to each person 16 years and older in their sample. Although the authors and others have interpreted their results as measuring the extent of mobility out of poverty, their income definition does not identify people in poor families because poverty should be measured on the basis of family, not personal, income. For example, a 16-year-old with a part-time job in an affluent family may well fall in the lowest quintile of personal income in the initial year. But this person is clearly not poor nor at the bottom of the distribution based on the family's total income. The fact that 16 years later this child is observed as a 32-year-old adult, possibly with substantial personal income, tells nothing about mobility out of poverty, which is defined in terms of total family income adjusted by family size.

To adjust for family size, we calculate total family income divided by the poverty line (which increases with family size)—the income-to-needs ratio—for the family in which the individual resides in each year. For example, consider a 20-year-old who lives on his own in year 1 and with his wife in year 2. In year 1, his income is divided by the poverty line for a single person. In year 2, his income and that of his wife are summed and divided by the poverty line for a two-person family.

Accounting Period

The length of the accounting period affects the extent of mobility as well as the degree of inequality. Inasmuch as measures of inequality at a point in time reflect transitory changes in income that are offset over longer periods, inequality is reduced as the accounting period is lengthened. Mobility is also reduced when the accounting period is lengthened. For example, consider how mobility would be measured for a person who receives roughly the same total income each year, but who experiences large month-to-month fluctuations. Mobility measured on a monthly basis would be larger than mobility measured on an annual basis because fluctuations within any year would cancel out.

What is the appropriate accounting period? A standard economic model of utility-maximizing agents with access to capital markets and full information implies that individuals can offset shortfalls in income in one period by drawing down savings or by borrowing to smooth consumption. Under these assumptions, families with low income in one period do not necessarily experience economic hardship. What matters is the average multiperiod (or permanent) income to which they have access.[14]

This model implies that longer accounting periods provide more appropriate inequality and mobility measures. However, this assumes that families can smooth transitory fluctuations in income by lending or borrowing. This may be a reasonable assumption for high income families who can rely on savings or who have access to capital markets to smooth transitory fluctuations. However, for low income or young families with little or no savings and limited access to capital markets to smooth consumption, the appropriate accounting period would be shorter, certainly not many years, and possibly even shorter than a year.[15]

In our empirical work reported below, we use two different accounting periods to show the sensitivity of our results to changes in this parameter. Because the data set we use does not measure income over periods shorter than a year, our shortest accounting period is annual income. We also measure inequality and mobility using a three-year accounting period. Extending the accounting period to three years eliminates most of the effects of short-term income fluctuations.

Absolute Versus Relative Mobility

As discussed above, economic growth and mobility are conceptually distinct concepts. Growth refers to changes in the absolute level of the mean of the income distribution in each year; mobility refers to the extent to which people change relative positions across years. However, the term mobility is sometimes used in the media or in policy discourse to refer to changes in the level of absolute income, rather than to changes in relative income.

Consider the statement that "prosperity brings upward mobility." As commonly used, this implies that economic booms raise average living standards across the income distribution. However, it reveals little about mobility (or about inequality) because it does not indicate whether those at the bottom of the distribution stayed there or whether they moved up relative to other families. Such statements are almost always about changes in the mean of the income distribution, not about the degree of persistence in income.

We stress that economic growth should not be confused with mobility. Nonetheless, an analysis of absolute changes in income for families starting at different points in the distribution may be of interest in its own right. Therefore, we provide measures of "absolute mobility" that show changes in income levels for those starting at various points in the distribution. Consider, for example, how mobility would be measured if rapid economic growth produced a doubling in the real income of every family. An absolute measure of mobility would indicate that low and high income families had experienced upward mobility as they all moved into higher income categories. These family income increases reflect economic growth, not relative mobility. As a result, our empirical work emphasizes measures of relative mobility that change only when people change their relative position in the income distribution.

Measures of Relative Mobility

Several alternative measures of mobility have been proposed.[16] Some measures, such as the proportion of people changing quintiles or the intertemporal correlation coefficient, summarize mobility as a single number. These summary measures, however, provide limited information and do not reveal where in the distribution transitions have taken place. For example, transitions may not be symmetric—a greater percentage of people may experience mobility out of the bottom decile than out of the top decile.[17] To preserve information, we present the full transition matrix wherever possible. These contingency tables show the proportion of people in income group i in year t who moved to income group j in year t+k. These tables not only show the proportion of people changing categories, but they also provide information on the magnitude of the movement. For example, a different picture emerges if all those leaving the lowest quintile move into the second lowest quintile or if they move into the highest quintile.

To measure relative mobility, we classify people in each year into quintiles based on their family income-to-needs ratios and tabulate the proportion of people in quintile i in year t who move to quintile j in year t+k. By definition, 20 percent of the population are placed in each quintile in each year. These transition matrices reflect only changes in relative positions. For every person who moves out of any quintile, another person must move into that quintile.

In contrast, measures of absolute mobility use fixed, initial-year quintile cutoffs to determine the rankings in both year t and year t+k. For example, if the lowest quintile in 1968 includes individuals in families with income-to-needs ratios below 1.3, then this same cutoff value is used to define groups in the terminal year. Because the real income levels used to define the quintiles are fixed, the percentage of people in each income group in the terminal year will vary, depending on growth in the mean, changes in inequality, and changes in relative mobility.

Although transition matrices provide a rich picture of economic mobility, they capture only movements across groups, not family income changes within the same group. These movements can be captured by making the groupings smaller (e.g., deciles instead of quintiles), but at the cost of higher sampling variability. Our choice of quintiles reflects this trade-off.

DATA SET, SAMPLE, AND VARIABLE DEFINITIONS

Because we are interested in both the extent of and the changes in mobility, we must use a sufficiently long panel to observe how income transition matrices have changed over time. We analyze data on total money income from all sources and all family members from the Panel Study of Income Dynamics (PSID). The PSID offers the longest continuous income data on a nationally representative sample of families, starting in 1968 and continuing to the present. We use data through 1991, the most recent year for which data were available when we began our empirical work.

There are two problems with the PSID data for our purposes. First, income is measured only on a yearly basis, which we have suggested may be too long an accounting period for people who are credit constrained. However, alternative longitudinal data sets that gather information on monthly income, such as the Survey of Income and Program Participation (SIPP), cover too short a period to analyze long-term income dynamics or changes in mobility during the 1970s and 1980s.

A second potential problem is that roughly one-half of the original panel members were no longer in the sample by the end of the 1980s. Whether this attrition biases estimates of mobility depends on whether the families continuing to participate in the study have mobility rates that are representative of the entire population. Although the amount of attrition in the PSID is substantial, Fitzgerald, Gottschalk, and Moffitt conclude that using sample weights can largely overcome any biasing effects of attrition on the variables they examine.[18]

Our sample consists of all those between the ages of 22 and 62 with valid income-to-needs ratios at the beginning and end of the periods being analyzed. For example, to construct the 1979-89 transition matrix, we included all people between the ages of 22 and 52 in 1979 who had valid income-to-needs ratios in 1979 and 1989. By 1989, these people were between the ages of 32 and 62. We excluded those under age 22 to avoid including intergenerational mobility effects associated with children leaving their parental homes and setting up their own households. We excluded those over 62 because the elderly may have lower income but higher consumption when they draw down their assets after retirement.

EXTENT OF MOBILITY

We start by describing the extent of mobility using both relative and absolute definitions. Then we examine whether these mobility rates have changed in recent years.

Relative Mobility

Table 1 presents the extent of single-year income mobility between 1990 and 1991. It shows that 75.1 percent of people in the lowest quintile in 1990 were also in the lowest quintile in 1991. Of the remaining 24.9 percent who moved out of the lowest quintile, about 80 percent (19.5/24.9) moved into the second quintile. In other words, 94.6 percent (75.1 plus 19.5 percent) of individuals who started in the lowest quintile

TABLE 1

SHORT-TERM RELATIVE MOBILITY: ONE-YEAR TRANSITION PROBABILITIES BETWEEN 1990 AND 1991 (%)

1990 Quintiles	1991 Quintiles					
	1st Quintile	2nd Quintile	3rd Quintile	4th Quintile	5th Quintile	Total
1st Quintile	75.1	19.5	3.3	1.4	0.7	100.0
2nd Quintile	18.0	57.0	20.5	3.3	1.2	100.0
3rd Quintile	4.0	17.0	57.9	19.1	1.9	100.0
4th Quintile	1.9	5.2	15.6	60.4	17.0	100.0
5th Quintile	1.0	1.4	2.9	15.6	79.2	100.0
Total	100.0	100.0	100.0	100.0	100.0	100.0

Note: All tables are based on weighted data; totals may not add to 100.0 because of rounding; unweighted n = 12,242.

Source: For all tables, computations by authors from Panel Study of Income Dynamics microdata. Data are used through 1991, the most recent year for which data were available when the authors began their empirical work.

of family income-to-needs ratios in 1990 ended up in the first or second quintile one year later.

There was also relatively little mobility out of the highest quintile. Of those in the top quintile in 1990, 79.2 percent remained there and 94.8 percent ended up in one of the top two quintiles.

Mobility out of the middle three quintiles was larger, as people starting in the middle can move either up or down. In contrast, those in the lowest quintile who experience income declines cannot fall further; those in the top quintile who experience increases cannot move higher.[19] About 60 percent of people in each of the middle three quintiles stayed in the same quintile; less than 8 percent moved up or down more than one quintile.

Although mobility rates between 1990 and 1991 for all people were relatively low, there were substantial differences across demographic groups. Table 2 shows mobility rates out of the lowest and highest quintiles for people classified by race and education (college graduate or less). The data also show mobility rates for people who are often assumed to be mired in poverty—women with less than a college education who are family heads and who receive cash welfare.

Individuals with these demographic attributes have very different prospects for mobility. Consistent with Table 1, 24.9 percent of all people

TABLE 2

PROBABILITY OF MOVING OUT OF LOWEST AND HIGHEST QUINTILES BETWEEN 1990 AND 1991 BY CHARACTERISTIC IN 1990

	Moving Up from Lowest Quintile (%)	n	Moving Down from Highest Quintile (%)	n
All	24.9	3,951	20.8	1,513
Nonwhite	14.4	2,075	26.9	202
White	29.7	1,876	20.5	1,311
Less than College	23.7	3,844	27.7	754
Welfare Recipients	7.5	578		
Nonwhite	7.8	383		
White	7.1	195		
College or More	41.8	107	14.8	759

Note: n is the number of unweighted observations in each group.

in the lowest quintile in 1990 moved into higher quintiles in 1991. Mobility was greater for whites than for nonwhites (29.7 versus 14.4 percent) and for college graduates than for those without college degrees (41.8 versus 23.7 percent).[20] Upward mobility was especially low for welfare recipients; only 7.5 percent of them left the lowest quintile.

People in demographic categories with higher probabilities of leaving the lowest quintile had smaller probabilities of leaving the highest quintile. For example, 20.5 percent of whites, but 26.9 percent of nonwhites, and 14.8 percent of college graduates, but 27.7 percent of those without a college degree, fell from the highest quintile.

Although the one-year transition rates indicate relatively little mobility, it is possible that, with more years to experience income changes, mobility measured across a longer period would be greater. For example, a person with high family income in the initial year might experience economic difficulties and, after a few years, might slowly fall from the top quintile, or a person might move slowly to successively higher quintiles, showing little change between adjacent years, but large changes across decades

To address longer-term mobility, Table 3 shows the probabilities of changing quintiles between 1968 and 1991 for people who were between the ages of 22 and 39 in 1968 (and hence, between 45 and 62 in 1991).[21] Over this 23-year period, more changes in relative positions occurred than over a 2-year period. For example, 46.9 percent of the people in the

TABLE 3

**LONG-TERM RELATIVE MOBILITY: TRANSITION PROBABILITIES
BETWEEN 1968 AND 1991 BASED ON ANNUAL INCOME (%)**

1968 Quintiles	1991 Quintiles					
	1st Quintile	2nd Quintile	3rd Quintile	4th Quintile	5th Quintile	Total
1st Quintile	46.9	25.1	17.7	9.0	1.3	100.0
2nd Quintile	24.2	24.8	22.3	19.1	9.7	100.0
3rd Quintile	10.8	20.5	20.5	27.0	21.2	100.0
4th Quintile	10.4	16.4	27.0	20.4	25.9	100.0
5th Quintile	7.5	13.0	13.7	24.2	41.6	100.0
Total	100.0	100.0	100.0	100.0	100.0	100.0

Note: The sample includes 1,909 unweighted persons who had valid income observations in both 1968 and 1991 and who were between the ages of 22 and 39 in 1968; totals may not add to 100.0 due to rounding.

lowest quintile in 1968 were still in the lowest quintile in 1991. Nearly one-half of those who had moved up landed in the second quintile (25.1/53.1), and 1.3 percent had made it all the way to the top quintile.

Whether this represents a little or a lot of mobility for those starting at the bottom is akin to asking whether a bottle is half full or half empty. The fact that 46.9 percent of those in the bottom quintile were still there and another 25.1 percent stayed near the bottom over a 23-year period indicates substantial immobility. However, the fact that about a quarter of those who were in the bottom quintile in 1968 moved above the 40th percentile by 1991 (the top of the second quintile) shows that many low income people do not remain persistently at the bottom of the distribution.

Movements out of the top quintile also show substantial long-term mobility. Of those in the top quintile in 1968, 41.6 percent were still there in 1991. Most of those moving down ended up in the second or third highest quintile, but about 13 percent of the movers (7.5/58.4) had fallen to the bottom quintile. Likewise, the probability of moving out of the middle three quintiles over this 23-year period was substantially higher than the one-year exit probabilities shown in Table 1.

So far we have placed individuals into quintiles in each year based on the annual income-to-needs ratio of their families. As discussed above, lengthening the accounting period has the advantage of reducing the effects of transitory income fluctuations, which can be smoothed by people with access to capital markets.

Table 4 illustrates the effect of lengthening the accounting period. In this table, people are classified into quintiles based on average income for 1968, 1969, and 1970 in the initial period and for 1989, 1990, and 1991 in the final period. As expected, mobility of three-year average income was somewhat lower than mobility based on single-year income. The differences, however, were small. When the probabilities from Table 3 (which are based on one-year income) are compared with the corresponding ones from Table 4 (which are based on three-year average income), the proportion remaining in the lowest quintile increases from 46.9 to 53.8 percent. Likewise, the proportion of people staying in the top quintile increases from 41.6 to 46.1 percent.

Table 5, similar to Table 2, shows the probability of moving out of the lowest and highest quintiles for people classified by their demographic characteristics and using three-year average income. Again, nonwhite individuals are substantially less likely than whites to move up from the lowest quintile, but they are less likely to move down from the highest quintile.[22] People with less than a college education are also much less likely to escape from the bottom, but much more likely to fall from the top, than college graduates. Likewise, women with less than a college education who received welfare in the 1968 period had a low probability of escaping from the bottom quintile.

Absolute Mobility

Absolute mobility is measured as the probability that a person starting in a given quintile has an income outside the fixed (inflation-ad-

---

TABLE 4

LONG-TERM RELATIVE MOBILITY: TRANSITION PROBABILITIES BETWEEN 1968 AND 1991 BASED ON THREE-YEAR AVERAGE INCOME (%)

1968-70 Quintiles	1989-91 Quintiles					
	1st Quintile	2nd Quintile	3rd Quintile	4th Quintile	5th Quintile	Total
1st Quintile	53.8	21.8	18.8	4.8	0.9	100.0
2nd Quintile	22.7	25.4	18.5	25.8	7.7	100.0
3rd Quintile	11.1	21.4	24.4	27.8	15.4	100.0
4th Quintile	5.3	22.6	23.0	19.3	29.8	100.0
5th Quintile	7.0	8.6	16.2	22.2	46.1	100.0
Total	100.0	100.0	100.0	100.0	100.0	100.0

Note: Income is averaged over the 1968 to 1970 period for the row quintiles and 1989 to 1991 for the column quintiles; totals may not add to 100.0 because of rounding; unweighted n = 1,840.

TABLE 5

**PROBABILITY OF MOVING OUT OF LOWEST AND HIGHEST QUINTILES
BASED ON THREE-YEAR AVERAGE INCOME (1968-70 AND 1989-91)
BY CHARACTERISTIC IN 1968**

| | Three-Year Average Income | | | |
	Moving Up from Lowest Quintile (%)	n	Moving Down from Highest Quintile (%)	n
All	46.2	647	53.9	260
Nonwhite	28.0	409	37.5	24
White	53.6	238	55.4	236
Less than College	45.5	638	65.2	145
Welfare Recipients	22.2	177		
Nonwhite	17.2	140		
White	27.6	37		
College or More	78.2	9	41.7	115

Note: n is the number of unweighted observations in each group.

justed) bounds of that quintile in a subsequent period. For example, we present the probability that a person in the lowest quintile in 1968 had an income in 1991 that exceeded the 1968 boundary between the first and second quintiles. Absolute mobility is affected by increases in income associated with the aging of the cohort, by increases in income due to economic growth, and by changes in income inequality, as well as by relative mobility.

The transition matrix shown in Table 6 is based on the 1968-70 average income-to-needs ratios of respondents between the ages of 22 and 39 in 1968. The 1989-91 cutoffs are the same (inflation adjusted) as those used to divide the sample into quintiles in the 1968-70 period. The columns are labeled "groups" rather than "quintiles" because this formulation does not require that 20 percent of the sample fall into each group in the terminal period, as shown by the percentages in the bottom row.

Slow economic growth over these two decades and the aging of the sample reduced the percentage of people whose income-to-needs ratio was below the base year cutoff by half. By definition, 20 percent of the entire sample fell below the first quintile threshold in the late 1960s.[23] By the early 1990s, 10.0 percent of the sample had real incomes below this fixed threshold (bottom row of first column), and 51.0 percent of the

TABLE 6

LONG-TERM ABSOLUTE MOBILITY: TRANSITION PROBABILITIES BASED ON THREE-YEAR AVERAGE INCOME USING 1968-70 INCOME CUTOFFS (%)

1968-70 Quintiles	1989-91 Groupings					
	Group 1	Group 2	Group 3	Group 4	Group 5	Total
1st Quintile	31.0	25.4	11.1	21.1	11.4	100.0
2nd Quintile	9.5	14.6	17.0	16.3	42.5	100.0
3rd Quintile	4.5	8.2	12.7	17.4	57.1	100.0
4th Quintile	1.6	4.9	13.2	16.6	63.7	100.0
5th Quintile	3.6	5.2	4.4	6.8	80.1	100.0
Total	10.0	11.7	11.7	15.6	51.0	100.0

Note: Income is averaged over the 1968 to 1970 period for the row quintiles and 1989 to 1991 for the column groupings; unweighted n = 1,840 and includes persons between the ages of 22 and 39 in 1968.

sample had incomes above the 80th percentile two decades earlier (bottom row of fifth column).

The extent of this absolute mobility is impressive. Transitions across these boundaries, however, differ substantially by initial quintile. Of those who started in the lowest quintile in the late 1960s, 31 percent still had incomes below that fixed threshold two decades later, even though they were more than 20 years older. This represents a substantial persistence of low income over a period of positive, but slow economic growth and rising inequality. An additional 25.4 percent of those who started in the lowest quintile moved only into the next higher group.

On the other hand, some individuals who started in the lowest quintile made substantial absolute progress—11.4 percent ended up in the highest group.[24] Eighty percent of those in the top quintile in the late 1960s were still in the highest group two decades later. Among those who were in the highest income group in the early 1990s, more than one-half were also in the two highest quintiles in the late 1960s, and only 4.5 percent started from the lowest quintile in the late 1960s.[25]

Cross-National Comparisons[26]

One basis on which to judge whether mobility in the United States is high or low is to compare it with mobility in other industrialized countries. The United States has substantially more inequality than other Organization for Economic Cooperation and Development (OECD) countries. However, it is not an outlier with respect to income mobility.[27] One-year U.S. mobility rates resemble those of countries as different as France, Italy, and the Nordic countries. Of course, the United States, as well as each of these countries, has less inequality when a longer accounting period is used. However, because countries differ little in their extent of mobility, the rankings of countries in terms of inequality remain similar whether we use a multiyear or an annual accounting period.

The fact that the United States has a less regulated, more decentralized labor market than the Nordic countries or Germany has not generated greater economic mobility here, either in earnings or in family income. Similarly, the more extensive systems of social protection in the European countries have yielded lower poverty and lower family income inequality, but not at the cost of lower mobility.

HAS INCOME MOBILITY INCREASED?

Some analysts argue that because a substantial number of Americans move across income quintiles over time, there should not be too much concern about the well-documented increase in income inequality. Such a conclusion is inappropriate.[28] As we demonstrated earlier, only increases in mobility can offset increased income inequality. If the extent of mobility has stayed roughly constant over the past two decades, then increases in annual income inequality will translate directly into increased inequality using a multiple-year accounting period.[29]

Therefore, we have analyzed the trend in family income mobility to see if the extent of mobility has changed. Chart 1 focuses on relative mobility. It plots the probability that a person remained in the same quintile in adjacent years. For example, 62.7 percent of all people were in the same quintile in 1968 and 1969.[30] This annual probability declined to about 60.5 percent between 1974 and 1975, and then rose steadily through the 1980s, reaching a high of 65.9 percent between 1990 and 1991.

That the probability of staying in the same quintile increased into the early 1990s indicates that mobility was declining somewhat, not increasing, during the same period in which income inequality was rising.[31] This refutes the notion that enhanced mobility has offset increased family income inequality.

Chart 1 does not distinguish between people falling out of the top quintile and people rising out of the bottom quintile. U.S. social policies are concerned primarily with increasing mobility out of the bottom; thus, Chart 2 plots the probability of moving out of the lowest quintile in each pair of years (shaded line) as well as the probability of falling from the highest quintile. The probability of staying in the lowest and highest quintiles decreased moderately during the 1970s, indicating an increase in downward mobility for those who started at the top and an increase in upward mobility for those who started at the bottom. However, the patterns were reversed in the late 1970s. The probability that a

CHART 1

PERCENT STAYING IN SAME QUINTILE IN EACH PAIR OF YEARS, 1968-69 TO 1990-91

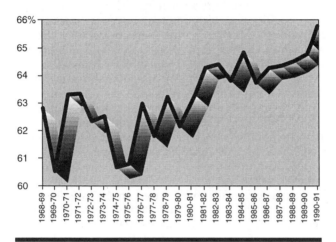

CHART 2

PERCENT STAYING IN THE LOWEST AND HIGHEST QUINTILES IN EACH PAIR OF YEARS, 1968-69 TO 1990-91

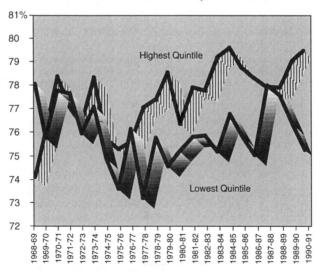

person in the lowest quintile would still be in the lowest quintile in the following year reached a low of 73 percent in 1978 and was above 75 percent by 1990. Similarly, the probability of staying in the highest quintile increased from 75 percent in 1975 to 79 percent in 1990. Thus, there is no evidence that short-term mobility increased during the 1980s. If anything, mobility was declining for people starting at the bottom.

The probability of changing quintiles between adjacent years is, by definition, based on one-year incomes. To illustrate mobility over longer periods, Table 7 shows measures of mobility across the decade-long periods 1969-79 and 1979-89, first using annual income, then using a three-year accounting period. With a one-year accounting period (columns 1 and 2), mobility shows a modest decline. For example, the probability of remaining in the lowest quintile remains virtually constant, but the probability of staying in the second quintile increased from 26.3 percent over the 1969-79 decade to 33.8 percent over the 1979-89 decade. The probability of remaining in the highest quintile increased from 49.1 to 51.3 percent.

The pattern in columns 3 and 4, based on the three-year accounting period, is somewhat stronger, with mobility declining in all five quintiles. Taken together, there is no evidence that mobility increased. Thus, the rise in income inequality was not offset by increased mobility.

CONCLUSIONS

Many of the chapters in this volume document that the quarter century since the early 1970s has been one of slow growth in family income and rising earnings and income inequality. In this chapter, we

TABLE 7

PROPORTION REMAINING IN SAME QUINTILE BETWEEN 1969 AND 1979 AND BETWEEN 1979 AND 1989, ONE- AND THREE-YEAR INCOME MEASURES (%)

Initial-Year Quintile	Annual Income in Each Year			Three-Year Average Income		
	(1) 1969-79	(2) 1979-89	Percentage Point Difference	(3) 1969-79	(4) 1979-89	Percentage Point Difference
1st Quintile	55.8	55.2	−0.6	62.6	63.2	0.6
2nd Quintile	26.3	33.8	7.5	34.5	36.8	2.3
3rd Quintile	25.9	25.1	−0.9	28.7	30.1	1.4
4th Quintile	28.4	28.9	0.5	31.3	33.9	2.6
5th Quintile	49.1	51.3	2.2	55.8	61.0	5.2

have examined mobility using a one-year and a three-year accounting period. We have examined mobility measured across adjacent years, across decades, and across a 23-year period. In all cases, we have shown that even though there is substantial income mobility, the extent of mobility has not increased over this period. As a result, the gaps between those at the top and those at the bottom have widened and have remained at least as persistent as they were in the 1970s.

There is no evidence that the growth in the economy since the mid-1980s has significantly reduced inequality or increased mobility. If America is to offset the detrimental effects of the rise in inequality over the past two decades, it will need to enhance labor market and income supplementation policies to shore up the incomes of those who have not been benefiting from economic growth—especially less educated workers and inner-city residents. The hope that mobility is sufficiently large or growing fast enough to offset the rise in inequality is inconsistent with the data presented in this chapter.

NOTES

The empirical results reported here were supported in part by a grant from the Russell Sage Foundation. Katherine Lang and Michael Hansen provided outstanding research assistance, and Pauline Lonergan, clerical assistance. We thank Isabel Sawhill, Lawrence Katz, Joseph Quinn, Robert Haveman, Markus Jantti, Barbara Wolfe, Eugene Smolensky, and Greg Duncan for constructive suggestions on a previous draft.

1. Giovanni A. Cornia and Sheldon Danziger, eds., *Child Poverty and Deprivation in the Industrialized Countries, 1944-1995* (Oxford: Clarendon Press, 1997); and Peter Gottschalk and Timothy M. Smeeding, in "Cross-National Comparisons of Earnings and Income Inequality," *Journal of Economic Literature*, Vol. 35, No. 2 (1997), pp. 633-687, present poverty rates for more than a dozen industrialized countries using a relative poverty line. The United States also has higher poverty rates than many countries with similar income levels even when absolute poverty thresholds are used.

2. For a discussion of the relationship between inequality and poverty, see Peter Gottschalk and Sheldon Danziger, "A Framework for Evaluating the Effects of Economic Growth and Transfers on Poverty," *American Economic Review*, Vol. 75, No. 1 (1985), pp. 153-161; and Sheldon Danziger and Peter Gottschalk, *America Unequal* (Cambridge, MA: Harvard University Press, 1995), Chap. 5.

3. For a review of the literature on earnings mobility, see Anthony B. Atkinson, Francis Bourguignon, and Christian Morrison, "Empirical Studies of Earnings Mobility," in *Fundamentals of Pure and Applied Economics*, ed. Jasques Lesourne and Hugo Sommenschien, Vol. 52 (Philadelphia: Harwood Academic Publishers, 1992). Family income mobility studies are more limited. They include Thomas Hungerford, "U.S. Income Mobility in the Seventies and Eighties," *Review of Income and Wealth*, Vol. 39, No. 4 (1993), pp. 403-417; Greg Duncan and Willard Rodgers, "Has Children's Poverty Become More Persistent?" *American Sociological Review*, Vol. 56, No. 4 (1991), pp. 538-550; Mark Condon and Isabel Sawhill, "Income Mobility and Permanent Income Inequality," Washington: Urban Institute, 1992, mimeo; and Greg Duncan, Timothy M. Smeeding, and Willard Rodgers, "W(h)ither the Middle Class? A Dynamic View," in *Poverty and Prosperity in the USA in the Late Twentieth Century*, ed. Dimitri Papadimitriou and Edward Wolff (New York: St. Martin's Press, 1993), pp. 240-271. Mary Jo Bane and David T. Ellwood, "Slipping into and out of Poverty: The Dynamics of Spells,"

Journal of Human Resources, Vol. 21, No. 1 (1986), pp. 1-23, focus on transitions into and out of poverty.

4. Robert Moffitt and Peter Gottschalk, "Trends in the Autocovariance Structure of Earnings in the U.S.," Johns Hopkins University, 1995, mimeo, examine changes in earnings mobility.

5. This analogy has been attributed to Joseph Schumpeter and was used by Condon and Sawhill, "Income Mobility and Permanent Income Inequality."

6. Throughout this chapter, the term economic growth refers to increases in the mean of income across all families. Because each family may experience life cycle increases in income, and because we do not adjust for age, these life cycle changes affect our measures of mobility. Such life cycle changes also affect cross-sectional measures of inequality, as families are at different points in their life cycles. Inasmuch as families can borrow early in their lives to offset low income when they are young, such life cycle effects tend to overstate inequality and mobility. To partially address this issue, we provide mobility measures of income averaged across a number of years.

7. Unless otherwise stated, we use the term poverty to mean income below a fixed real threshold. The poverty threshold, therefore, is not increased when real mean incomes grow.

8. This section assumes knowledge of basic statistics. It provides an alternative to the intuitive presentation provided earlier.

9. Assume income is measured in log form so that changes in scale do not affect measures of variances or covariances.

10. This term is an average covariance because the K by K covariance matrix has K^2 elements, K of which are variances.

11. It can be shown that the variance of multiple period income can never be larger than the average variance of single period income. This reflects the fact that the correlation between family income in any adjacent years must lie between −1 and 1.

12. Unrelated individuals are considered "one-person families."

13. Michael Cox and Richard Alm, "By Our Own Bootstraps: Economic Opportunity and the Dynamics of Income Distribution," *Federal Reserve Bank of Dallas Annual Report,* 1995.

14. In this case, all life cycle changes are eliminated.

15. Official measures of inequality and most academic studies use an annual accounting period, even though this is too short a period for families that can smooth consumption over multiple years and too long for families that are credit constrained.

16. See Atkinson, Bourguignon, and Morrison, "Empirical Studies of Earnings Mobility."

17. The form of the asymmetry may be more subtle. For example, probabilities of transitions out of the bottom may be similar to those out of the top. However, the extent of the fall of those leaving the top may be smaller than the rise of those leaving the bottom category.

18. John Fitzgerald, Peter Gottschalk, and Robert Moffitt, "An Analysis of Sample Attrition 1998 in Panel Data: The Michigan Panel Study of Income Dynamics," *Journal of Human Resources,* 1998 in press.

19. An exception to this would occur if people not in the lowest quintile lost sufficient income to put them below people previously in the lowest quintile, who were thereby pushed into a higher quintile. These effects are small because almost all transition matrices show greater persistence in the bottom and top groups than in the intermediate groups.

20. Duncan, Smeeding, and Rodgers, "W(h)ither the Middle Class?" show that part, but not all, of these differences reflect the fact that the mean income of blacks in the lowest decile is lower than that of whites in that decile, placing them further from the border.

21. Note that increases in income associated with the aging of this cohort do not necessarily imply greater mobility because the cutoffs in 1991 are based on the distribution of income for this cohort in 1991.

22. However, note the very small numbers of nonwhites in the highest quintile, n = 24.

23. All statements refer to the weighted sample.

24. This absolute upward mobility is largely a reflection of holding the thresholds fixed. The relative mobility matrix (Table 4) indicates that only 0.9 percent of the same sample had made it into the top group, whereas the thresholds classify 20 percent of persons into each quintile in the terminal year.

25. Because 20 percent of all people are in the first row, 11.4 percent of the 20 percent of all people who started in the lowest quintile ended up in the highest quintile. This is 4.5 percent of the 51 percent of all people who ended up in the highest quintile.

26. This section is based largely on Peter Gottschalk, "Inequality, Income Growth, and Mobility: The Basic Facts," *Journal of Economic Perspectives*, Vol. 11, No. 2 (1997), pp. 21-40.

27. For evidence on cross-national differences, see Rolfe Aaberg, Andres Björklund, Markus Jäntti et al., "Income Inequality and Income Mobility in the Scandinavian Countries Compared to the United States," University of Stockholm, Discussion Paper, January 1996; Richard V. Burkhauser, Douglas Holts-Eakim, and Stephen Rhody, "Mobility and Inequality in the 1980s: A Cross-National Comparison of the United States and Germany," in *The Distribution of Welfare and Household Production: International Perspectives*, ed. Stephen Jenkins, Arie Kapteyn, and Bernard van Praag (Cambridge: Cambridge University Press, 1996); " Organization for Economic Cooperation and Development (OECD), "Earnings Inequality, Low-Paid Employment and Earnings Mobility," *Employment Outlook, July 1996*, pp. 59-108; and Greg Duncan, Björn Gustafson, Richard Hauser et al., "Poverty Dynamics in Eight Countries," *Journal of Population Economics*, Vol. 6, No. 3 (1993), pp. 215-234.

28. See Cox and Alm, "By Our Own Bootstraps," for an example of this mistake.

29. See equation 2, page 95. If the average variance increases, then the variance of average income also increases, unless there is an offsetting change in the average covariance.

30. This is the sum of the diagonal elements in the 1968-69 transition matrix that is similar to the Table 1 matrix.

31. Trends in earnings mobility and income mobility seem to differ because Moffitt and Gottschalk, "Trends in the Autocovariance Structure of Earnings in the U.S," do not find such an upward trend in earnings mobility over a similar time frame.

Chapter 8

Income Disparity and Unionism: The Workplace Influences of Post-1965 Immigration Policy

◆

by Vernon M. Briggs, Jr.

AT THE TIME OF ITS PASSAGE, the Immigration Act of 1965 was called "the most far-reaching revision of immigration policy" in the United States since the imposition of the first numerical quotas in 1921.[1] Unknowingly, this legislation would lead directly to the revival of the phenomenon of "mass immigration" from the nation's distant past.[2] Immigration had been of declining significance to the size and composition of the nation's population and labor force for more than 50 years. Indeed, in 1965, only 4.4 percent of the population was foreign born, the lowest percentage since before the Civil War. In the years that have followed, these trends have been sharply reversed.

By the 1980s, a comprehensive study of U.S. society by an international panel of social science scholars observed that "America's biggest import is people" and concluded that "at the time when attention is directed to the general decline in American exceptionalism, American immigration continues to flow at a rate unknown elsewhere in the world."[3] Because of policies already in place, the 1990s should sustain the largest infusion of immigrants in any 10-year period in the nation's history. Moreover, as the noted demographer Leon Bouvier has observed, the post-1965 wave of mass immigration—unlike earlier waves—shows "no sign of imminent decline."[4]

Paralleling the years in which the scale and cumulative effects of mass immigration again became significant (i.e., since the late 1970s), the issue of widening income disparity also emerged as a national issue. As former U.S. Secretary of Labor Robert Reich said in his farewell speech in January 1997 before returning to private life, "Over 15 years ago, inequality of income, wealth, and opportunity began to widen, and the gap today is wider than at anytime in living memory."[5]

Because mass immigration has significant labor market implications and the labor market is the principal source of national income, immigration policy has contributed to the evolving income distribution trends. Declining union membership has also been linked to the growth in income inequality. Union membership trends have historically moved in the opposite direction of immigration trends; rising immigration has meant falling union membership. Hence, workplace remedies intended to address the issues of income disparity and the decline of unionism must include significant immigration reform if they are to be taken seriously.

A STORY OF UNINTENDED CONSEQUENCES

Unlike most public policy interventions designed to influence labor market outcomes, immigration policy is a special case. The admission of immigrants to the United States is purely a discretionary act of the federal government. The nation is under no obligation to allow foreign nationals into the country on either a temporary or a permanent basis to live or to work. There is no right to immigrate. Indeed, the word "immigration" or any reference to the concept is not to be found anywhere in the U.S. Constitution. Hence, how many immigrants are admitted annually and under what terms depend entirely on the immigration policy that Congress puts in place at any particular time and the funding levels it provides for its enforcement. As circumstances change, so must the nation's immigration policy if it is to serve the national interest and not confound it.

In the case of the Immigration Act of 1965, the primary motivation for its passage was to end the era of overt discrimination associated with the national origins admission system that had been embodied in the immigration laws since 1924.[6] The reform movement of that era was not seeking to raise the level of immigration. The paramount goal was to achieve a nondiscriminatory immigration policy. Indeed, the reformers "were so incensed with the ethnocentrism of the laws of the past that they spent virtually all of their energies seeking to eliminate the country of origin provisions" and, as a consequence, "they gave very little attention to the substance or long range implications of the policy that would replace them."[7]

A new admissions system was enacted based largely on the reunification of family members beyond immediate family members (whose numbers are unlimited) of each immigrant. Seventy-four percent of the available entry visas each year were reserved for this grouping (the percentage was increased to 80 percent in 1980). Family ties, not labor force needs, became "the cornerstone" of U.S. immigration policy. This new admissions system remains in place to this day. It is designed to serve private interests, not the national interest. Most future citizens are admitted not because they have needed skills, talents, or abilities or are willing to locate where workers are needed, but because they have relatives who are already citizens or permanent resident aliens.

Perhaps the nation could afford the luxury of a nepotistic immigration system if immigration levels had remained low. However, these levels have soared since 1965. Thus, despite contemporary platitudes about its merits, the post-1965 revival of mass immigration was a completely unexpected event.

There was no shortage of labor in 1965 that required an increase in immigration. Indeed, the postwar baby boomers were just entering the labor market. One million more people had turned 18 years old (the primary labor force entry age for seeking full-time jobs) the year before, and that high level of new entrants persisted for the next 16 years. Already worried about the adverse effects of foreign workers on the welfare of citizen workers, the Johnson administration (following through on a Kennedy administration initiative) had terminated the Mexican Labor Program (i.e., the infamous "bracero program") only 10 months before the Immigration Act of 1965 was signed. Moreover, in the presidential campaign of 1964, the Republican Party had raised the specter of massive job displacement if the proposed immigration legislation was enacted by the Johnson administration after the election.[8] Congress, therefore, was sensitive to the charge of adverse employment impacts. For that reason, it significantly tightened the labor certification requirements that applied to all nonfamily and nonrefugee admissions provided by the Immigration Act of 1965.

In addition, the Immigration Act of 1965 was passed the same year that the equal employment opportunity provisions (i.e., Title VII) of the Civil Rights Act of 1964 went into effect (on July 1, 1965). In fact, a strong case can be made that the passage of the Immigration Act of 1965 was itself another civil rights achievement of that era.[9] Having passed legislation to end overt discrimination within the country, Congress's logical next step was to end similar discriminatory policies that affected the nation's relations with the international community. No one foresaw the possibility that the Immigration Act of 1965 would subsequently undermine the original objectives of the Civil Rights Act of 1964—namely, the enhancement of economic opportunities for African Americans.

Indeed, none of the subsequent ramifications of the Immigration Act of 1965 were foreseen by its proponents. In testimony in favor of its passage, then Secretary of State Dean Rusk stated that "the significance of immigration for the United States now depends less on numbers than on the quality of the immigrants."[10] Senator Edward Kennedy (D-MA), the floor manager of the bill in the Senate, stated, "This bill is not concerned with increasing immigration to this country, nor will it lower any of the high standards we apply in the selection of immigrants."[11] Kennedy also said that "our cities will not be flooded with a million immigrants annually," that "the ethnic mix of this country will not be upset," and that "[the pending bill] would not cause American workers to lose their jobs."[12] None of these assurances has proved to be valid.

Subsequent actions by Congress have perpetuated and enhanced the scale of this social and economic phenomenon. The Refugee Act of 1980 enlarged the definition of eligible refugees, created a separate admission system for refugees that is uncapped, increased substantially the number of refugees annually admitted over the legislative level first set in 1965, and enacted the first political asylum policy in the nation's history, a policy that has been extensively used (and abused) for entry since then. The Immigration Reform and Control Act of 1986 provided for the legalization of status for more than 2.5 million formerly illegal immigrants. The Immigration Act of 1990 raised legal immigration by 35 percent over the levels in existence at that time. In addition to these expansionary actions, the mass violation of the nation's immigration laws by illegal immigrants continues and grows unabated by the half-hearted deterrence policies that Congress has enacted to date. As of October 1996, the "official" estimate of the number of illegal immigrants residing in the United States was 5 million, with an additional annual inflow of 275,000 illegal entrants.[13]

THE ECONOMIC CONSEQUENCES OF POST-1965 IMMIGRATION

The most obvious of the unexpected effects of the changes in immigration policy adopted in 1965 has been a significant increase in the foreign-born population. The foreign-born population grew from 4.4 percent of the total population in 1965 to 8.7 percent of the population in 1994 (or about 1 of every 11 people in the population). In absolute terms, the foreign-born population increased from 8.6 million people in 1965 to 22.8 million people in 1994 (an increase of 165 percent). If an allowance is made for the undercount of illegal immigrants in official data, the actual inflow has certainly exceeded a million people a year throughout most of the 1980s and all of the 1990s to date. The inflow, however, has been exceedingly uneven in terms of where the immigrants have come from. Twenty-eight percent of the nation's entire foreign-born population in 1994 came from only one country—Mexico.

The immigrant population is younger than the native-born population and contains more men than women; hence, the impact of immigration on the labor force is significantly greater than population statistics reveal. Indeed, in October 1994, the foreign born accounted for 10.9 percent of the labor force (or one of every nine members of the U.S. labor force).[14] These figures must also be viewed as minimal rates because of the acknowledged sizable undercount of the number of illegal immigrants in the country.[15]

If the revival of mass immigration since 1965 had been evenly distributed across the country, the incongruity of the subsequent immigrant inflow would have been less dramatic than it has been. A key feature of the post-1965 mass immigration, however, has been its geographic concentration. In 1994, five states (California, New York, Florida, Texas, and Illinois) accounted for 65 percent of the entire foreign-born population and 66 percent of the entire foreign-born labor force. The foreign born are also overwhelmingly concentrated in only a handful of urban areas. But these particular labor markets are among the nation's largest in size, which greatly increases the significance of their concentration. These five metropolitan areas in October 1994 were Los Angeles, New York, San Francisco, Miami, and Chicago. Collectively, they accounted for 51 percent of all foreign-born workers in October 1994. The concentration in the central cities of the nation is even more extreme. According to the 1990 census, the foreign born made up 60 percent of the population in

Miami, 28 percent in New York City, 38 percent in Los Angeles, 34 percent in San Francisco, and 17 percent in Chicago. The percentage of the labor force that was foreign born, of course, was higher in each of these cities than these population percentages show.

The flow of immigrants into the United States has tended to be bimodal in terms of their human capital attributes (as measured by educational attainment), but the highest concentration by far is in the lowest end of the nation's human capital distribution. It is this feature of the immigration inflow that has the most significant impact on contemporary wage inequality and income disparity trends. The 1990 census revealed that the 25 percent of foreign-born adults 25 years and older had less than a ninth-grade education (compared with only 10 percent of native-born adults) and that 42 percent of foreign-born adults did not have a high school diploma (compared with 23 percent of native-born adults). Thus, it is the low skilled, low wage sectors of urban labor markets that are the most affected by immigrant job seekers. Not only do low skilled immigrants compete with each other for whatever opportunities exist at the bottom of the nation's job hierarchy, but they also compete with the low skilled native-born workers.

On the other hand, the percentage of both foreign-born and native-born adults with a bachelor's degree or higher was the same (20.3 percent and 20.4 percent, respectively), whereas more foreign-born adults than native-born adults had graduate degrees (3.8 percent versus 2.4 percent). It is unclear, however, exactly how immigrants with graduate degrees from foreign educational institutions transfer their educational training into actual employment experiences. There is significant variation in the quality of many foreign universities—especially with respect to their graduate programs. Moreover, those with training in law, medicine, and education do not automatically qualify for comparable employment when they enter the U.S. labor force. They must become licensed or certified before they can practice their professions. In some instances, they must wait until they become naturalized citizens before they can be employed in such jobs. Their ability to communicate fluently in English also affects skill transferability. Hence, it is likely that there is some degree of downward occupational mobility in the employment of foreign-born workers that is not readily apparent from a mere examination of their educational attainment statistics.

The effects of the human capital variation between the foreign born and the native born are reflected in a comparison of their October 1994 occupational distributions.[16] Twenty-five percent of the foreign-born labor force were employed in the low skilled and semiskilled occupations of operatives, laborers, and farm workers (compared with 18 percent of native-born workers). Moreover, 20 percent of the foreign-born labor force are employed in low skilled service occupations (compared with 13 percent of native-born workers).

The disproportionate concentration of foreign born who lack even a high school diploma is also reflected in their unemployment experiences.[17] The overall unemployment rate of foreign-born workers in October 1994 was 7.4 percent, whereas the comparable national unemployment rate was 5.5 percent. The unemployment rate for foreign-born workers with less than a ninth-grade education in 1994 was 9.4 percent; for those with some high school education but with no diploma, it was 14.4 percent. The comparable rates for native-born workers were 10.3 percent and 13.3 percent, respectively. Consequently, immigration's greatest impact on the labor market is in the sector that is already having the greatest difficulty finding employment—the least skilled segment of the labor force (using educational attainment as the usual proxy for skill) is bearing the brunt of the direct job competition with immigrant workers. There certainly is no shortage of unskilled native-born workers, as indicated by their high unemployment rates and by the high number of adult illiterates in the nation's population and labor force (estimated at more than 30 million).

As for the racial and ethnic composition of the post-1965 inflow, immigrants from Asia and Latin America overwhelmingly dominate. They account for about 80 percent of the post-1965 immigrants and more than 85 percent of the post-1980 immigrants. Indeed, in the 1990s, Asia has emerged as the primary immigrant source region. As of 1994, 62 percent of the Asian population in the United States were foreign born, with 92 percent having entered the United States since 1970. Regarding the Hispanic population, 39 percent were foreign born in 1994, with 51.2 percent of the Hispanic labor force being foreign born. In contrast, only 3 percent of the non-Hispanic white labor force was foreign born, and only 4 percent of the non-Hispanic black labor force was foreign born in 1994. Thus, the most distinguishing feature of the Asian and Hispanic labor forces is the inordinately high proportion of both groups who are foreign born.

The 1990 census also disclosed that 79.1 percent of the foreign-born population five years old and over speak a language other than English (compared with 7.8 percent of the native born) and that 47.0 percent of the foreign born five years old and over reported that they do not speak English "very well." The ability to speak English in an increasingly service-oriented economy has been definitively linked to the ability to advance in the U.S. labor market of the post-1965 era.[18]

For these and other reasons, it should come as no great revelation that the incidence of poverty among families of the foreign-born population in 1990 was 50 percent higher than that of native-born families, or that 25 percent of families with a foreign-born householder who entered the country since 1980 were living in poverty in 1990. Nor is it surprising that immigrant families in the early 1990s made significantly greater use of both cash and noncash welfare programs than did native-born families.[19]

The human capital deficiencies of adult immigrants have dire intergenerational consequences on the preparation of their children to become future workers. About 2 million immigrant youth enrolled in U.S. public schools in the 1980s. Many more have come in the 1990s. Studies of these immigrant children indicate that they are "twice as likely to be poor as compared to all students, thereby straining local school resources."[20] Moreover, "many immigrants, including those of high school age, have had little or no schooling and are illiterate even in their native languages."[21]

New demands for the creation of bilingual programs and special education classes have significantly added to the costs of urban education and have frequently led to the diversion of funds from other important educational programs for needy native-born children.[22] Overcrowding of urban school systems, already confronting enormous educational burdens, has frequently occurred, with devastating effects on the educational process.[23] Other educational costs are more subtle but are as significant as the financial concerns. Namely, the societal goal of desegregated urban schools has been greatly retarded by the arrival of immigrant children because they have increased the racial isolation of inner-city black children.[24]

The adverse effects of immigration on the quality of the labor force and future income distribution patterns can also be seen by examining differential school enrollment data.[25] As of October 1994, only 43 percent of foreign-born youths between the ages of 16 and 24 were enrolled in school compared with 54 percent of native-born youths. Within the Hispanic population, the differential was acute, with only 28 percent of foreign-born Hispanic youths enrolled in school versus 51 percent of native-born Hispanic youths. With respect to secondary school enrollment rates (i.e., those youths 16-19 years old), the native born attended school at a 56 percent rate versus a 48 percent rate for the foreign born. Postsecondary enrollment rates reflect a similar pattern. The major explanation for the differential rates in both secondary and postsecondary enrollment between the native born and the foreign born is the much lower enrollment rates by foreign-born Hispanics.

There is also the issue of job competition. Logic indicates that if immigrants are disproportionately concentrated in the nation's largest urban labor markets and if foreign-born workers are disproportionately lacking in human capital attributes, and if they are overwhelmingly minority group members themselves, similarly situated native-born workers (actual and potential) will experience the greatest competition with immigrants for jobs. But developing a methodology to measure job displacement is a difficult task. Not only is it impossible to prove that if one person is hired someone else has been displaced, but even if such a straightforward approach were feasible, it would not settle the issue. Which native-born workers might have moved to the high immigrant impact cities if the immigrants were not pouring into those same labor markets? Moreover, there are people who leave these same high immigrant labor markets in despair who might otherwise have retained their jobs or had higher wages and incomes if not for the continual inflow of immigrants.

In fact, research on these labor mobility issues has found that the internal immigration patterns of native-born workers in the urban areas where immigrants are concentrated have been reduced.[26] The higher the concentration of immigrants in a local labor market, the less attractive in economic terms the locality is to native-born workers. Other research has found that immigrants are less likely to move out of states where they are concentrated than are the native born.[27] Both features accentuate the employment and wage impacts on labor markets where immigrants are concentrated. Furthermore, research shows that cities in California that have experienced quantum increases in immigration have seen the flight of low income, poorly educated native-born workers out of their former communities to the outer fringes of their metropolitan areas or to other states.[28] This means that these workers have lost the competitive struggle for jobs with low skilled, poorly educated immigrants and that the other labor markets now have to accommodate the outflows of unskilled citizen and resident alien job seekers.

The same can be said of wage rates. If immigrants had not entered the same local labor markets in substantial numbers, wages would have risen, which should have attracted citizens to move to or stay in those cities. Instead, the wages for low skilled workers—especially workers without a high school education—were significantly reduced in those localities.[29] The exodus of low income native-born workers from high immigrant impact communities may also be a response to the extensive employment discrimination against native-born workers—especially African Americans—by the growing number of immigrant-owned businesses in those urban areas.[30]

RECOGNITION THAT IMMIGRATION POLICY HAD GONE AWRY

As discussed, the reemergence of mass immigration began as a gradual process in the late 1960s. But by the late 1970s, its cumulative effects had already become sufficiently worrisome to warrant the creation by Congress of a special commission to study what had happened and to recommend policy changes. Officially known as the Select Commission on Immigration and Refugee Policy (SCIRP), it was composed of 16 members and chaired by a nonpolitician, the Reverend Theodore Hesburgh, who at the time was president of the University of Notre Dame. In its final report in March 1981, SCIRP concluded that immigration was "out of control" and that comprehensive reforms were essential.[31] It called for a "cautious approach" in reforming the immigration system and concluded that "this is not the time for a large-scale expansion in legal immigration."[32]

Congress's ensuing response to SCIRP's recommendations for reform is a long and frustrating tale that cannot be told here.[33] To summarize the story, Congress passed legislation in 1986 designed to reduce illegal immigration, but it was full of enforcement loopholes and its deterrence measures were poorly funded. With regard to legal immigration, in 1990 Congress dramatically increased admissions by 35 percent over existing levels, in direct contradiction of SCIRP's earlier recommendations.

To monitor the impact of the 1990 legislation, another congressionally created commission was created in 1991. Known as the U.S. Commission on Immigration Reform (CIR), it was a nine-member commission that was chaired by former congresswoman Barbara Jordan from 1993 until her death in January 1996 (at the time she was a professor of public policy at the University of Texas). CIR's final report was released on September 30, 1997, but it also had issued a series of earlier interim reports. In 1994, CIR identified illegal immigration as the "most immediate need" for policy action.[34] In 1995, CIR recommended the nation's first legislative reductions in the level of legal immigration.[35] The reductions would be accomplished by eliminating most of the extended family preferences that are so prominent in the existing admissions system. The recommended new system would make the nuclear family the mainstay of family admissions. The commission also recommended that no unskilled immigrants be admitted under any of the employment-based admission preferences and that the new "diversity immigrant" admission category created by the 1990 legislation be eliminated. It also called for including refugee admissions in the overall legal immigration ceiling that would be in effect each year. CIR's report concluded with the statement that the current immigration system "must undergo major reform" and that it requires "a significant redefinition of priorities."[36]

In 1995, Congress initiated efforts to respond to CIR's recommendations and to the public outcry for changes.[37] Unfortunately, by the time the legislative smoke cleared, comprehensive immigration reform was dead.[38] Special interest groups succeeded in separating (and thereby killing) all reforms pertaining to legal immigration, while illegal immigration reforms were bundled into an omnibus appropriation bill that was passed by the 104th Congress just before it adjourned. Although the bipartisan legislation did substantially increase funding for deterrence, the final bill passed in 1996 had been stripped of its most important policy reforms—the establishment of a viable verification system of worker eligibility to be employed in the United States. Thus, meaningful immigration reform was postponed once again.

THE PARALLEL EMERGENCE OF THE INCOME DISPARITY ISSUE

Appearing roughly at the same time that SCIRP was finding that extant immigration policy was not serving the national interest were the first signs that the nation was experiencing widening disparity in its wage and income distributions. Since the 1970s, these patterns have become ongoing trends. As Robert Reich said in 1997, the repeated findings of accumulating inequality year after year proves that "this is not a statistical fluke."[39]

As shown in Chart 1, the cumulative change in real wages for adult full-time weekly workers between 1980 and 1996 (after adjusting for inflation) reveals a 10.7 percent increase in real wages for workers in the top 10 percent of the wage distribution (i.e., the 90th percentile) and a 9.6 percent

CHART 1

CUMULATIVE CHANGE IN REAL WAGES, 1980-96

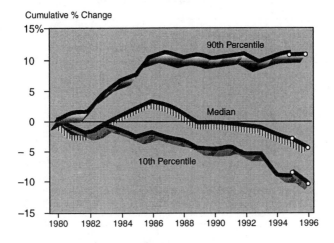

Note: 1996 data are for the first three quarters of that year.

Sources: Data are from the Technical Appendix, Robert B. Reich, "The Unfinished Agenda," speech before the Council on Excellence in Government, Washington, D.C., January 9, 1997, as reprinted in the *Daily Labor Report*, January 10, 1997, pp. E-14 and E-15; and U.S. Bureau of Labor Statistics.

decline in real wages for those in the bottom 10 percent of the wage distribution (i.e., the 10th percentile). The median for all adult workers shows that adjusted wages fell by 3.6 percent over this timespan.[40]

The changes are even more dramatic with respect to family income disparity. Chart 2 shows that for the years 1950 to 1978, real family income for the bottom 20 percent of the population increased substantially more than that of the top 20 percent (a 138 percent increase for the former versus 99 percent for the latter). Chart 3, however, shows the same data for the period 1979 to 1995, and it reveals precisely the opposite trend—namely, the inflation-adjusted income of the top 20 percent of the distribution grew by 26 percent while that of the poorest 20 percent fell by 9 percent. Even more telling is the fact that in 1995, the richest 5 percent of U.S. families received 20 percent of the nation's total income, while the bottom 40 percent received only 14.6 percent of the nation's total income.

The U.S. Bureau of the Census has studied the distribution of income since the late 1940s. It has reported that from 1947 to 1968 there was a perceptible decline of 7.4 percent in family income inequality in the

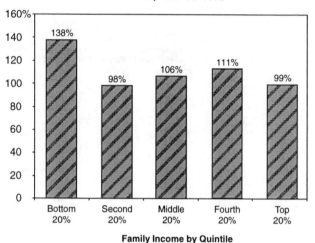

CHART 2

GROWING TOGETHER: GROWTH OF FAMILY INCOME BY QUINTILE, 1950 TO 1978

Family Income by Quintile

Source: See Chart 1.

United States. But since 1968, income inequality among families has increased. By 1982, inequality was back to the same level it was in 1947, and by 1994, family income inequality had increased by 22.4 percent over the distribution that existed in 1968.[41] It is worthy of note that 1968 was the year in which the changes contained in the Immigration Act of 1965 went into full effect.

THE IMMIGRATION LINKAGE

It is no easy task to specify the causes of mounting income inequality in the United States since the late 1960s. Even the Census Bureau acknowledged in 1996 that "the root causes are still not entirely understood."[42] Nonetheless, immigration has been identified as being among the constellation of adverse influences. The President's Council of Economic Advisers (CEA) noted a relationship in its 1994 annual report: "Immigration has increased the relative supply of less educated labor and appears to have contributed to the increasing inequality of income."[43] Although the report claims that the aggregate effect on the overall distribution of income is "small," immigration is a major factor in the deterioration of wages and incomes at the lower end of the distribution. Indeed, a 1995 study by the Bureau of Labor Statistics found that "immigration accounted for approximately 20 to 25 percent

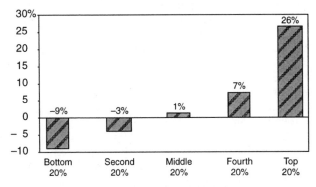

CHART 3

**GROWING APART: GROWTH OF FAMILY INCOME
BY QUINTILE, 1979 TO 1995**

Source: See Chart 1.

of the increase in the wage gap between low and high skilled workers during the 1980s in the 50 largest metropolitan areas of the United States."[44] The same study revealed that half of the decline in real wages for native-born high school dropouts over the decade can be attributed to the impact of unskilled foreign workers.[45] Thus, the critical issue that is so often overlooked is not only that a disproportionate number of the immigrants themselves are unskilled and poor, but that, by their presence, they also impoverish similarly situated native-born workers and their families.

Mass immigration affects wages, employment, labor mobility, and unemployment—all of which adversely and disproportionately affect the income patterns of workers at the bottom of the economic ladder. Given the geographic concentration of the foreign-born population, it is the urban labor force and its disproportionately large minority populations that are the most adversely affected.[46] Therefore, just because the effects of immigration are dissipated when the perspective is at the aggregate national level does not mean that they are insignificant. Indeed, in many of the nation's major urban labor markets, immigration and its effects are dominating factors in interpreting wage, employment, and income trends.

THE UNIONISM LINKAGE

In its 1995 analysis of the causes of mounting wage inequality since the 1970s, the CEA cited the decline of unionism as being a significant explanatory factor. According to the CEA, "Empirical evidence suggests that unions tend to raise wages for workers who would otherwise be in the bottom half of the wage distribution."[47] It noted that 26 percent of the employed labor force were union members in 1973 but that the percentage had fallen to 16 percent by 1995. Moreover, the decline in union membership has been greatest for workers in the private sector where foreign-born workers are disproportionately employed (in 1995, only 11 percent of private sector workers belonged to unions). The CEA indicated that perhaps as much as 20 percent of the increase in wage inequality—"especially of men"—could be attributed to this decline in union membership.[48]

Although the CEA did not itself draw the linkage between the decline in union membership and the increase in immigration, it has been historically true that the two phenomena have been inversely related. In the first decade of the 20th century, only about 5 percent of the employed labor force were union members. Mass immigration was also at its highest levels until that time. Only with the outbreak of World War I in 1914 did immigration levels begin to fall and union membership begin to rise. From the mid-1930s to the early 1960s, union membership had its most sustained period of growth. In 1945, it reached its zenith when union membership accounted for about 36 percent of the employed nonagricultural labor force. Even as late as 1962, more than 30 percent of the employed labor force were union members. During this lengthy period of union growth, immigration levels declined continually and significantly. As indicated earlier, the percentage of the population that was foreign born in the mid-1960s had fallen to a low level that had not been experienced in more than 100 years. The revival of mass immigration in the late 1960s exactly parallels the decline in union membership that has occurred since then. Obviously, many factors adversely affect both union membership and wage inequality trends, and immigration is one of them.

From the very beginnings of the American labor movement, immigration has been one of the most troublesome issues the movement has had to confront. For while the immigration flow has been historically dominated by working people (i.e., wage earners), the union movement traditionally regarded immigrants as a short-term threat, even though in the long run they might contribute to growth in the ranks of working people. But the American labor movement has traditionally been short-term oriented, preferring "bread and butter in the here and now rather than pie in the sky in the sweet bye and bye." Hence, until recently, organized labor was generally opposed to large and continual increases in immigration.

In 1864, when the nation passed its first major immigration legislation—the Act to Encourage Immigration—the National Labor Union (NLU) vigorously opposed its implementation and was successful in gaining its repeal only four years later in 1868.[49] Likewise, the NLU—at the behest of many working people—fought for the repeal of the Burlingame Treaty of 1868, which extended to immigrants from China the same entry rights as immigrants from other countries. In 1872, one of organized labor's most effective tools to enhance unionization, the use of the union label as a boycott measure, was first introduced by union workers to distinguish the products they produced from those made by nonunion immigrant workers.[50] At its founding convention in 1881, the Federation of Organized Trades and Labor Unions (which in 1886 became the American Federation of Labor) passed a convention resolution that called for "the use of our best efforts to get rid of this monstrous immigration."[51] The resolution was specifically addressed at Chinese immigration, and similar resolutions were also adopted by the rival labor organization at the time, the Knights of Labor, as well as by various socialist labor groups.[52] These efforts culminated in the enactment of the Chinese Exclusion Act of 1882, which represented the first legislative action by Congress to exclude all immigrants from a specific country. The Knights of Labor were also instrumental in the passage of the Alien Contract Labor Act of 1885, the first legislation ever enacted to restrict immigration of would-be workers from Europe.[53] At its early conventions, the American Federation of Labor (AFL) constantly criticized the nation's immigration policies. But it was not until its 1896 convention that resolutions endorsing restrictions on immigration in general were finally adopted.[54] At that same convention, Samuel Gompers, then president of the AFL and probably the most influential labor leader in U.S. history, stated that "immigration is working a great injury to the people of our country."[55] The following year, the AFL passed a resolution favoring the use of a literacy test to screen and reduce the inflow of unskilled workers into the U.S. labor force. Legislation accomplishing this purpose was ultimately enacted by the Immigration Act of 1917 with strong AFL support.[56]

The culmination of organized labor's efforts to end the era of virtually unrestricted immigration came with the passage of the Immigration Acts of 1921 and 1924. This legislation not only placed a low ceiling on total immigration from the Eastern Hemisphere but also imposed separate quotas on each nation. These country quotas greatly favored western and northern European nations and greatly disfavored immigrants from eastern and southern European nations. It was, as the noted labor historian Philip Taft wrote, "the adverse influence of the immigrant upon the labor market rather than opposition based on race or religion which accounts for the attitude of organized labor" in supporting the restrictionist movement.[57] After all, many labor leaders of that era—including Gompers himself—were immigrants, as were many of their union members. Even socialist unions such as those in Milwaukee, Wisconsin, made it clear that their support for the worldwide solidarity of labor did not mean that workers in other countries had a right to come to Milwaukee to seek jobs.[58]

In fact, subsequent studies of the impact of the mass immigration of the era before quotas were imposed have validated the economic concerns of union leaders at that time. As one examination of that period concluded: "Yet to a very great extent the traditional viewpoint of native-born labor, especially the organized segment of it, appears to have been substantiated by experience. In many cases, labor markets were flooded, the labor supply was made more redundant, and wages in consequence were undermined."[59]

The same study concluded that the dramatic increase in workers' real earnings that occurred in the 1920s, and that lasted until the onset of the Great Depression, was a significant result of the imposition of immigration quotas in 1921 and 1924.[60] Moreover, the decrease in immigration during that decade was found to have contributed to "a new interest" by employers "in developing employee goodwill and in training workers."[61]

In the 1960s, the AFL-CIO joined in the efforts to end the use of national origin as the basis for the nation's immigration policy. At its 1963 convention, it specifically endorsed the two proposed bills that would later become the Immigration Act of 1965. Its resolution of support stated that "an intelligent and balanced immigration policy ought to rest on practical considerations of desired skills."[62] There is no indication in the resolution that the labor movement anticipated that the subsequently adopted legislation would launch another era of sustained mass immigration—especially of unskilled workers—which continues to this day.

In the 1980s, the AFL-CIO supported the legislative efforts to reduce illegal immigration that culminated in the passage of the Immigration Reform and Control Act of 1986.[63] But when the subject of legal immigration reform arose in 1989, the AFL-CIO indicated that it supported family reunification as the principal admission condition, opposed any reduction in legal immigration levels, and preferred not to use immigration as a means of acquiring skilled workers because it would cause a "brain drain" in other countries and it would be better to train and educate U.S. workers for such jobs.[64] Strangely, there was no parallel concern for protecting jobs for unskilled and semiskilled citizen workers, who were the most adversely affected by the policy then in place.

In the legislative debates preceding passage of the Immigration Act of 1990, the AFL-CIO did not oppose the dramatic increase in immigration that it provided. The AFL-CIO's only concern for restrictions pertained to its successful effort to impose a cap on the number of foreign workers who could temporarily be employed in the United States as professional athletes and entertainers.

During the subsequent 1995 and 1996 debates over what has happened since the Immigration Act of 1990 took effect, the AFL-CIO joined the coalition of special interest groups that succeeded in deleting all of the proposed changes in legal immigration from the pending bills.[65] This tactical move effectively killed those initiatives. The proposed changes, as discussed earlier, called for a reduction in legal immigration back to levels that approximated those in existence prior to the passage of the

Immigration Act of 1990. These reductions would have been accomplished by reducing various entry categories for adult family members who were relatives of U.S. citizens or permanent resident aliens and by capping annual refugee admissions. It also would have closed the door to the entry of all unskilled workers who were not family members and would have eliminated the "diversity immigrant" admissions category. As mentioned earlier, all of these were changes that the CIR had recommended the year before by an overwhelming 8-1 vote.

As for illegal immigration, the AFL-CIO opposed the creation of a national database to verify the identities of job seekers and their eligibility for employment. The CIR had recommended such a system, and it was included in the original bill. However, during the floor debate in the House of Representatives, the verification provisions were stripped from the bill that was finally passed—the Illegal Immigration Reform and Immigrant Responsibility Act of 1996—as part of an omnibus appropriation act.

Thus, over the past decade, the AFL-CIO has altered its position. Judging by its conduct, the AFL-CIO no longer seems to consider mass immigration a threat to unionism in particular and to the economic well-being of low skilled workers in general. There is, unfortunately, extensive evidence to the contrary.[66]

CONCLUDING OBSERVATIONS

It should be stressed that it is post-1965 immigration policy, not immigrants per se, that is causing concern about the adverse effects of immigration on income inequality and the declining state of unionism. Immigrants are only availing themselves of the opportunities that existing immigration policy permits or tolerates. Immigration to the United States is a policy-driven phenomenon. Post-1965 immigration policy had unexpected consequences, and its terms have been massively abused by illegal immigration. Rather than correcting those outcomes so that immigration can serve the national interest—as two distinguished expert commissions have advocated—Congress has chosen to rationalize what it has created. In the meantime, special interest groups that have benefited from what has happened or that wish to play "rainbow coalition" politics have rallied to defend the existing system despite its demonstrated conflict with the well-being of the nation and its workers.

A complete statement of needed reforms is beyond the scope of this undertaking,[67] but the broad outlines can be indicated. The focus of the legal immigration system must be shifted away from family reunification. As long as the preponderance of immigrant inflow is admitted on the basis of family ties, it is impossible to ensure that immigrants' human capital attributes are congruent with emerging labor market needs of the nation. If immigration levels were low, the entry of unskilled, poorly educated, and non-English-speaking immigrants probably could be accommodated. But the levels are enormous—indeed, they exceed those of any other period in U.S. history. Moreover, at this stage of the nation's economic development, the nation must have a high wage and highly productive labor force if it is to survive in today's service-oriented, high technology, and globally competitive economy.[68]

As the noted immigration scholar John Higham has pointed out, family reunification serves to "reinforce and perpetuate existing patterns of immigration" that instead "of opening a way for prospective leaders, striking out on their own to make a new life, grants preference to followers, pursuing the family chain."[69] Higham also notes that, just as with the earlier supporters of the national origins admission system, "the family preference scheme [has] a stubborn constituency in the ethnic groups that believe they benefit from it."[70] Nonetheless, if the current undesirable outcomes of immigration policy are to be changed, family reunification—as the CIR made clear—must be deemphasized as an entry criterion.

As for the annual level of immigration, it should be made flexible, as it is in other immigrant-receiving nations such as Australia and Canada. There is no magic in any particular number. The current practice in the United States is to engrave a number in legislative stone that is unable to respond to changing conditions in the U.S. economy over long periods. This practice makes no sense. The annual admission number should be set administratively, not legislatively.

Furthermore, responsibility for the administration of immigration policy should be returned to the U.S. Department of Labor (DOL), as was the case from the time it was created as an independent agency in 1913 until 1940, when, for national security reasons, immigration was shifted to the U.S. Department of Justice (DOJ) as a wartime emergency measure.[71] The move was supposedly temporary, but it has remained to this day. The DOL is far better positioned to make immigration policy consistent with the employment needs of the country than is DOJ with its individualistic and legalistic orientations.

Of course, no policy reforms will be of consequence if the immigration policy that is adopted continues to be massively abused by illegal immigration. The gaping loophole in the current system of deterrence is the proliferation of counterfeit documents used to secure access to jobs. A national system to verify the authenticity of documents used to comply with existing law must be established. As Theodore Hesburgh has observed:

> Identification systems to be used upon application for a job and for work purposes are no different from other forms of identification required by our society today and readily accepted by millions of Americans: credit cards, which must be checked by merchants; identification cards other than driver's licenses for cashing checks; social security numbers to open bank accounts, register for school, or obtain employment. . . . .

Raising the specter of "Big Brotherdom," calling a work identification system totalitarian or labeling it "the computer taboo" does not further the debate on U.S. immigration policy: it only poisons it.[72]

Similarly, it is essential that sufficient funding and adequate personnel be provided for enforcement of the immigration policies that are in effect. This effort should include not only enhanced border management but also increased enforcement of the battery of workplace sanctions that prohibit the employment of illegal immigrants, protect fair labor standards, and monitor safety and health conditions.

The fact that prevailing immigration policy is linked to mounting income disparity within the populace and that it is associated with declining union membership should provide additional support for its overhaul. Immigration reform is an issue that will not go away.

NOTES

1. Elizabeth Harper, *Immigration Laws of the United States* (Indianapolis: Bobbs Merrill, 1975), p. 38. It should be noted that the Immigration Act of 1921 was a temporary piece of legislation. It was enacted for a one-year period, but it was subsequently extended until 1924, when permanent legislation, the Immigration Act of 1924, was passed.

2. Vernon M. Briggs, Jr., *Mass Immigration and the National Interest*, 2nd ed. (Armonk, NY: M.E. Sharpe, Inc., 1996), Chap. 7.

3. Oxford Analytica, *America in Perspective* (Boston: Houghton-Mifflin, 1986), p. 20.

4. Leon Bouvier, *Peaceful Invasion: Immigration and Changing America* (Washington: Center for Immigration Studies, 1991), p. 18.

5. Robert B. Reich, "The Unfinished Agenda," speech before the Council on Excellence in Government, Washington, D.C., January 9, 1997, as reprinted in the *Daily Labor Report*, January 10, 1997, p. E-13.

6. Briggs, *Mass Immigration*, Chap. 6.

7. David North and Marion F. Houstoun, *The Characteristics and Role of Illegal Aliens in the U.S. Labor Market: An Exploratory Study* (Washington: Linton and Company, Inc., 1976), p. 5.

8. For example, see "Should the Gates Be Opened Wider," *Business Week*, October 17, 1964, p. 114.

9. Briggs, *Mass Immigration*, pp. 106-109.

10. "Department Urges Congress to Revise Immigration Laws," *Department of State Bulletin*, August 24, 1965, p. 276.

11. *Congressional Record*, 89th Congress, 1st Session, September 17, 1965, pp. 24, 225.

12. U.S. Congress, Senate Committee on the Judiciary, Hearings before a Subcommittee on Immigration and Naturalization, 89th Congress, 1st Session, 1965, pp. 1-3.

13. U.S. Immigration and Naturalization Service (INS),"Estimates of the Unauthorized Immigrant Population Residing in the United States: October 1996," *Backgrounder* (January 1997), p. 1.

14. U.S. Department of Labor (DOL), *Labor Force, School Enrollment, and Educational Attainment Statistics for the Foreign-Born Using the October 1994 Current Population Survey,* Bulletin No. 3, Division of Immigration Policy and Research, Bureau of International Labor Affairs, May 1996, Table 1.

15. INS, "Estimates of the Unauthorized Immigrant Population." For comments on the undercount of illegal immigrants as it relates to employment data, see Paul Flaim, "How Many Jobs Since 1982? Data from Two Surveys Differ," *Monthly Labor Review* (August 1989), pp. 10-15.

16. DOL, *Labor Force, School Enrollment, and Educational Attainment Statistics,* Table 4.

17. Ibid., Table 1.

18. Barry R. Chiswick, ed., *Immigration, Language, and Ethnicity: Canada and the United States* (Washington: American Enterprise Institute, 1992).

19. "Immigrant Provisions of the New Welfare Bill," *Research Perspectives on Migration,* Vol. 1, No. 1 (September-October 1996), pp. 8-11.

20. U.S. General Accounting Office, statement of Linda Morra, Director of Education and Employment Issues, Health, Education, and Human Services Division, to U.S. Senate Committee on Labor and Human Resources," Immigration Education, GAD/T-HEHS 94-1946, April 14, 1994, p. 2.

21. Ibid.

22. Francisco L. Rivera-Batiz, "Immigrants and Schools: The Case of the Big Apple," *Forum for Applied Research and Public Policy* (Fall 1995), pp. 84-89.

23. David Firestone, "Crowded Schools in Queens Find Class Spaces in Unusual Places," *New York Times,* June 8, 1994, p. A-2.

24. For example, see E. Fiske, "Racial Shifts Challenge U.S. Schools," *New York Times,* June 23, 1988, p. A-16. See also Jeffrey A. Raffel, William Lowe Boyd, Vernon M. Briggs, Jr., Eugene E. Eubanks, and Roberto Fernandez, "Policy Dilemmas in Urban Education: Addressing the Needs of Poor, at Risk Children," *Journal of Urban Affairs,* Vol. 14, Nos. 3 and 4 (1992), pp. 263-290.

25. DOL, *Labor Force, School Enrollment, and Educational Attainment Statistics,* p. 1 and Supplementary Table.

26. Robert Walker, Mark Ellis, and Richard Barff, "Linked Migration Systems: Immigration and Internal Labor Flows in the United States," *Economic Geography* (July 1992), pp. 234-248. See also Randall K. Filer, "The Effect of Immigrant Arrivals on Migratory Patterns of Native Workers," in *Immigration and the Work Force,* ed. George J. Borjas and Richard B. Freeman (Chicago: University of Chicago Press, 1992), pp. 245-269.

27. Mary Kritz and June Marie Nogle, "Nativity Concentration and Internal Migration Among the Foreign-Born," *Demography* (August 1994), pp. 1-16.

28. William H. Frey, "Immigration and Internal Migration," *Population and Environment* (March 1995), pp. 353-375; and Frey, "Immigration, Domestic Migration, and Demographic Balkanization in America: New Evidence for the 1990s," *Population and Development Review* (December 1996), pp. 741-763.

29. For example, see George J. Borjas, Richard B. Freeman, and Lawrence F. Katz, "On the Labor Market Effects of Immigration and Trade," in *Immigration and the Work Force,* pp. 213-244.

30. For example, see Elizabeth Bogen, *Immigration in New York* (New York: Praeger, 1987), p. 91; Jonathan Kaufman, "Help Unwanted: Immigrant Businesses Often Refuse to Hire Blacks

in Inner City," *Wall Street Journal,* June 6, 1995, pp. A-1 and A-8; and discussion of the issue in Briggs, *Mass Immigration,* pp. 238-240.

31. Select Commission on Immigration and Refugee Policy, *U.S. Immigration Policy and the National Interest* (Washington: U.S. Government Printing Office [GPO], 1981), p. 5.

32. Ibid., p. 8.

33. For a discussion of the evolution of post-1965 immigration policy, see Briggs, *Mass Immigration,* Chaps. 7 and 9.

34. U.S. Commission on Immigration Reform, *U.S. Immigration Policy: Restoring Credibility* (Washington: U.S. Commission on Immigration Reform, 1994).

35. U.S. Commission on Immigration Reform, *Legal Immigration: Setting Priorities* (Washington: U.S. Commission on Immigration Reform, 1996).

36. Ibid., Letter of Transmittal, p. I.

37. For elaboration, see Briggs, *Mass Immigration,* pp. 246-248.

38. For an exceptionally frank discussion of how the national interest was undermined by special interests and political maneuvering, see John B. Judis, "Huddled Elites: Bipartisan Law v. Good Law," *The New Republic,* December 23, 1996, pp. 23-28.

39. Reich, "The Unfinished Agenda," p. E-13.

40. The figures cited in this and the next paragraph are from the Technical Appendix to Reich, "The Unfinished Agenda," pp. E-14 and E-15. For related discussion and elaboration of these trends, see also Paul Ryscavage, "A Surge in Growing Income Inequality," *Monthly Labor Review* (August 1995), pp. 51-61.

41. U.S. Bureau of the Census, *A Brief Look at Postwar U.S. Income Inequality,* Current Population Reports, Series P-60, No. 191 (Washington: GPO, 1996), p. 1.

42. Ibid.

43. Council of Economic Advisers, *Economic Report of the President, 1994* (Washington: GPO, 1994), p. 120.

44. David A. Jaeger, *Skill Differences and the Effect of Immigrants on the Wages of Natives,* BLS Working Paper No. 273 (Washington: DOL, Bureau of Labor Statistics, December 1995), p. 21.

45. Ibid.

46. Randall W. Eberts, *Urban Labor Markets,* Staff Working Paper No. 95-32 (Kalamazoo, MI: W.E. Upjohn Institute for Employment Research, January 1995).

47. Council of Economic Advisers, *Economic Report of the President, 1995* (Washington: GPO, 1995), p. 182. For supporting findings, see Francine D. Blau and Lawrence M. Kahn, *Wage Inequality* (Washington: American Enterprise Institute, 1996), pp. 8-9.

48. *Economic Report of the President, 1994,* p. 120.

49. Joseph G. Rayback, *A History of American Labor* (New York: Free Press, 1966), pp. 119-120.

50. Philip Taft, *Organized Labor in American History* (New York: Harper and Row, 1964), p. 304.

51. Ibid., p. 303.

52. Ibid.

53. Ibid., p. 305.

54. Ibid., p. 306.

55. Ibid.

56. A.T. Lane, "American Trade Unions, Mass Immigration, and the Literacy Test, 1900-1917," *Labor History* (Winter 1984), pp. 5-25.

57. Taft, *Organized Labor in American History*, p. 306.

58. Ibid., p. 308.

59. Harry A. Millis and Royal E. Montgomery, *Labor's Progress and Some Basic Labor Problems* (New York: McGraw-Hill, 1938), p. 31. See also Jefferey G. Williamson, *The Impact of Immigration on American Labor Markets Prior to the Quotas*, NBER Working Paper Series, No. 5185 (Cambridge, MA: National Bureau of Economic Research, 1995).

60. Millis and Montgomery, *Labor's Progress*, p. 211.

61. Ibid., p. 32.

62. "Resolution 172 Immigration Reform," *Proceedings of the Fifth Constitutional Convention of the AFL-CIO*, Vol. 1 (Washington: AFL-CIO, 1963), p. 353.

63. *Proceedings of the Sixteenth Constitutional Convention of the AFL-CIO*, Vol. 2 (Washington: AFL-CIO, 1985), pp. 173-175.

64. *Proceedings of the Eighteenth Constitutional Convention of the AFL-CIO* (Washington: AFL-CIO, 1989), pp. 278-279.

65. "Legislative Alert," open letter from Peggy Taylor, Department of Legislation, AFL-CIO, to Senator Orrin Hatch, U.S. Senate Committee on the Judiciary, March 26, 1996, pp. 1-2. See also "Policy Resolutions Adopted October 1995 by the AFL-CIO Convention," *Stand Up* (1995), pp. 68-70.

66. For example, see Richard Mines and Jeffrey Avina, "Immigrants and Labor Standards: The Case of California Janitors," in *U.S.-Mexico Relations: Labor Market Interdependence*, ed. Jorge A. Bustamante et al. (Stanford: Stanford University Press, 1992), pp. 429-448.

67. See Briggs, *Mass Immigration*, Chap. 9, for a more complete discussion of needed reforms.

68. Commission on the Skills of the American Workforce, *America's Choice: High Skills or Low Wages* (Rochester, NY: National Center on Education and the Economy, 1990).

69. John Higham, "The Purpose of Legal Immigration in the 1990s and Beyond," *The Social Contract* (Winter 1990-91), p. 64.

70. Ibid.

71. For details, see Briggs, *Mass Immigration*, pp. 86-89.

72. Theodore Hesburgh, "Nothing Totalitarian About a Worker's ID Card," *New York Times*, September 24, 1982, p. A-26.

Chapter 9

Growing Income Inequality in American Society: A Political Economy Perspective

◆

by James H. Johnson, Jr., and Walter C. Farrell, Jr.

T HE GROWING SCHISM between the haves and the have-nots in American society reflects policies implemented at the federal, state, and local levels of government in the post-1980 period to foster the competitiveness of U.S. businesses and communities in the global marketplace.[1] This chapter presents snapshots of contemporary inequality in American society and analyzes the determinants of the observed disparities, using data from Los Angeles, California, a bellwether city in the emerging social and demographic trends of the 21st century. To set the context for the empirical analyses that follow, we begin by providing a general overview of the role of policies in selected domains in generating income inequality.

CRITICAL BACKGROUND

In an effort to shed light on the causes and consequences of growing income inequality in American society, we employ a political economy perspective, focusing specifically on the impact of policies enacted in four domains: (1) business and local economic development; (2) employment and training; (3) education; and (4) crime and criminal justice.

Business Policy and Local Economic Development

It is generally agreed that policy-driven changes on both the demand side and the supply side of the U.S. labor market have contributed to growing income inequality in American society over the past two decades.[2] Specific policies undergird recent structural changes in the American economy.

One of the key contributing factors on the demand side, according to Grant and Johnson, was the Reagan administration's efforts during the 1980s to "create a deregulated business environment in order to facilitate the competitiveness of U.S. firms in the global marketplace."[3] Grant and Johnson note that these business policy developments altered the structure of economic opportunity in several ways. First, they accelerated the decline of highly unionized, high wage, central city manufacturing employment, a process referred to as deindustrialization.[4] More than 1.1

million manufacturing jobs disappeared from the U.S. economy in the 1980s, predominantly from large cities.[5] Second, these policies fostered organizational changes in production methods in the rapidly growing sectors of the economy—high technology manufacturing and craft specialty industries.[6] Firms in these high growth sectors, as well as in some of the traditional manufacturing industries (e.g., auto manufacturing), shifted from the so-called Fordist mode of production (i.e., the assembly line) to more flexible modes of production. This shift has been described as follows:

> Unlike mass production activities which are typically rigid in structure, the new forms of production are generally characterized by the ability to change process and product configurations with great rapidity—an ability that is frequently much enhanced by the use of computerized technologies. They are also typically situated in networks of extremely malleable external linkages and labor market relations. By the same token, they tend so far as possible to externalize production processes by buying in services and products that might otherwise be supplied internally, and this sometimes leads in turn to concomitant downsizing of individual establishments.[7]

Grant and Johnson suggest that two features of this shift are key to understanding how it has contributed to growing income inequality in American society.[8] The first is that firms shifting to more flexible modes of production have consciously sought "alternative locational environments uncontaminated by previous historical experience of large scale manufacturing activity and Fordist employment relations (i.e., unionization)."[9] Grant and Johnson also argue that this "has resulted in the emergence of new industrial spaces on the U.S. landscape—most often in places where there are few blacks in the local labor market and few within reasonable commuting distance."[10] Some of these new industrial spaces are in large metropolitan areas in older metropolitan regions, such as inner-city enclaves of craft specialty industries in New York and the suburban high technology complexes in the western suburbs of Boston. Others have emerged in communities that historically were on the geographic margins of the U.S. manufacturing core. They include the high technology centers in the Sun Belt cities of Albuquerque, Austin, Boulder, and Colorado Springs and the suburban complexes in Orange County and Silicon Valley, California.[11]

According to Grant and Johnson, "To the extent that suburban, exurban, and nonmetropolitan communities with significant black populations have inherited new economic activities, they typically have been noxious industries that pose a threat to public health and safety."[12] As an example, they cite Cancer Alley—a 90-mile stretch between New Orleans and Baton Rouge, Louisiana, where blacks share residential space with one of the highest concentrations of petrochemical plants in the United States, and possibly the world. Describing this area, Grant and Johnson assert that:

> blacks in this region reap few of the benefits—for example, few are employed in full time, well paying jobs in the industry—and incur most of the risks—that is, they are burdened by high incidences of cancer-related deaths and illnesses as a consequence of exposure to deadly toxic releases from the petrochemical plants. The enormous inequality inherent in this type of situation is yet another manifestation of the federal government's failure during the 1980s to enforce workplace standards and environmental regulations—all under the guise of fostering our economic competitiveness in the global marketplace—which has been dubbed "environmental racism."[13]

The second factor, in their view, pertains to the way in which these flexible production facilities meet the demand for low skilled labor:

> U.S. firms shifting to more flexible modes of production contend that their survival in the marketplace hinges on the extent to which their prices remain competitive vis a vis national and international firms. Thus, in an attempt to keep labor costs down, this type of work is either farmed out to subcontractors or the demand is met by preferential hiring practices. Owing to the federal government's lax enforcement of workplace wage and safety laws, such firms, especially those in the craft specialty sector, typically offer very low wages, have unattractive working conditions, and structure their workforces illegally—usually by hiring foreign and undocumented labor or women.[14]

At the same time that employers have been carving out new industrial spaces on the U.S. landscape, the evidence indicates that, in an effort to lure international capital to cities, local officials have been pursuing, consciously and aggressively, a strategy of downtown redevelopment at the expense of the poorer residential neighborhoods nearby. As a consequence of this redevelopment strategy, many large U.S. cities have become transactional centers that now house the headquarters of multinational corporations and other advanced service sector employers.[15]

Jobs in these revitalized downtown areas typically require high levels of education and technical training—the ability to do "head work" as opposed to "hand work." The primary low skill employment opportunities that exist in these downtown redevelopment zones are low level service and custodial jobs that typically are filled by newly arrived immigrants and that pay, at best, the minimum wage.[16] Thus, these downtown redevelopment policies are partly responsible for the polarization of urban labor markets into high wage and low wage sectors and, by extension, growing income inequality in U.S. society.

With respect to changes on the supply side of the U.S. labor market, growing income inequality reflects the growing presence of women in the U.S. labor market and the failure of U.S. businesses to develop family-friendly policies to accommodate them.[17] The dramatic increase in female labor force participation since World War II is attributable to the women's rights movement, which in turn led to the enactment of equal opportunity laws designed to protect and enhance their status in the employment arena. In terms of broadening understanding of growing income inequality, it is useful to divide those women who were born after World War II and who have entered the civilian labor market into three groups.

The first group, the baby boomers, were raised by parents whose "ability to finance a college education for their sons and daughters was unprecedented."[18] Many of the women in this group earned graduate degrees and then joined the professional and managerial ranks in both the public and the private sectors. According to Bianchi:

> They inundated executive offices, law firms, hospitals, and finally the armed forces, voicing great skepticism as to whether they would be the exception rather than the rule. If they worked assertively, diligently, and continuously, the inherently sexist, unfair system would somehow recognize their individual talent and would promote them as readily as their equally well trained male counterparts. . . . The gamble that unfairness and discrimination would not impede their progress—or at least would deter them much less than it had in the past—ultimately paid off.[19]

Bianchi notes that, during the 1980s, "there was a narrowing of the gender wage gap partly as a function of this baby boom generation of young women moving into mid-career and partly as a result of their mothers', who were paid much less than their daughters, retirement from the labor market."[20]

In contrast to the baby boomers, for the second group of women—working women with a high school education or less—life did not seem so fair during the 1980s. These women were concentrated principally in the expanding service sector of the economy (particularly in health care). Working long hours (much longer than their male counterparts) in mainly part-time and temporary jobs, these women and their families have become members of the working poor in America, that growing class of individuals and families whose earnings are insufficient to lift them above the official poverty line.[21]

Single mothers with dependent children, who are disconnected from the labor market and who rely primarily on welfare for survival, constitute the third group of women. Findings from recent studies show that most of these women possess neither the "hard" human capital skills nor the "soft" cultural capital skills to compete for jobs in the contemporary labor market.[22] Nevertheless, they are the target of the recently enacted welfare reform legislation that seeks to change welfare as we know it by transitioning these women into the world of work. It should be noted here that by removing these individuals from the welfare rolls and pushing them into the labor market without adequate skills to compete in the advanced industrial economy, the federal government is, in essence, flooding the labor market with additional low skilled job seekers, which in turn will further exacerbate existing income disparities.

Some of the difficulties that women face in the U.S. labor market stem from the fact that, despite recent changes in social norms, they remain either principally (two-parent families) or solely (single-parent families) responsible for child care in their households. As Apter points out in her provocatively titled book *Working Women Don't Have Wives*, this reality represents a major barrier to female labor force participation and to the occupational mobility of women when they manage to secure employment because of the failure of both public and private sector employers to adjust workplace rules to accommodate women's primary roles as homemakers and caretakers of children.[23]

Previous research indicates that lack of access to affordable child care is one of the reasons women are more likely to work part time or to drop out of the labor force from time to time. Further, studies show that such family-related breaks in employment adversely affect wages, other types of compensation, and occupational advancement.[24]

Recent reforms of U.S. immigration laws also have played a major role in the growing income disparities in the American society. It is well documented that the origin, size, and composition of the legal immigration stream changed dramatically as a consequence of the Hart-Cellar Act of 1965 and more recent amendments to it (especially the Immigration Reform and Control Act of 1986 [IRCA] and the Immigration Act of 1990). Between 1961 and 1992, legal immigration to the United States averaged 561,000 people per year, compared with an average of 206,000 per year between 1921 and 1960.[25]

Along with those entering by means of the hemispheric quota and family/occupation preference provisions established in the Hart-Cellar Act of 1965, the new arrivals over the past 30 years have also included a significant number of refugees, parolees, and asylum seekers fleeing political persecution in their home countries and a substantial number of illegal immigrants searching for jobs and an improved quality of life. Between 1961 and 1993, according to the Immigration and Naturalization Service (INS), 2,149,369 refugees, parolees, and asylees were allowed to settle in the United States (roughly 65,000 annually). It has been estimated that between 300,000 and 400,000 unauthorized immigrants have entered the United States each year over the past two decades. However, the actual number of undocumented immigrants who have settled permanently in the United States remains unknown, partly because their illegal status makes it difficult to enumerate them and partly because an undetermined proportion enter and exit the country on a daily (e.g., Mexican day laborers) or seasonal (e.g., migrant farm workers) basis.[26]

In terms of the impact of illegal immigration on the U.S. civilian labor pool, the number of unauthorized aliens granted amnesty under the IRCA of 1986 is probably the best indicator. Any illegal immigrant who could demonstrate that he or she had lived in the United States before 1982 was eligible to apply for citizenship under this act. Three million undocumented immigrants took advantage of this opportunity to become U.S. citizens.[27]

The view was that if amnesty was granted to such a large number of people who were residing in the United States illegally, these new legal workers would saturate domestic labor demand and thereby stem the illegal flow. In an effort to further stem the tide, the IRCA of 1986 also introduced sanctions designed to prohibit employers from hiring undocumented or unauthorized workers and allocated additional resources to beef up control of the U.S.-Mexico border.[28]

These reforms have been largely ineffective and have contributed to growing income inequality in American society. Their ineffectiveness is partially rooted in the initial framing of the legislation, which involved a strange ideological convergence of two otherwise politically opposite groups: market-oriented expansionists, comprising mainly business people on the political right, and rights-oriented expansionists, comprising primarily human rights advocates and members of ethnic minority groups on the political left.[29] In the debate over the illegal immigrant problem and U.S. immigration policy that led up to the enactment of the 1986 IRCA, both of these groups advocated expanded immigration, but for radically different reasons.

Reflecting the resurgence of free market economics in American politics during the 1980s, the market-oriented expansionists advocated the "free flow of goods, technology, capital, and people across international borders."[30] In support of a robust immigration policy, they praised immigrants for their propensity to start new businesses and for keeping U.S. businesses competitive in the international marketplace. Using this argument, they were able to secure, through the 1986 IRCA, "sharp increases in employer-sponsored and skilled-worker visas, as well as cheap labor for the agricultural, garment, and hotel sectors."[31]

Building on the legacy of the civil rights movement in American politics, rights-oriented expansionists sought to gain entry and protection for powerless immigrant groups, especially nonwhite illegal immigrants and refugees. Through the 1986 reform legislation, they were able to "secure a generous amnesty program for illegal aliens, a new civil rights agency charged with combating job discrimination against aliens, a new protection for temporary farm workers, generous allocation of family reunification visas, and the removal of many ideological and sexual-orientation restrictions."[32]

Largely because of the political coalition between these otherwise strange bedfellows, the 1986 reforms have been counterproductive. First, as Andreas notes, above and beyond the Mexican immigrants who were living in the United States illegally, many of their counterparts who had returned to Mexico actually came back to the United States to claim their legalization papers after the 1986 law was enacted.[33] It is noteworthy that these immigrants were able to reenter the United States illegally even though the federal government, pursuant to the reform legislation, nearly doubled the number of border control agents—from 2,500 to 4,800 in 1986—in an effort to significantly tighten control of the border. It was assumed that beefed up control would increase the number of apprehensions, which in turn would serve as a deterrent to continued illegal immigration.

But, as Andreas points out, this has been an ineffective strategy: "Many illegal immigrants make regular trips between the United States and Mexico, but often stay in the U.S. only long enough to earn a fixed amount of money. Stricter border control, however, induces them to stay longer; the more difficult it is to cross the border, the more expensive the journey becomes. As border controls are tightened, illegal immigrants rely on 'coyote' professional smugglers to take them across the U.S. for a fee."[34]

Andreas states further that, "in effect, tighter border controls may reduce the number of trips made by illegal immigrants, but they increase the incentive to cross the border and, once across, to stay longer. Moreover, by forcing illegal immigrants to depend more on smugglers, border enforcement has helped to create a profitable and increasingly sophisticated business in 'human trafficking'."[35]

In addition, research shows that when surveillance is tightened in one area, new ports of illegal entry are established elsewhere along the border. As one INS official said: "We call it the balloon effect. You squeeze it here, it goes over there."[36]

Similarly, the employer sanctions component of the IRCA of 1986 has been largely ineffective. In deliberations surrounding this act, neither the market-oriented expansionists on the right nor the civil rights-oriented expansionists on the left supported the creation of a new counterfeit- and tamper-resistant employer identification card that would have made it easier for the federal government to monitor workplace hiring practices. In the absence of support for the use of such a card, the IRCA of 1986 permitted undocumented immigrants to use a wide range of documents to demonstrate that they had lived in the United States before 1982. Moreover, because of the political left's concerns about violations of civil liberties and the potential for discrimination in hiring decisions and because of the political right's concerns about the undue burden that the document requirements would place on businesses from the political right, small businesses were exempt from the document requirements altogether. Other employers were required only to attest to the face validity of the documents and to their authenticity. Further, the enforcement of these sanctions has been very lax.[37]

Andreas concludes that fewer than 5 percent of U.S. workplaces have been inspected since sanctions were initiated.[38] In addition, field research suggests that since the implementation of IRCA, the "use of fraudulent documents by unauthorized workers is widespread."[39] It has been estimated that "at least one-half, and perhaps substantially more, of the unauthorized hires made after the passage of the IRCA may have involved fraudulent documents."[40]

Thus, partly because of the aforementioned flaws or unanticipated effects and partly because of the state of the U.S. economy when it was enacted, the 1986 law may have contributed to the increased flow of illegal immigrants into the U.S. labor market instead of stemming the tide as originally intended. When the law was implemented, the U.S. economy was booming, and the demand for cheap unskilled and semi-skilled labor, especially in the craft specialty and hospitality service industries, served as a strong magnet for continued illegal immigration into the United States. Further, the flow was facilitated and enhanced by the unanticipated effects of beefed up border controls, lax enforcement of employer sanctions, and, most important, the granting of legal status to 3 million formerly undocumented and mostly Mexican immigrants. Commenting on the unanticipated impact of the amnesty provision of the 1986 law, Andreas notes that "those who were granted legal status and thus allowed to work provided a more permanent base for the social networks that facilitate the arrival of new [illegal and legal] immigrants."[41]

Not unlike what happened with the IRCA of 1986, the reforms implemented by the Immigration Act of 1990 have been similarly counterproductive, and basically for the same reason: the invisible hands of the rights-oriented expansionists on the political left and the market-oriented expansionists on the political right. In the 1990 act, the former were successful in winning stays of deportation for family members of immigrants legalized under the IRCA of 1986, which heightened the flow of legal immigrants to the United States under the family preference provision. The latter succeeded in getting the cap raised on legal immigration by securing increases in employer-sponsored and skilled worker visas.[42]

That these reforms have been counterproductive and have contributed to growing income inequality is directly related to the timing of the law's enactment. These reforms were implemented precisely when the U.S. economy was experiencing a major downturn, characterized by massive layoffs, increasing job insecurity, and sharply declining wages, all of which figure heavily in the growing opposition among native-born Americans to U.S. immigration policy.[43] As a consequence, the large-scale influx of immigrants—legal and illegal—over the past three decades has created labor surplus environments, that is, labor market conditions in which there are far more job seekers than available jobs.[44] In the low wage sectors of the economy, this situation not only tends to depress wages, but it also affords employers maximum flexibility to pick and choose workers.

Studies by Kirschenman and Neckerman, among others, indicate that in such environments, employers display a strong preference for immigrant workers over native workers in general and over black job seekers in particular.[45] Black workers are perceived to be lazy, inarticulate, untrainable, and, most important, dangerous. Immigrant workers, especially those who are undocumented, are perceived to be more compliant and industrious and thus are highly preferred in the workplace.[46] Employers in rapidly growing industries such as garment manufacturing and hospitality services (e.g., hotels, motels, restaurants, fast food outlets, and taxicab companies) satisfy their labor demands either by tapping into informal networks of immigrant workers directly or by contracting with firms that have access to such networks.[47]

Although there is considerable disagreement in the literature on the actual labor market impacts of immigrants, there is growing evidence that displacement is occurring.[48] Mines reports how employers in the high rise office district of Los Angeles contracted with firms that tapped into networks of recent immigrants to hire janitors. Mines shows not only that the recently arrived immigrant workers displaced black janitors, but also that wage rates declined from $13 per hour to just over the minimum wage.[49]

Other research suggests that a similar displacement of veteran workers is occurring in industries such as garment manufacturing, frozen foods, construction and construction clean-up, and hospitality services, all of which previously had large numbers of black workers. In the Los Angeles garment industry, for example, an estimated 90 percent of the workforce is foreign born, mainly undocumented immigrants from Mexico.[50] At the upper end of the labor market, employers use temporary work visas and employment-based provisions of the immigration law to bring in foreign workers for professional-level jobs that might otherwise go to native-born Americans. This is thought to be a common practice in the United States in multinational corporations, universities, and computer and movie companies.[51]

Current immigration law permits foreigners with specialized skills to work in the United States for six years. "The law even permits U.S. companies to fire American professionals and replace them with foreigners as long as the foreigners are paid 'comparable' wages to the departing Americans."[52] However, enforcement is difficult because the federal government acts only when foreigners complain, which they rarely do. Thus, it is not known how many companies pay foreigners below-market wages.

One recent case handled by the U.S. Department of Labor illustrates how employers have used the law to the detriment of American workers and how it has contributed to growing income inequality in American society.[53] A large insurance firm laid off its entire management information services department staff of 250 programmers and replaced them with foreign programmers brought from India on H-1B visas. The firm that the insurance company contracted with to provide the computing services was accused of paying the 40 programmers from India below-market wages.[54] To settle the case, the contractor was forced to pay $77,000 in back wages to the

40 foreign programmers, to hire 40 American programmers in the next year, and to spend $1 million to train U.S. workers in the latest software techniques. The company also agreed not to bring any more foreign programmers into the United States for 90 days.[55]

Complaints about these kinds of practices have led a group of Austin, Texas, programmers to form a political action committee to protect their jobs.[56] These and other concerned groups have encouraged members of Congress to press for cuts in the number of foreign workers allowed into the United States under this provision of the immigration law from 65,000 to 30,000 annually. Moreover, a bill was introduced in Congress that sought to discourage the practice by requiring foreigners to be paid 10 percent more than their American predecessors.[57]

Employment and Training Policy

Over the past 15 years, some individuals and groups have been constrained by the employment and job training assistance policies enacted in the 1980s from gaining the skills that would qualify them for well-paying jobs in the high growth sectors of the U.S. economy. The Job Training and Partnership Act of 1981 (JTPA), which replaced the Comprehensive Employment and Training Act of 1973 (CETA), represented the Reagan administration's programmatic response to the growing mismatch between skills and jobs in the U.S. economy. Fitzgerald and McGregor summarize how the JTPA program contributed to growing income inequality in American society during the 1980s:

> The limited effectiveness of JTPA is related to the need to meet federal regulations. The goal is to place applicants as quickly as possible, without respect to quality of employment. Job placement assistance is preferred over training, because it is the shortest, and thus the cheapest, service. Fifty percent of enrollees receive placement assistance only. Evidence suggests that the JTPA program creams off the most employable individuals for the most effective types of training in order to meet placement criteria. Specifically, white males seem to be channeled into on-the-job training programs, which provide the highest reemployment opportunities, while women, minorities, the long-term unemployed, and public assistance recipients are more likely to receive classroom than on-the-job training [with little or no guarantee of employment upon completion].[58]

More specifically, the latter groups were more likely to be directed into general equivalency diploma (GED) programs. Commenting on the labor market experiences of these individuals, Fitzgerald and McGregor "frequently find that there is no demand for their newly acquired skills in the local labor market," a finding supported by other research that documents the modest economic returns to securing a GED.[59]

In addition to the discrimination inherent in program implementation, Grant and Johnson point out that the Reagan administration substantially cut the federal budget for job training and employment assistance.[60] Fitzgerald and McGregor estimate that "real per capita funding for federal employment and job training programs declined by nearly 80% between 1979 and 1986."[61]

Education Policy

Several studies point out that the growing income inequality in American society is partly related to recently implemented policies designed to remedy what is increasingly being perceived as a failing public education system. In dissecting and challenging the "crisis" in American public education, researchers contend that analysts and policymakers have instituted a series of "get-tough" education policies— such as tracking by ability, grade retention, increasing reliance on standardized tests as the ultimate arbiter of educational success, and extreme disciplinary sanctions—that have disenfranchised large numbers of black and other minority youth.[62]

With respect to tracking, Oliver and Johnson cite data indicating that black youth are underrepresented in the gifted and talented or college-bound tracks and overrepresented in the vocational, general education, and special education or noncollege-bound tracks. Moreover, they note that individuals who have little or no training in child development often do this tracking. Pursuant to the adverse effects of tracking, they also show how school officials have tightened requirements for both high school graduation and college admission without paying proper attention to whether qualified teachers and the necessary facilities are available at the primary and secondary school levels. These developments, they contend, have been especially problematic for urban blacks from impoverished backgrounds who attend economically and educationally inferior schools.[63]

Oliver and Johnson also cite the increased reliance on standardized general and subject-specific tests as yet another barrier—consistent with well-established biases that characterize these tests in predicting black (and other minority) student academic success in higher education. Finally, they draw attention to research showing that blacks generally, and black males specifically, are more likely than their white counterparts to be subjected to extreme disciplinary sanctions, including permanent expulsion from school.[64] A number of studies confirm that these and related get-tough education policies are directly responsible for the recent rise in the dropout rate and the decrease in the college-attendance rate of black youth, especially black males. Johnson and Oliver argue that because many of those who drop out of high school or fail to qualify for admission to a college or university do not possess the skills to compete for jobs in the rapidly growing high wage sectors of the U.S.

economy, these policies have further exacerbated joblessness and eroded the earning power of young black males.[65]

Crime Policy and Criminal Justice

State governments' anticrime policies also have contributed to growing income inequality in American society. According to Petersilia and others, for nearly three decades, states have pursued a policy of resolving the problems of the inner city through the criminal justice system.[66] California, once a leader in the rehabilitation of criminals, epitomizes this shift in anticrime policy. Describing this shift, Petersilia states that "In 1977 the California legislature enacted the Determinant Sentence Law, which, among other things, embraced punishment (and, explicitly, not rehabilitation) as the purpose of prison, required mandatory prison sentences for many offenses formerly eligible for probation, and dramatically increased the rate at which probation and parole violators were returned to prison."[67] As a consequence of this law, "the California prison population skyrocketed from 22,000 to 106,000 between 1980 and 1992, an increase of more than 400%."[68]

Following California's lead, a number of other states have enacted determinant sentence laws and also have gone on a prison construction binge to accommodate the resulting increase in their prison populations. Freeman notes that, as a consequence of this "lock-them-up-and-throw-away-the-key" approach to the crime problem, state spending on criminal justice has far outstripped total spending and spending on education.[69] According to Petersilia, over a five-year period, spending on the criminal justice system increased by 70 percent in California, approximately four times greater than total state spending, whereas state spending on education increased by only 10 percent.[70] Minorities, especially black males, have been affected disproportionately by these get-tough-on-crime policies.[71] In California, for example, two-thirds of the prison population is black or Hispanic, with blacks constituting 35 percent of the total.[72] Freeman estimates that nationally "In 1993, about 7 percent of black men over 18 were incarcerated. One black man was in prison for every 11 black men in the workforce; and approximately one was under the supervision of the criminal justice system for every three to four black men in the workforce. Combine race and age and you find that 12 percent of black men age 25-34 were incarcerated."[73]

What are the prospects of landing a job in general, and a good job in particular, if you have a criminal record? As Johnson and Oliver note, for the African American male, "incarceration breeds despair, and hopelessness, and in the employment arena, it is the 'Scarlet Letter' of unemployability."[74] Thus, interracial disparities in income are related, at least in part, to state-level anticrime policies that have been implemented over the past three decades.

THE RESEARCH CONTEXT

Nowhere in the United States have the effects of recent policy changes in the aforementioned domains been more evident than in metropolitan Los Angeles.[75] To set the context for the snapshots of income inequality presented here, we highlight the nature and magnitude of changes in the Los Angeles community that were wrought by conservative policy-making at the federal, state, and local levels of government.[76] It must be noted, however, that there are rapidly increasing manifestations of unequal economic and social circumstances between and within racial/ethnic, gender, and immigrant groups across America.[77]

It is well documented that to lure international capital to Los Angeles and to enhance the competitiveness of locally based firms, city officials have pursued, consciously and aggressively over the past quarter century, a strategy of downtown and Westside redevelopment at the expense of the neighborhoods and communities that make up south central Los Angeles.[78] This policy paid off handsomely in terms of job creation, at least during the 1980s, when more than 732,000 jobs were added to the Los Angeles economy. But undergirding this massive job growth were sectoral, organizational, and locational changes in economic activities that dramatically altered the structure of employment opportunities and the socioeconomic well-being of the population.

First, as Table 1 shows, most of the job growth was highly concentrated in two economic sectors—producer services (high wage jobs) and personal services (mainly low wage jobs). Second, most of the high wage job growth was concentrated in the downtown area, where city officials used tax increment financing and other financial incentives to encourage multinational corporations to establish their headquarters, and in new high technology manufacturing employment growth nodes, or "technopoles," that were established in the San Fernando Valley, in the San Gabriel Valley, in El Segundo near the airport in Los Angeles County, and in nearby Orange County, communities where the black and Hispanic populations were small or nonexistent.[79]

Third, between 1978 and 1989, in part as a function of the city's wholesale disinvestment in south central Los Angeles—the traditional industrial hub of the region—approximately 200,000 "good paying," unionized manufacturing jobs disappeared from the Los Angeles economy—a process known as deindustrialization—because of plant closings and capital flight to the U.S.-Mexico border region. During this period, an estimated 215 Los Angeles-based employers, including Hughes Aircraft, Northrop, Rockwell, and many smaller firms, established manufacturing facilities in the Mexican border towns of Tijuana, Ensenada, and Tecate, where labor is much cheaper than in Los Angeles. As noted elsewhere, this capital flight, in conjunction with the plant closings, "essentially denied the predominantly black and Hispanic residents of south central Los Angeles access to formerly well-paying, unionized jobs."[80]

TABLE 1

EMPLOYMENT CHANGE BY INDUSTRY, 1980-90

	Total Employment	Transfor-mative	Distributive	Producer Services	Personal Services	Social Services
			Industry			
Los Angeles County						
1980	3,471,764	1,038,751	948,524	492,278	254,320	694,150
1990	4,203,792	1,107,917	1,150,053	709,066	365,534	810,096
Change '80-'90	732,028	69,166	201,529	216,788	111,214	115,946
%	21.0	16.6	21.0	44.0	44.0	16.7
Los Angeles City						
1980	1,394,855	376,656	365,858	229,350	129,901	275,733
1990	1,670,488	405,447	437,548	315,409	184,850	302,367
Change '80-'90	275,633	28,791	71,690	86,059	54,949	26,634
%	19.7	7.6	19.6	37.5	42.3	9.7
Balance of County						
1980	2,076,909	662,095	582,666	262,928	124,419	418,417
1990	2,533,304	702,470	712,505	393,657	180,684	507,729
Change '80-'90	456,395	40,375	129,839	130,729	56,265	89,312
%	21.9	6.1	22.3	49.7	45.2	21.3

Source: Compiled by authors from the LASUI.

However, new employment opportunities have emerged within or near the traditional industrial core in south central Los Angeles,[81] but they are radically different from the manufacturing jobs that disappeared from the area. The new jobs are in the competitive sector of the economy, including the hospitality service industry and craft specialty industries such as clothing, jewelry, and furniture manufacturing, in which employers survive only to the extent that their prices remain nationally and internationally competitive. To remain competitive, they "often hire undocumented workers, offer unattractive working conditions, and pay, at best, the minimum wage."[82] The growth of the competitive sector of the Los Angeles economy has been fostered by the federal government's failure to control the flow of illegal immigrants into the Los Angeles region and to enforce laws governing employer recruitment, hiring, and compensation of undocumented workers.[83]

A number of studies have demonstrated how the foregoing developments helped widen the divide between the haves and the have-nots in

Los Angeles during the 1980s. Making matters worse, since 1990, the demand for labor in all sectors of the Los Angeles economy has been on a downward trajectory. This is generally a result of major federal cuts in defense spending and a growing trend in corporate America toward downsizing, reengineering, and capital flight, especially from California, in an effort to facilitate efficiency and competitiveness in the global marketplace.[84] Mainly as a consequence of these forces, it has been estimated that California lost 700,000 jobs at the onset of this decade. Much of this loss is attributable to business failures and capital flight from the Los Angeles metropolitan area. Unfortunately, these demand-side changes in the labor market did not stem the tide of job seekers arriving in Los Angeles, primarily from abroad. Between 1990 and 1995, the population of Los Angeles increased by nearly 25 percent because of a steady stream of legal and illegal immigrants into the area.[85]

Partly as a function of the city's wholesale economic disinvestment in south central Los Angeles, the area has become host to a disproportionate number of alcohol outlets and other locally unwanted land uses, which makes it an unattractive place for business development. Moreover, city officials' neglect of south central Los Angeles coincided with massive cuts in federal aid to cities.[86] Both of these developments occurred when the primary institutions in south central Los Angeles—families, schools, churches, and others—were being swamped with huge increases in the juvenile population. Partly as a function of these cuts in local and federal government assistance, the community's primary institutions started "to crumble at the very moment when they were needed to be towers of strength."[87]

At the state level during this same period, there was a dramatic reallocation of resources from the public education system to the criminal justice system. This reallocation process has been a double-edged sword for African American males in particular.[88] Cuts in education have contributed to their school failure, and the increased spending on "lock-them-up-and-throw-away-the-key" crime control policies has been used to brand them with the scarlet letter of unemployability.[89] It is emblematic of the state and national changes in crime control policy that both the Los Angeles Police Department and the Los Angeles Sheriff's Department have strategically targeted south central Los Angeles, the heart of Los Angeles's black community, and young African American males within this community in their war on gangs and drugs.[90]

THE DATA

In 1992, we undertook a primary data-gathering initiative, the Los Angeles Survey of Urban Inequality (LASUI), in an effort to gauge the impact of these and other developments on the social and economic well-being of the residents of metropolitan Los Angeles. The LASUI is part of a larger interdisciplinary research initiative, the Multi-City Survey of Urban Inequality (MCSUI). Through surveys of large samples of households (8,600) and employers (4,000) in Atlanta, Boston, Detroit, and Los Angeles, the MCSUI sought to gather data that would enable researchers to determine the extent to which three sets of forces—changing labor market dynamics, racial attitudes and polarization, and residential segregation—contributed, singularly and in concert, to the growing gap between the haves and the have-nots that has been observed in urban America over the past two decades.

In the remainder of this chapter, we use data from the LASUI to illustrate the nature and magnitude of income inequality in Los Angeles and to identify some of the factors contributing to the growing disparities in income that emanate from the policy choices and options adopted at the federal, state, and local levels of government. The LASUI sample is large and highly representative not only of the dominant ethnic groups—Asians, African Americans, Hispanics, and non-Hispanic whites—in the local labor market, but also of the population residing in both poor and nonpoor neighborhoods in Los Angeles (see Table 2).

For the purpose of this research, we relied on self-reports of 1992 pretax income from all sources for individuals captured in the LASUI who were employed either part time or full time, temporarily laid off, on maternity leave, on sick leave, or unemployed. To facilitate our efforts to develop a profile or portrait of income inequality in Los Angeles, we grouped these individuals by race/ethnic identity (white, black, or Hispanic), gender, and immigrant status (undocumented immigrant or green card holder). Because of problems in coding and verifying the data for Asians, a process still under way, they are excluded from this analysis. We selected four sets of variables from the LASUI that we believe capture the effects of conservative policymaking during the past 20 years on income distribution in Los Angeles.

The first set of variables seeks to document changes in the structure of employment opportunities that have accompanied the government's efforts to create a deregulated business environment to foster the competitiveness of U.S. firms (see business policy variables in Table 3). It includes indicators of the type (full-time versus part-time), quantity (hours worked per week, weeks worked per year), and quality (e.g., whether the job is covered by a union contract or a collective bargaining agreement) of work that is available to workers and job seekers in Los Angeles. One school of thought posits that growing income inequality reflects the fact that an increasing number of jobs are concentrated in the contingent economy, characterized by part-time and temporary work, jobs with no benefits, and few, if any, prospects for upward mobility.[91] The data reveal how prevalent these kinds of jobs are in the Los Angeles economy and how they affect the income distribution.

The second set of variables seeks to assess the effects of policies implemented to improve the human capital skills of workers and job seekers (see employment and training variables in Table 3). It also seeks to elucidate the consequences of policies designed to improve the competitiveness of urban communities in the global marketplace, including

TABLE 2

COMPARISON OF LASUI DATA WITH 1990 CENSUS OF POPULATION AND HOUSING DATA

Neighborhood Poverty Status

Neighborhood Poverty Level	LASUI RAW Sample	LASUI Weighted Sample	L.A. County Eligibles*	L.A. County Total
<20%	52.7	75.2	72.6	70
20-40%	31.5	22.2	24.7	27
>40%	15.8	2.6	2.6	3
Total	4,025	3,133	6,108,478	8,863,164

COMPARISON OF LASUI DATA WITH 1990 CENSUS OF POPULATION AND HOUSING DATA

Race and Ethnicity

Group	LASUI RAW	LASUI Weighted	L.A. County Eligibles*	L.A. County Total
White	21.4	43.2	49.4	47.0
Black	27.8	11.0	10.9	10.3
Asian	26.2	7.7	6.5	6.2
Hispanic	24.5	38.1	33.2	31.5
Other	—	—	—	5.0
Total	4,025	4,025	5,787,991	6,090,712

*Population 21 years of age or older.

Source: U.S. Bureau of the Census, 1990 Census of Population and Housing, STF3A.

the get-tough-on-crime policies implemented at the various levels of government (see criminal justice variable in Table 3).

A third set of variables focuses on the federal, state, and local governments' disinvestment in urban communities. In part because of the dismantling of the social safety net in the inner city, many urban communities are socially isolated and economically marginalized from mainstream networks of information about educational and employment opportunities, as well as other resources (e.g., access to affordable child care) needed to compete successfully in the labor market. Three specific variables are included in this analysis.[92]

TABLE 3

**MEANS AND STANDARD DEVIATIONS FOR VARIABLES
USED IN LASUI ANALYSES**

Type of Variable	Policy Domain	Concept	Specific Measure	Mean	Standard Deviation
Independent	Equal opportunity	Race/ethnic identity	Black (yes)	.342	.475
			Hispanic (yes)	.307	.461
		Gender	Female (yes)	.547	.498
		Immigration	Green card (yes)	.091	.287
			Undocumented (yes)	.070	.256
			English proficiency (yes)	.858	.349
	Human capital	Hard skills	Education (years)	12.8	3.3
			Age (<35)	.451	.498
			Years of work experience	17.1	12.6
	Employment and training	Skills enhancement	Job training (yes)	.350	.477
			GED (yes)	.012	.111
	Social	Public assistance	AFDC (yes)	.138	.345
			Child care	.132	.339
	Business	Job quality	Job w/benefits (yes)	.646	.478
			Hours worked/week	39.5	11.4
			Weeks worked/92	37.7	19.8
	Criminal justice	Criminal record	Reform school, detention center, jail, prison (yes)	.107	.309
	Urban	Social capital	Race bridge (yes)	.267	.442
			Education bridge (yes)	.653	.467
Dependent	Income	Disparity	Natural log of 1992 pretax income as a percent of metro average income	.605	.473

Source: Compiled by authors from the LASUI.

The first pertains to the effects on income of being embedded in homogeneous versus heterogeneous networks (see social capital variables in Table 3). The LASUI included several questions regarding networks and social functioning that were introduced with the following statement: "From time to time, most people discuss important matters with other people. Looking back over the last six months, who are the people, other than people living in your household, with whom you discussed matters important to you?" For the first three names given, data were recorded on race or ethnicity; sex; level of education completed; relationship to respondent; marital status; whether they lived in the respondent's neighborhood, had a steady job, and received public aid or welfare; and whether these individuals assisted with everyday activities and could be relied on for help in a major crisis.

From these data, we created two indicators of the degree to which the individual was embedded in a homogeneous or heterogeneous network. If any member of a respondent's network was of a different race, then the respondent was assumed to have a race bridge—that is, to be embedded in a racially diverse network. If at least one person in the network had more than a high school education, then the respondent was assumed to have an education bridge—that is, to be embedded in a diverse network based on the years of school completed by the various members.

The third and fourth variables are, respectively, a self-reported measure of child care constraints and whether the individual was a recipient of public assistance income. Previous research has shown lack of access to affordable and quality child care and receipt of public assistance to be major impediments to full-time employment for women, especially those who live in spatially and socially isolated, ghetto poor, or concentrated poverty communities.[93]

In addition to the foregoing variables, we included three standard human capital measures that are typically included in analyses of income inequality: education, age, and work experience.

ANALYSES AND FINDINGS

Snapshots of Income Inequality

To illustrate the nature and depth of income inequality in Los Angeles, we used the pretax 1992 mean annual income ($20,465) for all residents of metropolitan Los Angeles, the standard or benchmark against which the mean annual incomes of the various race/ethnic, gender, and immigrant groups would be compared. The results are presented in Chart 1.

Using the metropolitanwide mean income as the benchmark, we see that white males constitute a major outlier at the upper end of the distribution. On average, they earned 84 percent more than the average resident of the Los Angeles metropolitan area in 1992. The incomes of

CHART 1

INCOME COMPARISON BY RACE/ETHNICITY, GENDER, AND IMMIGRANT STATUS, PRETAX INCOME, 1992

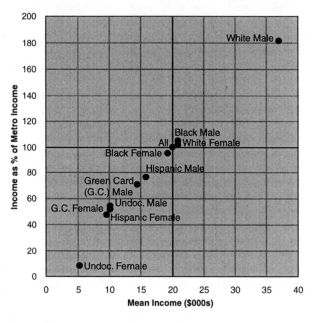

Source: Compiled by authors from the LASUI.

the other race/ethnic, gender, and immigrant groups tended to cluster in four distinct patterns. The mean annual incomes of black males, white females, and black females hovered around the mean income level for the Los Angeles metropolitan area. The mean annual incomes of these groups ranged from 96 percent to 104 percent of the metropolitanwide average. A second cluster comprised Hispanic males and recent male immigrants who had green cards; their mean incomes were 79 percent and 72 percent, respectively, of the metropolitan average. Male undocumented workers, female immigrants who had green cards, and Hispanic females made up the third cluster, with annual incomes ranging between 48 percent and 54 percent of the metropolitan average.

Finally, not unlike white males at the upper end of the income distribution, female undocumented workers constitute a major outlier at the lower end of the Los Angeles distribution. In 1992, their mean annual income ($4,481) was only 22 percent of the metropolitan average. Hispanic males and male immigrants who had green cards earned, on average, 43 percent and 39 percent, respectively, of what the average white male in Los Angeles earned in 1992. The incomes of undocumented male workers, immigrant females with green cards, and Hispanic females were 26 percent to 29 percent of the mean income of white males. Female immigrants living in Los Angeles illegally had an average income in 1992 that was only 12 percent of that of the average white male.

Factors Contributing to Income Disparities

Are the foregoing disparities in income a function of discrimination in the Los Angeles labor market based on race/ethnicity, gender, and immigrant status, or are other factors operating to account for these differences? The data in Charts 2 through 12 provide preliminary answers to this question.

Bivariate Associations

Employment

Chart 2 presents data on the levels of full-time work, part-time work, and nonwork as well as mean incomes by race/ethnicity, gender, and immigrant status. These data suggest that income disparities are related in part to the high levels of underemployment that exist in the Los Angeles labor market. In this study, underemployment is defined as the percentage of individuals in the Los Angeles labor market who either were not working or were working part-time involuntarily. Included in the involuntary part-time work category were individuals who indicated that they could find only part-time work, that they could not find enough work, or that their hours had been reduced. As Chart 2 shows, this is an especially acute problem for undocumented immigrants and Hispanics, whose rates of involuntary part-time employment in 1992 were consistently above the metropolitanwide average. This pattern, it should be noted, held across gender lines.

Combining the involuntary part-time workers with those who were not working reveals that more than one-half of all undocumented workers and more than 40 percent of black and Hispanic workers were underemployed compared with less than one-third of white workers. The pattern is basically the same when the data are disaggregated by gender. The main difference is that the rates of underemployment were much higher for females across all race/ethnic and immigrant status groups than they were for males.

Also contributing to income disparities were differences in average weeks worked and average hours worked per week, which varied by race/ethnicity, gender, and immigrant status (see Table 4). In Los Angeles, the average worker was employed for 37.7 weeks in 1992. White males (40.1 weeks), white females (38.0 weeks), Hispanic males (42.8 weeks), immigrant males with green cards (42.3 weeks), and undocu-

CHART 2

EMPLOYMENT AND INCOME COMPARISON BY RACE/ETHNICITY, GENDER, AND IMMIGRANT STATUS, PRETAX INCOME, 1992
(% Employment Status)

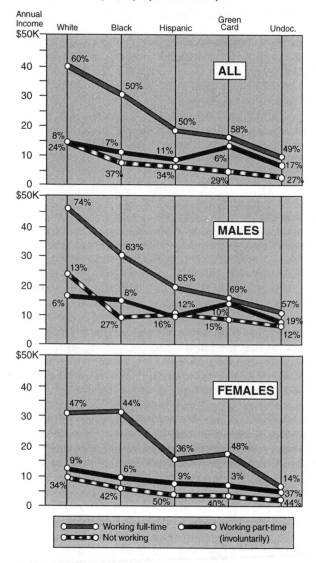

Note: Percentages do not total 100% because some individuals did not report income from any source in 1992.

Source: Compiled by authors from the LASUI.

TABLE 4

**AVERAGE WEEKS WORKED AND AVERAGE HOURS WORKED
PER WEEK IN 1992 BY RACE/ETHNICITY, GENDER, AND
IMMIGRANT STATUS**

Respondent	N	Average Weeks Worked	Average Hours Worked/Week
All	2,232	37.7	39.6
Male	1,061	40.4	41.5
Female	1,171	35.4	37.9
White	660	39.1	40.1
Male	341	40.1	43.1
Female	314	38.0	36.8
Black	763	35.6	38.8
Male	275	36.6	40.8
Female	488	35.1	37.7
Hispanic	809	38.6	39.9
Male	445	42.8	40.6
Female	364	33.5	39.0
Green card holder	187	37.0	38.7
Male	82	42.3	39.7
Female	105	32.9	38.0
Undocumented workers	189	36.9	40.2
Male	105	41.9	40.7
Female	84	30.6	39.4

Source: Compiled by authors from the LASUI.

mented male workers (41.9 weeks) all exceeded the metropolitan average for weeks worked in 1992 (37.7 weeks). In contrast, black males (36.6 weeks), black females (35.1 weeks), Hispanic females (33.5 weeks), female immigrants with green cards (32.9 weeks), and female undocumented immigrants (30.6 weeks) all worked less than the metropolitanwide average.

Similar disparities exist in average hours worked per week. In 1992, the typical worker in Los Angeles worked 39.6 hours per week on average. White males (43.1 hours), black males (40.8 hours), Hispanic males (40.6 hours), male immigrants with green cards (39.7 hours), and both male (40.7 hours) and female (39.4 hours) undocumented workers worked at or above the metropolitanwide average. White females (36.8

hours), black females (37.7 hours), Hispanic females (39.0 hours), and female immigrants with green cards (38.0 hours) all worked slightly fewer hours per week than the metropolitan average. The most vivid finding to emerge from this analysis of average weeks worked and average hours worked per week pertains to white male workers. On both of these indicators, white males exceeded the metropolitanwide averages, which partly explains the wide gap between their incomes and those of the rest of the Los Angeles population.

Job Quality

Further insights into the income disparity puzzle can be gained from Chart 3, which contains data on pretax 1992 mean income and job quality by race/ethnicity, gender, and immigrant status in Los Angeles. "Good" jobs are defined as those that provide health benefits to workers and their families, paid vacation leave, and retirement benefits. Two salient findings emerge.

The first is that whites are employed in the good jobs at a much higher rate than are members of the other race/ethnic and immigrant status groups. Moreover, this finding holds even after controlling for gender. Roughly 70 percent of white men and white women in Los Angeles were employed in good jobs in 1992. In the case of both black males (69.0 percent) and black females (63.5 percent), their concentration in good jobs hovered slightly above the metropolitanwide average; for green card holders, the proportion in good jobs was slightly below the metropolitan average. However, the pattern for undocumented workers was the reverse of that for the other groups. Only 24.6 percent of all undocumented workers, 32 percent of all male undocumented workers, and 16 percent of all female undocumented workers were employed in good jobs as defined here.

The second salient finding in Chart 3 is that statistically significant differences exist in the mean incomes of people employed in good jobs and those who were not. Individuals employed in good jobs had incomes, on average, of $6,000 to $12,000 higher than incomes of their counterparts who were not employed in good jobs. Black males and undocumented females were the only two groups for whom these findings did not hold.

Unionization

Whether a job is covered by a union contract or collective bargaining agreement is also a critical factor in understanding growing income inequality in American society over the past two decades. As Chart 4 shows, black women, Hispanic men and women, and male immigrants with green cards whose jobs were covered by these types of worker protections reported significantly higher pretax incomes in 1992 than did their counterparts who did not have such coverage or backing. For

CHART 3

JOB QUALITY AND INCOME COMPARISON BY RACE/ETHNICITY, GENDER, AND IMMIGRANT STATUS, PRETAX INCOME, 1992

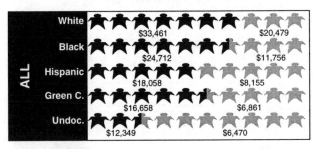

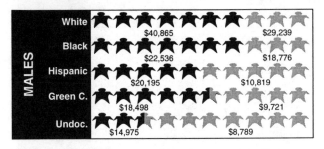

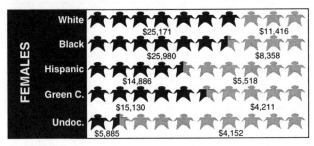

"Do you have a good job?" 🦅 **Yes**   🦅 **No**

(Yes/No per 10 respondents)

Source: Compiled by authors from the LASUI.

black females, the mean income differential was almost $17,000; for Hispanic males it was $5,000; for Hispanic females it was $10,000; and for male immigrants with green cards it was almost $6,000.

CHART 4

**A COMPARISON OF UNION AND NONUNION INCOME
BY RACE/ETHNICITY, GENDER, AND IMMIGRANT STATUS,
PRETAX INCOME, 1992**

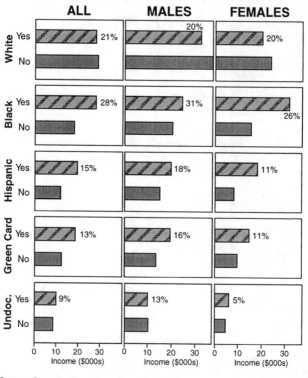

Source: Compiled by authors from the LASUI.

Education

In the extant literature, considerable attention has been devoted to the different human capital skill endowments that individuals and groups bring to the labor market as a major determinant of growing income inequality in U.S. society. More specifically, the research points to the poor performance of individuals with less than a high school education as a major source of the income inequality problem. The data in Chart 5 support this finding. Across race/ethnicity, gender, and immigrant status lines, with only one exception (undocumented female

CHART 5

EDUCATION AND INCOME COMPARISON BY RACE/ETHNICITY, GENDER, AND IMMIGRANT STATUS, PRETAX INCOME, 1992

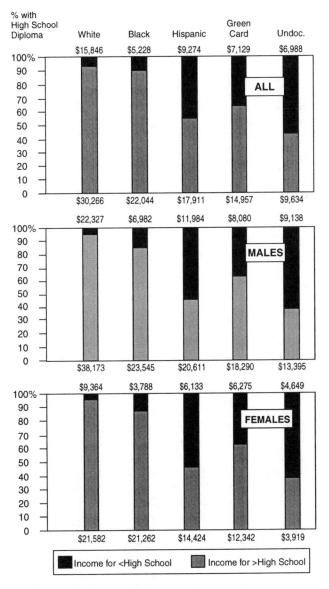

Source: Compiled by authors from the LASUI.

workers), the incomes of individuals with less than a high school education were significantly less than those of their counterparts who had more education. It is noteworthy that for black men, the income differential was almost $17,000.

At all levels of government, efforts have been made over the past 15 years to improve the human capital skills of the most disadvantaged (i.e., high school dropouts) through a wide array of education and job training programs, including encouraging young men and women who dropped out of high school to obtain a GED. Consistent with the findings of other researchers, the findings here suggest that GED programs have done little to narrow the income gap in metropolitan Los Angeles (see Chart 6). Undocumented immigrant males appear to be the only group for whom the GED has generated a statistically significant improvement in pretax mean income.

Job Training

Job training programs appear to have been similarly ineffective in closing the income gap between the haves and the have-nots (see Chart 7). Those programs are significant only for Hispanic females, and they are marginally significant for black females. Hispanic women who had job training reported incomes that were, on average, $5,242 more than their female counterparts who had not participated in a job training program. Black women with job training experience reported incomes that were, on average, $8,017 more than incomes reported by their counterparts who lacked job training experience.

Criminal Justice

Several researchers have argued that the get-tough-on-crime policies launched during the 1980s systematically targeted African American males for discriminatory treatment.[94] Further, the research suggests that in so doing, the policies have exerted a negative effect on both their access to jobs and their earnings if they are lucky enough to secure a job after having contact with the criminal justice system. The data in Chart 8 lend support to both arguments. As shown, more black males in the sample had criminal records (27.0 percent) than any other race/ethnic, gender, or immigrant status group. Thus, although the incomes of white females appear to have been hurt by their criminality, black males appear to be more adversely affected based on sheer numbers.

English Proficiency

As more and more jobs in the restructured economy require direct interface with the public, a premium is placed in the labor market on the ability to speak standard English. What impact, if any, does English proficiency have on incomes in the Los Angeles labor market? The data

CHART 6

GED COMPLETION AND INCOME COMPARISON BY RACE/ETHNICITY, GENDER, AND IMMIGRANT STATUS, PRETAX INCOME, 1992

(% shown of group that completed a GED)

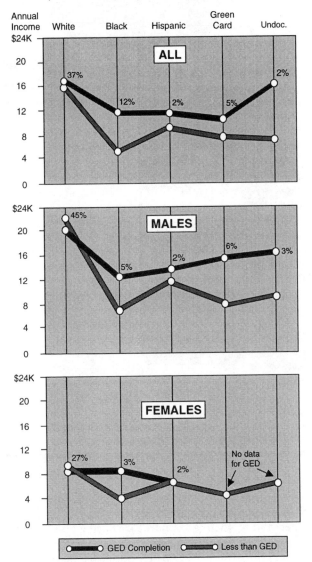

Source: Compiled by authors from the LASUI.

CHART 7

JOB TRAINING AND INCOME COMPARISON BY RACE/ETHNICITY, GENDER,* AND IMMIGRANT STATUS, PRETAX INCOME, 1992

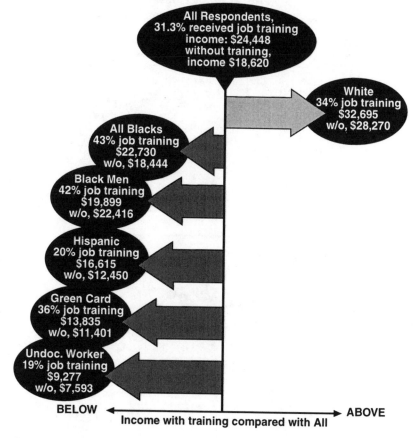

*Gender shown for black men only.

Source: Compiled by authors from the LASUI.

indicate that it has a statistically significant impact on the incomes of Hispanic men and women (see Chart 9). Those who were proficient in the English language reported pretax mean annual incomes that were $8,662 (Hispanic men) and $7,565 (Hispanic women) higher than the reported incomes of their counterparts who were not proficient in English.

CHART 8

CRIMINAL RECORD AND INCOME COMPARISON BY RACE/ETHNICITY, GENDER, AND IMMIGRANT STATUS, PRETAX INCOME, 1992

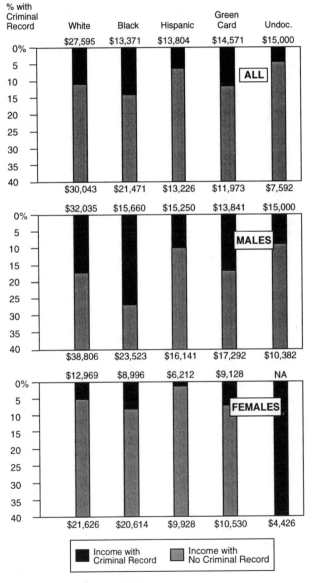

Source: Compiled by authors from the LASUI.

CHART 9

ENGLISH PROFICIENCY AND INCOME COMPARISON BY RACE/ETHNICITY, GENDER, AND IMMIGRANT STATUS, PRETAX INCOME, 1992

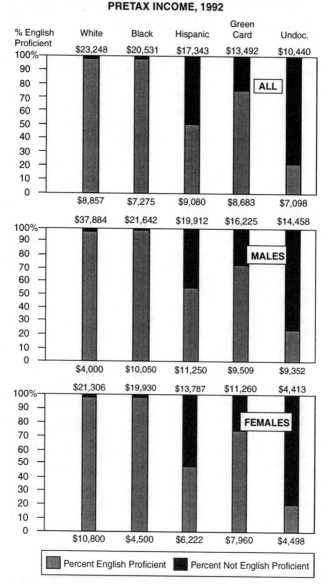

Percent English Proficient   Percent Not English Proficient

Note: Amounts at top of columns are incomes of English proficient. Amounts at bottom of columns are incomes of not English proficient.

Source: Compiled by authors from the LASUI.

Child Care Constraints

What impact do child care constraints have on female incomes? Across all race/ethnic and immigrant status groups, females who reported child care constraints as a major impediment to their participation in the labor market reported significantly smaller incomes than their counterparts who did not report such constraints (see Chart 10). The income differential ranged from a high of $12,000 for black females to a low of about $3,000 for undocumented female workers.

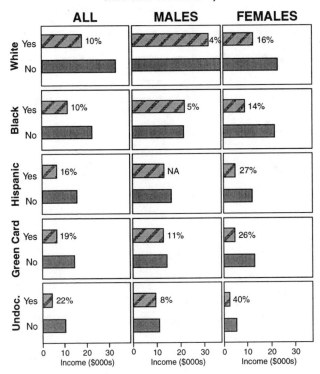

CHART 10

**CHILD CARE CONSTRAINTS AND INCOME COMPARISON
BY RACE/ETHNICITY, GENDER, AND IMMIGRANT STATUS,
PRETAX INCOME, 1992**

**(% shown are those answering "Yes" to having
child care constraints)**

Source: Compiled by authors from the LASUI.

Racially and Educationally Diverse Networks

The final two charts were assembled in an effort to assess the effects of social and spatial isolation on annual incomes of the sample of Los Angeles residents. Being embedded in a racially diverse network had a significantly positive effect on the incomes of both African American and Hispanic men and women in the sample (see Chart 11). The data suggest that racially heterogeneous or diverse networks are especially beneficial to black women. There was a $24,213 difference in the incomes

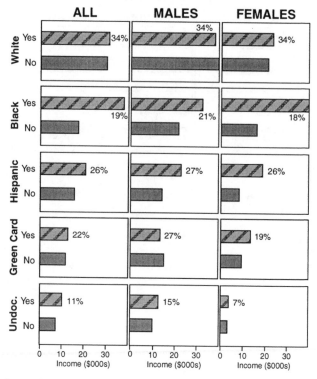

CHART 11

**COMPARISON OF RACIAL COMPOSITION OF NETWORKS
AND INCOME BY RACE/ETHNICITY, GENDER, AND
IMMIGRANT STATUS, PRETAX INCOME, 1992**

**(% shown are those answering "Yes"
to race bridge question)**

Source: Compiled by authors from the LASUI.

of those with a race bridge and those without such network ties. For Hispanic women, the difference was $10,700, and for Hispanic men and black men, the differences were $8,278 and $11,995, respectively. The findings were similar for those who were embedded in educationally diverse networks (see Chart 12). White females, black males, Hispanic males, Hispanic females, and immigrant females with and without green cards who were embedded in educationally diverse networks reported higher annual incomes than their counterparts who were embedded in homogeneous networks.

Multivariate Analysis

How much of the variance in observed income disparities in Los Angeles is accounted for by the factors highlighted in Charts 2 through 12? To answer this question, we fitted an ordinary least squares (OLS) regression model to the data extracted from the LASUI. For this analysis, we used as the dependent variable the pretax 1992 mean annual income of the survey respondents expressed as a percent of the mean income for the Los Angeles metropolitan area as a whole. To satisfy the data requirements of the OLS model, it was necessary to transform this variable so that it approached a normal distribution. The natural log transformation eliminated most of the skewness in the raw distribution.

We estimated the effects of the race/ethnicity identity measures and the gender, immigration status, human capital, employment and training, business policy, crime, and social capital variables listed in Table 3. We entered these variables into the model in blocks in serial order, beginning with the race/ethnicity identity measures. The percentage of the variance in our measure of income disparity that these variables explained, singularly and in concert, for the total sample, all whites, all blacks, all Hispanics, all males, and all females is summarized in Table 5.

For the total sample, the model accounts for 59 percent of the variance in the observed income disparity in Los Angeles in 1992. As Table 5 shows, the business policy variables, that is, those factors that undergird recent changes in the demand side of the labor market, account for the largest proportion of the explained variance (36.4 percent). The race/ethnicity identity indicators constitute the second most important set of determinants, accounting for 7.1 percent of the explained variance, followed by human capital factors, which account for 6.0 percent of the disparity in mean income in Los Angeles. Gender (4.0 percent) and immigration status (3.5 percent) account for small but nevertheless significant proportions of the explained variance. The remaining independent variables—employment and training (1.3 percent), crime (0.0 percent), and social capital (0.1 percent)—explain none or a relatively insignificant amount of the variance in the income disparity that existed in Los Angeles in 1992.

As these results reveal, both race/ethnic identity and gender characteristics of the survey respondents are critical determinants of contem-

CHART 12

COMPARISON OF EDUCATIONAL COMPOSITION AND INCOME BY RACE/ETHNICITY, GENDER, AND IMMIGRANT STATUS, PRETAX INCOME, 1992

(% shown are those answering "Yes" to education bridge question)

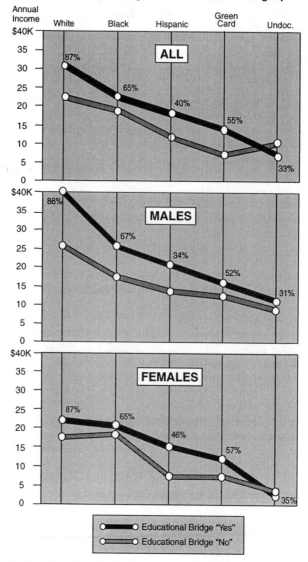

Source: Compiled by authors from the LASUI.

TABLE 5
DETERMINANTS OF INCOME DISPARITIES IN LOS ANGELES USING THE PRETAX 1992 MEAN INCOME OF THE LOS ANGELES METROPOLITAN AREA AS THE BENCHMARK

Policy Domains	(1) Total Sample			(2) All Whites			(3) All Blacks			(4) All Hispanics			(5) All Males			(6) All Females		
	R^2 %	R^2 Change %	F	R^2 %	R^2 Change %	F	R^2 %	R^2 Change %	F	R^2 %	R^2 Change %	F	R^2 %	R^2 Change %	F	R^2 %	R^2 Change %	F
Race/ethnicity	—	7.1	59.0	—	—	—	—	—	—	—	—	—	9.5	—	37.1	5.0	—	22.9
Gender	11.1	4.0	64.0	6.1	—	34.9	1.9	—	10.8	5.1	—	25.7	—	—	—	—	—	—
Immigration	14.6	3.5	44.2	7.8	1.7	12.1	3.1	1.2	5.1	18.8	13.7	27.5	12.6	3.1	20.8	9.0	4.0	17.3
Human capital	20.6	6.0	44.7	13.6	5.9	12.8	18.2	15.1	17.4	23.2	4.5	20.9	16.7	4.1	18.1	18.4	9.4	24.4
Employment and training	21.9	1.3	33.5	14.3	0.7	9.0	18.5	0.3	11.7	26.5	3.2	16.0	17.0	0.3	12.6	20.8	2.4	19.0
Business	58.3	36.4	132.9	54.9	40.6	46.7	59.7	41.2	55.7	58.4	31.9	47.0	51.9	34.9	50.2	63.7	42.9	97.8
Crime	58.3	0.0	125.0	54.8	-0.1	43.5	59.6	-0.1	51.9	58.4	0.0	43.8	51.9	0.0	47.0	63.7	0.0	91.8
Social capital	58.5	0.1	113.2	54.8	0.0	38.6	60.1	0.5	46.7	59.0	0.6	39.8	51.9	0.0	42.0	64.2	0.5	83.4

Note: All F-statistics are statistically significant at the $p = .0000$.

Source: Compiled by authors from the LASUI.

porary income inequality in Los Angeles. Do the effects of the remaining independent variables change when statistical controls for race/ethnicity and gender are introduced into the regression model? Columns 2 through 6 of Table 5 provide answers to this question.

With respect to the results controlling for the race/ethnic identity of the survey respondents, the model explains 54.8 percent, 60.1 percent, and 59.0 percent of the explained variance in income inequality among whites, blacks, and Hispanics, respectively, in Los Angeles. As in the case of the results for the total sample, the business policy variables account for the greatest proportion of the explained variance. These variables are significantly more important for blacks (41.2 percent) and whites (40.6 percent) than for Hispanics (31.9 percent). Human capital variables capture a larger proportion of the variance in the case of blacks (15.1 percent) than in the cases of whites (5.9 percent) and Hispanics (4.5 percent). As expected, immigrant status is more important for Hispanics (13.7 percent) than for either whites (1.7 percent) or blacks (1.2 percent). None of the other independent variables—employment and training, social capital, and crime—account for much of the explained variance in income inequality among whites, blacks, and Hispanics in Los Angeles.

When statistical controls for gender were introduced, the model explained 51.9 percent of the variance in income inequality among males and 64.2 percent among females in Los Angeles. Consistent with the findings for the total sample and for whites, blacks, and Hispanics, the business policy variables were the strongest predictors of income inequality among males and females in Los Angeles; however, these variables accounted for a larger share of the explained variance in the case of females (42.9 percent) than in the case of males (34.9 percent). Moreover, whereas human capital variables played a more significant role in explaining income inequality among females (9.4 percent versus 4.1 percent for males), race was a more important determinant in the case of males (9.5 percent versus 5.0 percent for females).

Table 6 presents the specific independent variables that proved to be statistically significant determinants of income inequality in Los Angeles. The corresponding beta values represent the unique effect of each variable that is, after controlling for all of the other variables in the model. For the total sample (see column 1 in Table 6), the results indicate that job quality (a good job), that is, having a job with benefits (β=.113), is the most important determinant of income inequality. Because of the positive sign of the coefficient, this variable captures most of the individuals who were clustered at the upper end of the Los Angeles income distribution in 1992. The next five variables to enter the model identified individuals who were concentrated at the lower end of the Los Angeles income distribution in 1992: Hispanic (β=.108), age (β=.084), female (β=.100), undocumented worker (β=.076), and green card holder (β=.055). That all of these variables exerted a negative effect on the dependent variable lends empirical support to the labor surplus hypothesis; the hypothesis, as noted previously, posits that the growing supply of women and immigrants (most of whom tend to be relatively young) in the civilian labor force over the past two decades has depressed wages in the restructured American economy and thus accounts, at least in part, for growing income inequality.

As columns 2 through 4 in Table 6 show, however, the mix of variables that accounts for the income disparity that existed in Los Angeles in 1992 varies from one race/ethnic group to the next. For blacks, the disparity was attributable to individuals who were well educated (β=.043), embedded in racially diverse networks (β=.063), and employed in good jobs (β=.074) who earned relatively high incomes, on the one hand, and to the presence of young (β=.094) and female (β=.069) workers who earned relatively low incomes, on the other hand. Among Hispanics, the concentration of individuals in good jobs (β=.153) earning above the metropolitan average income and of young (β=.108) workers who were female (β=.056), undocumented (β=.062), or green card holders (β=.086) earning below the metropolitan average income accounted for most of the explained variance in income inequality. For whites, most of the variance in income inequality was attributable to a high concentration of well-educated workers (β=.046) who were employed in good jobs (β=.120) generating above average incomes and of female labor force participants (β=.163) earning below average incomes.

Among men in Los Angeles, the income disparity was related to the presence of Hispanic (β=.172) and black (β=.119) workers in the labor market, which accounted for the lower end of the income distribution. It was also related to the presence of white males who were concentrated in good jobs (β=.111), which accounted for the upper end of the Los Angeles income distribution. Among women, embeddedness in racially (β=.045) and educationally (β=.058) diverse networks and concentration in good jobs (β=.137) accounted for the upper end of the income distribution, and the clustering of young female entrants (β=.083) in the Los Angeles labor market accounted for much of the lower end of the income distribution.

In the foregoing analysis, the natural log of the survey respondents' 1992 pretax income expressed as a percent of the Los Angeles metropolitan area mean income served as our measure of income inequality. To further document or demonstrate the unique contribution of each of the independent variables to income inequality as a final step in this research, we computed the antilog of their corresponding beta values, transformed them into 1992 dollar equivalents, and then calculated the difference between the dollar value equivalents of the parameter estimates and the metropolitan area mean income. The results, presented in Table 7, are estimates of the economic costs (negative beta coefficients) or returns (positive beta coefficients) associated with each of the independent variables emerging from our regression model as statistically significant determinants of income inequality in Los Angeles.

Conservative social policy analysts and opponents of affirmative action for minorities and women contend that the economic playing

TABLE 6
ORDINARY LEAST SQUARES REGRESSION RESULTS USING PRETAX 1992 MEAN INCOME OF LOS ANGELES METROPOLITAN AREA AS THE BENCHMARK

Independent Variables	(1) Total Sample		(2) All Blacks		(3) All Whites		(4) All Hispanics		(5) All Men		(6) All Women	
	β	T	β	T	β	T	β	T	β	T	β	T
Constant	-.436 (.062)	-7.00	-.721 (.147)	-4.91	-.853 (.213)	-4.00	-.220 (.077)	-2.86	-5.81 (.112)	-5.22	-.454 (.066)	-6.84
Black	-.064 (.020)	-3.14	—	—	—	—	—	—	-.119 (.037)	-3.25		NS
Hispanic	-.108 (.025)	-4.38	—	—	—	—	—	—	-.172 (.041)	-4.17		NS
Female	-.100 (.017)	-5.83	-.069 (.028)	-2.46	-.163 (.034)	-4.77	-.056 (.025)	-2.29	—	—	—	—
Green card	-.055 (.029)	-1.92		NS		NS	-.086 (.034)	-2.49		NS		NS
Undocumented	-.076 (.036)	2.11		NS		NS	-.062 (.031)	-2.46		NS		NS
Education	.027 (.003)	8.52	.043 (.007)	6.39	.046 (.007)	6.27	.012 (.003)	-3.59	.029 (.005)	5.66	.024 (.004)	6.30
Years of work experience		NS		NS	.003 (.002)	1.95		NS		NS		NS
Age	-.084 (.023)	-3.65	-.094 (.038)	-2.47		NS	-.108 (.033)	-3.29	-.076 (.041)	-4.40	-.083 (.026)	-3.23
Job training		NS		NS		NS		NS		NS		NS
GED		NS		NS		NS		NS		NS		NS

TABLE 6 (Continued)

Independent Variables	(1) Total Sample		(2) All Blacks		(3) All Whites		(4) All Hispanics		(5) All Men		(6) All Women	
	β	T	β	T	β	T	β	T	β	T	β	T
Public assistance	NS		NS		NS		NS		-.092 (.047)	-1.97	NS	
Child care	NS		NS		NS		NS		NS		NS	
Job quality	.113 (.018)	6.30	.074 (.031)	2.41	.120 (.036)	3.32	.153 (.025)	6.24	.111 (.030)	3.68	.137 (.021)	6.51
Hours worked/week	.006 (.0007)	7.80	.004 (.001)	3.21	.006 (.0001)	4.83	.003 (.001)	3.30	.006 (.001)	5.09	.005 (.0008)	5.63
Weeks worked/year	.013 (.0004)	31.40	.013 (.0006)	19.61	.016 (.0008)	18.80	.011 (.0006)	16.77	.015 (.0007)	20.19	.012 (.0004)	25.63
Crime record	NS		NS		NS		NS		NS		NS	
Race bridge	.044 (.018)	2.38	.063 (.033)	1.89	NS		.068 (.028)	2.45	NS		.045 (.021)	2.10
Education bridge	.042 (.019)	2.16	—		NS		—		NS		.058 (.022)	2.68
F	113.2		46.7		38.6		39.8		42.0		83.4	
R²	59.1		61.4		56.3		60.5		53.1		65.0	
Adjusted R²	58.5		60.1		54.8		59.0		51.9		64.2	

T = T-test.
NS = Not Significant.
Numbers in parentheses = Standard Error of Beta.
β = Beta value.

Source: Compiled by authors from the LASUI.

TABLE 7

ECONOMIC COSTS AND RETURNS OF SELECTED ATTRIBUTES

	Total Sample	Blacks	Whites	Hispanics	Males	Females
Black	−$3,274	NS	—	—	−$6,344	—
Hispanic	− 5,730	NS	—	−$2,865	− 9,823	—
Female	− 5,321	−$3,479	−$9,209	NS	—	—
Green card	− 2,660	NS	NS	− 4,502	NS	—
Undocumented	− 3,880	NS	NS	− 3,070	NS	—
Education	1,228	2,047	2,251	614	1,433	$1,228
Years of work experience	—	NS	205	NS	NS	—
Age	− 4,298	− 4,912	—	− 5,730	− 3,888	− 4,298
Job quality	6,140	3,684	6,549	8,595	5,935	7,572
Hours worked/week	205	205	205	205	205	205
Weeks worked/year	614	614	819	409	614	614
Race bridge	2,251	3,274	NS	3,479	NS	2,251
Education bridge	2,047	NS	NS	NS	NS	2,865

NS = Not Significant.

Source: Compiled by authors from the LASUI.

field is essentially level for all individuals who have played by society's rules (such as staying in school until graduation and avoiding trouble with the law).[95] The data in Table 7 do not support this proposition. Rather, they suggest that blacks, Hispanics, and women still encounter discrimination in the Los Angeles labor market.

After controlling for human capital skills and other critical factors hypothesized to influence income inequality, our data indicate that the income of blacks was, on average, $3,274 below the metropolitan mean in 1992; for black males, the disparity was even greater: $6,344 below the metropolitan average. A similar pattern emerges for Hispanics. They reported incomes, on average, $5,730 below the metropolitan average. As with blacks, the disparity was even greater for Hispanic males, whose 1992 incomes were, on average, $9,823 below the metropolitan mean. With respect to females, the gap between their incomes and the metropolitan mean ($5,321) falls between the gap for all blacks ($3,274) and all Hispanics ($5,730), but is narrower than the gap for black males ($6,344) and Hispanic males ($9,823).

Similar disparities exist in terms of immigrant status. The average income of green card holders was $2,660 below the metropolitan mean in 1992. For undocumented workers, the gap was wider, $3,880. Our data show that additional schooling, hours worked, and weeks worked, as well as being embedded in a racially diverse network and/or concentrated in a good job are all keys to narrowing the income gap. But it should be noted here that, in each case, the economic returns varied significantly by both race/ethnicity and gender. In the case of education, for example, for each additional year of schooling there was an average increase of $1,288 in annual income for all of the survey respondents in 1992. For whites, average income increased by $2,251 and for blacks by $2,047. However, Hispanics netted only $614 for each additional year of education.

These data suggest that race and gender inequality is inherent in the structure of the Los Angeles economy. Nowhere is this more apparent than in the role that network composition plays in economic well-being. As Table 7 shows, individuals who were embedded in a racially diverse network had incomes in 1992 that were $2,251 above the metropolitan average. This variable was not a statistically significant predictor in the model for whites, but it was highly significant for blacks and Hispanics as well as for females. Blacks and Hispanics who were embedded in racially diverse networks, which in most instances meant that at least one white person was in the network, had incomes that were $3,274 and $3,479, respectively, above the metropolitan average.

SUMMARY AND DISCUSSION

In this chapter, we have employed a political economy perspective in an effort to broaden the academic and scholarly debate about the causes of contemporary income inequality in American society. Scholars who embrace this research tradition typically "identify the early 1980s as the historical turning point that signaled the end of the post-World War II trend toward greater economic equality in the United States."[96] Using data from the LASUI, we have attempted to demonstrate how policies enacted in several key areas or domains have created disparities in income that vary by race/ethnicity, gender, and immigrant status. Moreover, as the 21st century approaches, these disparities are worsening.

Even more disturbing is that the growing distance between the haves and the have-nots in contemporary society is also confounded by race because minority youth and adults are at a distinct disadvantage in their attempts to access quality education, jobs, and other opportunities in mainstream society.[97] Concomitant with this escalating inequality is a concentration of African Americans and Hispanic Americans at the bottom rungs of the labor market. At the same time, employees' unions, which historically have provided livable and family-supporting wages and workplace benefits for low skilled workers, are in precipitous decline.

The apparent message emanating from government and the private sector is that every man, woman, and child must fend for himself or herself. In our view, the central policy issue is whether public and private sector policymakers will permit the growth in income disparity to continue into the next millennium. Can America hope to maintain a civil society when this disparity becomes even more pronounced along racial and ethnic lines?

Because minorities, in the aggregate, are projected to reach majority status in the early 21st century, will we be able to respond affirmatively to the question posed by Rodney King: "Can we all get along?" The answer may well determine the future stability and civility of American society.

NOTES

1. James H. Johnson, Jr., and Walter C. Farrell, Jr., "The Fire This Time: The Genesis of the Los Angeles Rebellion of 1992," in *Race, Poverty, and American Cities*, ed. J.C. Boger and J.W. Wegner (Chapel Hill, NC: UNC Press, 1996); David Grant and James H. Johnson, Jr., "Conservative Policymaking and Growing Urban Inequality in the 1980s," in *Research in Politics and Society*, ed. R. Ratcliff, Melvin L. Oliver, and T. Shapiro (Greenwich, CT: JAI Press); James H. Johnson, Jr., "The Real Issues for Reducing Poverty," in *Reducing Poverty in America: Views and Approaches*, ed. M. Darby (Thousand Oaks, CA: Sage Publications, 1996).

2. James H. Johnson, Jr., Melvin L. Oliver, and Lawrence D. Bobo, "Understanding the Contours of Deepening Urban Inequality," *Urban Geography*, Vol. 15 (1994), pp. 77-89; and Richard B. Freeman, "Toward an Apartheid Economy?" *Harvard Business Review* (September-October 1996), pp. 114-121.

3. Grant and Johnson, "Conservative Policymaking and Growing Urban Inequality," p. 135.

4. Barry Bluestone and Bennett Harrison, *The Deindustrialization of America* (New York: Basic Books, 1982).

5. John D. Kasarda, *The Severely Distressed in Economically Transforming Cities* (Center for Competitiveness and Employment Growth, Kenan Institute of Private Enterprise, University of North Carolina at Chapel Hill, March 1992).

6. Allen J. Scott, "Flexible Production Systems and Regional Development: The Rise of New Industrial Spaces in North America and Western Europe," *International Journal of Urban and Regional Research*, Vol. 12 (1988), pp. 171-186.

7. Ibid., p. 186.

8. Grant and Johnson, "Conservative Policymaking and Growing Urban Inequality."

9. Scott, "Flexible Production Systems and Regional Development," p. 186.

10. Grant and Johnson, "Conservative Policymaking and Growing Urban Inequality," pp. 135-136.

11. Ibid., p. 136.

12. Ibid.

13. Ibid.

14. Ibid.

15. Johnson, "The Real Issues for Reducing Poverty."

16. Johnson and Farrell, "The Fire This Time."

17. James H. Johnson, Jr., Elisa J. Bienenstock, and Walter C. Farrell, Jr., "Bridging Social Networks and Female Laborforce Participation in a Multi-Ethnic Metropolis," in *Faultlines in a Multiracial Metropolis: Race, Economics and Residential Space in Los Angeles,* ed. Lawrence D. Bobo and James H. Johnson, Jr. (New York: Russell Sage, 1998 in press).

18. Suzanne Bianchi, "Changing Economic Roles of Women and Men," in *State of the Union: America in the 1990s,* ed. R. Farley (New York: Russell Sage, 1995).

19. Ibid., p. 108.

20. Ibid.

21. Maria Cancian, Sheldon Danziger, and Peter Gottschalk, "Working Wives and Family Income Inequality Among Married Couples," in *Uneven Tides: Rising Inequality in America,* ed. Sheldon Danziger and Peter Gottschalk (New York: Russell Sage, 1993), pp. 195-221; Howard V. Hayghe and Suzanne Bianchi, "Married Mothers' Work Patterns: The Sub-Family Compromise," *Monthly Labor Review,* Vol. 117 (1994), pp. 24-30; Susan Sheenan, "Ain't No Middle Class," *The New Yorker,* December 11, 1995, pp. 82-93.

22. Jeffrey L. Katz, "GOP Welfare Plan: Self-Help, and Leave It to the States," *Congressional Quarterly,* Vol. 53 (1995), pp. 613-619.

23. Terri Apter, *Working Women Don't Have Wives: Professional Success in the 1990s* (New York: St. Martin's Press, 1993).

24. Johnson, Bienenstock, and Farrell, "Bridging Social Networks and Female Laborforce Participation"; Diane H. Fermelee, "Causes and Consequences of Women's Employment Discontinuity, 1967-1973," *Work and Occupations,* Vol. 22 (1995), pp. 167-187; David J. Maume, Child Care Expenditures and Women's Employment Turnover," *Social Forces,* Vol. 70 (1991), pp. 495-508; Jill Duerr Berrick, "Welfare and Child Care: The Intricacies of Competing Social Values," *Social Work,* Vol. 36 (1991), pp. 345-351.

25. James H. Johnson, Jr., Walter C. Farrell, Jr., and Chandre Guinn, "Immigration Reform and the Browning of America: Tensions, Conflicts, and Community Instability," *International Migration Review,* Vol. 31 (Winter 1997), pp. 1029-1069.

26. James H. Johnson and Melvin L. Oliver, "Interethnic Minority Conflict in Urban America: The Effects of Economic and Social Dislocations," *Urban Geography,* Vol. 10 (1989), pp. 449-463.

27. B.L. Lowell and Z. Jing, "Unauthorized Workers and Immigration Reform: What Can We Ascertain from Employers?" *International Migration Review,* Vol. 28 (1994), pp. 427-448.

28. P. Andreas, "Border Troubles: Free Trade, Immigration, and Cheap Labor," *The Ecologist,* Vol. 24 (1994), pp. 230-234.

29. D.J. Tichenor, "Immigration and Political Community in the United States," *Responsive Community,* Vol. 4 (1994), pp. 16-28.

30. Ibid., p. 18.

31. Ibid.

32. Ibid.

33. Andreas, "Border Troubles," p. 232.

34. Ibid.

35. Ibid.

36. Ibid.

37. Lowell and Jing, "Unauthorized Workers and Immigration Reform."

38. Andreas, "Border Troubles."

39. Lowell and Jing, "Unauthorized Workers and Immigration Reform," p. 443.

40. Ibid.

41. Andreas, "Border Troubles," p. 231.

42. Tichenor, "Immigration and Political Community."

43. Johnson, Farrell, and Guinn, "Immigration Reform and the Browning of America."

44. Richard B. Freeman, "Employment and Earnings of Disadvantaged Young Men in a Labor Shortage Economy," in *The Urban Underclass*, ed. C. Jencks and P. Peterson (Washington: Brookings Institution, 1991), pp. 103-121.

45. Joleen Kirschenman and Katherine Neckerman, "We'd Love to Hire Them But: The Meaning of Race for Employers," in Jencks and Peterson, *The Urban Underclass*; Katherine Neckerman and Joleen Kirchenman, "Hiring Strategies, Racial Bias, and Inner City Workers," *Social Problems*, Vol. 38 (1990), pp. 433-447; M. Turner, M. Fix, and R.J. Struyk, *Opportunities Denied, Opportunities Diminished: Racial Discrimination in Hiring*, Report No. 91-9 (Washington: Urban Institute Press, 1991).

46. Lowell and Jing, "Unauthorized Workers and Immigration Reform"; Johnson and Oliver, "Interethnic Conflict in an Urban Ghetto."

47. E. Soja, R. Morales, and G. Wolff, "Urban Restructuring: An Analysis of Social and Spatial Change in Los Angeles," *Economic Geography*, Vol. 58 (1983), pp. 221-235; S. Silverstein and N.C. Brooks, "Prop 187 Is Affecting Workplace: Immigration: More Companies Have Started Checking Job Candidates' Papers, and Employees Talk of Rising Tensions," *Los Angeles Times*, November 10, 1994, p. D1; U.S. General Accounting Office, "Janitors in the Los Angeles Area," *The Social Contract*, Vol. 5 (1995), pp. 258; A.Z. Nomani, F. Rose, and B. Ortega, "Labor Department Asks $5 Million for Alleged Worker Enslavement," *Wall Street Journal*, August 16, 1995, p. B6.

48. See, for example, G.J. Borjas, "Immigrants, Minorities, and Labor Market Competition," *Industrial and Labor Relations Review*, Vol. 40 (1987), pp. 382-392; B. Chiswick, C. Chiswick, and P. Miller, "Are Immigrants and Natives Perfect Substitutes in Production?" *International Migration Review*, Vol. 19 (1985), pp. 674-685; J.J. Jackson, "Competition Between Blacks and Immigrants," *The Social Contract*, Vol. 5 (1995), pp. 247-254.

49. U.S. Congress, Committee on Intergovernmental Relations, R. Mines, "Undocumented Immigrants and California Industries: Reflections and Research," November 15, 1985. Also see Vernon M. Briggs, Jr., "Income Disparity and Unionism: The Workplace Influences of Post-1965 Immigration Policy," Chap. 8 in this volume, *The Inequality Paradox: Growth of Income Disparity*.

50. Andreas, "Border Troubles."

51. G.P. Zachary, "U.S. Reaches Pact with Software Firm over Payment of Foreign Professionals," *Wall Street Journal*, August 16, 1995, p. A3.

52. Ibid.

53. Ibid.

54. L. Richards, "Middle Class Jobs on the Immigration Chopping Block," *The Social Contract*, Vol. 5 (1995), pp. 291-292.

55. Zachary, "U.S. Reaches Pact with Software Firm."

56. Richards, "Middle Class Jobs on the Immigration Chopping Block."

57. Zachary, "U.S. Reaches Pact with Software Firm."

58. J. Fitzgerald and A. McGregor, "Labor-Community Initiatives in Worker Training," *Economic Development Quarterly*, Vol. 7 (1993), pp. 160-171.

59. Ibid., p. 171; J. Heckman, "Is Job Training Oversold?" *The Public Interest* (Spring 1994), pp. 91-115.

60. Grant and Johnson, "Conservative Policymaking and Growing Urban Inequality."

61. Fitzgerald and McGregor, "Labor-Community Initiatives in Worker Training," p. 171.

62. Melvin L. Oliver and James H. Johnson, Jr., "The Challenge of Diversity in Higher Education," *The Urban Review*, Vol. 20 (1988); G. Orfield, Exclusion of the Majority: Shrinking College Access and Public Policy in Metropolitan Los Angeles," *The Urban Review*, Vol. 20 (1988); and G. Orfield and C. Ashkanize, *The Closing Door: Conservative Policy and Black Opportunity* (Chicago: University of Chicago Press, 1991).

63. Oliver and Johnson, "The Challenge of Diversity in Higher Education."

64. Ibid.

65. James H. Johnson, Jr., and Melvin L. Oliver, "Structural Changes in the Economy and Black Male Joblessness: A Reassessment," in *Urban Labor Markets and Job Opportunity*, ed. G.E. Peterson and W. Vroman (Washington: Urban Institute Press, 1992), pp. 113-147.

66. J. Petersilia, "Crime and Punishment in California: Full Cells, Empty Pockets, and Questionable Benefits," in *Urban America: Policy Choices for Los Angeles and the Nation*, ed. J. Steinberg, D. Lyon, and N. Vaiaina (Santa Monica: RAND Corporation, 1992), pp. 175-206; and Walter C. Farrell, Jr., and James H. Johnson, Jr., "Current Crime Policy Is Wrong-Headed," *Wisconsin Review* (July 1996), p. 21.

67. Petersilia, "Crime and Punishment in California," p. 176.

68. Ibid.

69. Richard B. Freeman, "Why So Many Young American Men Commit Crimes and What We Might Do About It," *Journal of Economic Perspectives*, Vol. 10 (1996), pp. 25-42.

70. Petersilia, "Crime and Punishment in California."

71. J. Miller, *Search and Destroy: African American Males and the U.S. Criminal Justice System* (New York: Cambridge University Press, 1996).

72. Farrell and Johnson, "Current Crime Policy Is Wrong-Headed."

73. Freeman, "Why So Many Young American Men Commit Crimes," p. 26.

74. Johnson and Oliver, "Structural Changes in the Economy and Black Male Joblessness," p. 144.

75. James H. Johnson, Jr., "Unraveling the Paradox of Deepening Urban Inequality: Theoretical Underpinnings, Research Design, and Preliminary Findings from a Multi-City Study," in *A Different Vision: Race and Public Policy*, ed. T.D. Boston (London: Routledge, 1997), pp. 77-89.

76. Grant and Johnson, "Conservative Policymaking and Growing Urban Inequality."

77. J.M. Braddock, II, and D. McPartland, "How Minorities Continue to Be Excluded from Equal Employment Opportunities: Research on Labor Markets and Institutional Barriers," *Journal of Social Issues*, Vol. 43 (1987), pp. 5-39; R.E. Coles and D.R. Deskins, "Racial Factors in Site Location and Employment Patterns of Japanese Auto Firms in America," *California Management Review*, Vol. 31 (1988), pp. 9-22; H. Cross, G. Kenny, J. Mell, and W. Zimmerman, *Employers Hiring Practices: Differential Treatment of Hispanics and Anglo Job Seekers*, Report No. 90-4 (Washington: Urban Institute Press, 1990); J. Culp and B.H. Denson, "Brothers of a

Different Color: A Preliminary Look at Employer Treatment of White and Black Youth," in *The Youth Employment Crisis*, ed. Richard B. Freeman and H.J. Holzer (Chicago: University of Chicago Press, 1986), pp. 233-259; H. Holzer and K. Ihlanfeld, "Customer Discrimination and Employment Outcomes for Minority Workers," unpublished manuscript (Michigan State University, 1996).

78. F. Clifford, R. Connell, S. Braun, and A. Ford, "L.A. Leaders Lose Feel for City in Crisis," *Los Angeles Times*, August 30, 1992, p. 22; Grant and Johnson, "Conservative Policymaking and Growing Urban Inequality"; and Johnson and Farrell, "The Fire This Time."

79. Johnson and Oliver, "Structural Changes in the Economy and Black Male Joblessness."

80. Johnson and Farrell, "The Fire This Time," p. 172.

81. Ibid.

82. Ibid., p. 173. See also William J. Wilson, *The Truly Disadvantaged* (Chicago: University of Chicago Press, 1987); and William J. Wilson, *When Work Disappears* (New York: Alfred A. Knopf, 1996).

83. Johnson, Farrell, and Guinn, "Immigration Reform and the Browning of America."

84. S. Head, "The New, Ruthless Economy," *New York Review of Books*, February 20, 1996, pp. 47-52.

85. W.H. Frey, "Immigration and Internal Migration Flight: A California Case Study," *Population and Environment*, Vol. 16 (1995), pp. 351-375; and S.A. Holmes, "Immigration Fueling Cities' Strong Growth," *New York Times*, January 1, 1998, pp. A1 and A13.

86. P. NiBlack and P. Stan, "Financing Public Services in Los Angeles," in *Urban America*, pp. 225-280.

87. W.J. Bennett, J.J. DiIulio, and J.P. Walters, *Body Count: Moral Poverty and How to Win America's War Against Crime and Drugs* (New York: Simon and Schuster, 1996), p. 14.

88. Johnson and Oliver, "Structural Changes in the Economy and Black Male Joblessness."

89. Farrell and Johnson, "Current Crime Policy Is Wrong-Headed."

90. M.W. Klein, *The American Street Gang: Its Nature, Prevalence, and Control* (New York: Oxford University Press, 1994).

91. Head, "The New, Ruthless Economy."

92. Johnson, Bienenstock, and Farrell, "Bridging Social Networks and Female Laborforce Participation."

93. Ibid.

94. Miller, *Search and Destroy*.

95. E. Gillespie and B. Schelhaus, eds., *Contract with America: The Bold Plan by Rep. Newt Gingrinch, Rep. Dick Armey, and the House Republicans to Change the Nation* (New York: Random House, 1994).

96. Grant and Johnson, "Conservative Policymaking and Growing Urban Inequality"; and J.L. Palmer and I.V. Sawhill, eds., *The Reagan Record* (Washington: Urban Institute Press, 1984).

97. See William J. Wilson, *When Work Disappears*; D. Massey and N. Denton, *American Apartheid: Segregation and the Making of the Underclass* (Cambridge, MA: Harvard University Press, 1993); and D. Massey, "The Age of Extremes: Concentrated Affluence and Poverty in the Twenty-first Century," *Demography*, Vol. 33 (1996), pp. 395-412.

PART IV
INCOME INEQUALITY IN OTHER NATIONS

Introduction

◆

by Dieter Dettke
Executive Director, Western Office of the
Friedrich Ebert Foundation

THIS PART BROADENS THE SCOPE of the study by looking at income inequality issues in nations other than the United States. Growing income inequality is not unique to the United States: Europe, Japan, and other countries have also had increases in income disparity in recent years.

The rise of income inequality is occurring at a time of relatively positive economic circumstances. For example, unemployment is relatively low in the United States, interest rates are moderate, and economic growth is solid. However, serious problems are occurring in Europe, where unemployment rates are high, and long-term unemployment is widespread. Although interest rates are low in continental Europe, job creation has not been strong. Thus far, the social system in Europe has dealt effectively with these problems. There is no social unrest in spite of the high unemployment levels, but this situation is obviously not sustainable in the long term.

The authors in this section examine the economic factors as well as the political and social variables that are involved in creating income inequality. They also explore possible solutions to the growth of economic disparity based on the experiences of other countries, particularly those in Europe. Even though it is sometimes difficult to borrow a solution that has worked in another country, there may be times when this is possible and desirable.

With the fall of communism, several models of capitalism have coexisted in recent years. The American model maximizes the use of market forces in the determination of wage levels, employment patterns, and prices. In the 1990s, the results of the U.S. model have been strong economic growth, as well as increased income disparity. The Asian model of "relationship" capitalism stresses long-term associations based on norms and informal codes of conduct. Given the recent crisis in Asian financial markets, however, it is realistic to expect that many Asian markets will soon be forced to act more like the American model, with a concomitant growth in income disparity. The European model uses more government regulations and interventions in markets than do the other models, but this path has created an expensive welfare state that is being reformed. Part of these reforms could lead to further income disparity in Europe.

Chapter 10

Income Inequality in Europe: What Can We Learn?

◆

by Reiner Hoffmann

LABOR MARKETS IN EUROPE are undergoing fundamental structural changes, characterized by new technologies and production concepts, as well as by ongoing globalization. The dramatic situation in European labor markets is illustrated by the fact that more than 20 million people are without jobs, long-term unemployment now seems here to stay, and more than 50 million people live below the poverty line. The rate at which new jobs are being created in industry and in the service sector has long been unable to compensate for the loss of employment in these traditional sectors. In addition, the projected growth in employment in the information society falls far short of the numbers needed to restore full employment. Moreover, experience since the beginning of the 1980s shows that high gross domestic product (GDP) growth rates are not enough to guarantee concomitant high employment.

THE EUROPEAN UNION: A COMMUNITY OF UNEQUAL PARTNERS

Although similar problems are encountered in different regions, there is no "single" economic area, nor is there a "single" labor market in the European Union (EU), even if the single market with its 340 million people has become a reality in the past few years. Further, within the single market, substantial differences exist among the economic performances of the EU member states (see Chart 1), and regional disparities have not eroded at all.

From an economic standpoint, what is important is the differences in labor productivity not only among the EU member states but also among the structures within the member countries. For example, islands of high productivity (individual companies or entire regions centered around major "conurbations" such as Barcelona) exist in countries with a generally weak economic structure. This situation can be seen, for instance, in Germany, particularly when rurally structured regions such as Upper Palatinate (Bavaria) or North Friesland (Lower Saxony) are compared with the industrialized areas of the Ruhr region (North Rhine-Westphalia) or the Rhine-Main region (Hesse). Regional disparities are especially clear with respect to unemployment rates (see Chart 2). An unemployment rate of

CHART 1

THE EUROPEAN UNION: UNEQUAL PARTNERS, 1996
GDP per Capita (Based on Purchasing Power Parities)

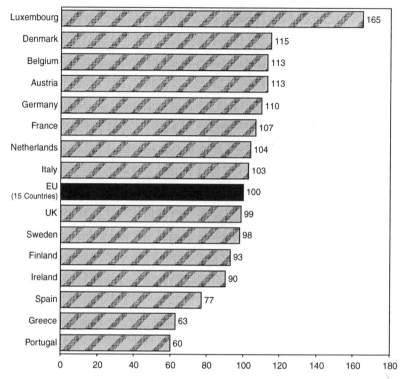

Source: Eurostat.

more than 20 percent in Spain (and in excess of 30 percent in Andalusia) contrasts with a 2 percent unemployment rate in Luxembourg or a still relatively moderate unemployment rate of 6 percent in Denmark. Other structural differences can be seen in the rate of inflation and in government indebtedness. Totally different regulatory systems can be added to the list of regional differences, most clearly evident in the ultra laissez-faire policy conducted in Great Britain and in the welfare state model in Scandinavia, still a social democratic-statist system.

Stubbornly high unemployment levels are not the only feature of structural change in European labor markets. A simultaneous change is the increasingly widespread differentiation in employment relationships. An important phenomenon in this area is the substantial growth

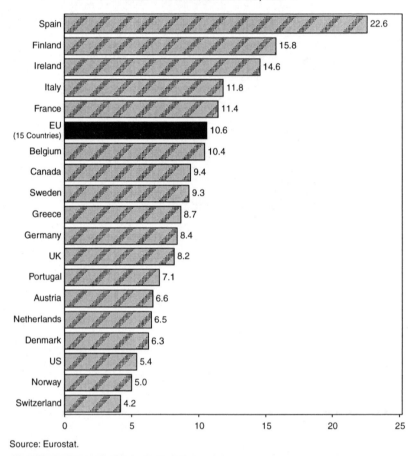

CHART 2

UNEMPLOYMENT RATES IN WESTERN EUROPE, CANADA, AND THE UNITED STATES, 1997

Country	Rate
Spain	22.6
Finland	15.8
Ireland	14.6
Italy	11.8
France	11.4
EU (15 Countries)	10.6
Belgium	10.4
Canada	9.4
Sweden	9.3
Greece	8.7
Germany	8.4
UK	8.2
Portugal	7.1
Austria	6.6
Netherlands	6.5
Denmark	6.3
US	5.4
Norway	5.0
Switzerland	4.2

Source: Eurostat.

in part-time work. Although in the 1970s the proportion of part-time workers was less than 10 percent, by the mid-1990s it had risen to more than 16 percent. Here, too, significant regional differentials exist. Whereas the proportion of part-timers in the Netherlands is about 30 percent, it is less than 10 percent in the southern European countries. In addition, part-time work in Europe is performed predominantly by women. The Netherlands again tops the list, with almost 70 percent of female workers in part-time jobs. The 1995 unemployment report of the European Commission (EC) indicates that most of the jobs newly created in the 1990s have been part-time jobs. Among men, 71 percent of new jobs fall in this category, while among women the figure is 85 percent. Further, a large proportion of newly created jobs are subject to fixed-term contracts. Although, on average, only 12 percent of European jobs are subject to fixed-term contracts, in 1995 more than 50 percent of previously unemployed workers entering employment were able to secure only limited contracts.[1]

There has been a significant increase in so-called atypical employment relationships, and this can be expected to considerably affect income distribution developments and to further swell the number of low income workers. The 1995 EC report did not include atypical employment relationships. However, studies conducted at national levels make it clear that the increasing tendency toward atypical employment relationships means an increase in the problems of the working poor.

A further characteristic of structural change in European labor markets is the increasing significance of small and medium sized enterprises. More than two-thirds of all employees work in companies with a workforce of less than 250. Because these workers are frequently not covered by collective bargaining agreements, more problems can be expected in this area regarding a fair distribution of earnings.

GENERAL BACKGROUND AFFECTING COLLECTIVE BARGAINING IN EUROPE

High unemployment rates and structural changes in labor markets have clearly exerted pressure on collective bargaining policy. Employers' associations never tire of saying that Europe is not competitive as a production site because of its high wages and social security benefits. Yet, the EC reached a different conclusion in its White Paper on growth, competitiveness, and employment, in which it argued against a low wage strategy within the EU, and thus against the policy followed by the United States.[2] The paper pointed out that labor costs are by no means the only decisive factor in international competitiveness. Compared with the newly industrialized countries, wage differentials in Europe are so huge that they can hardly be overcome by reducing wages or implementing a low wage strategy in attempting to gain any competitive advantage. Consequently, the EC has proposed a second path, one in "the spirit of the European social model," by which growth in real wages should remain one percentage point behind growth in labor productivity. However, the proposal fails to consider that the profitability of investments has been steadily rising throughout Europe since 1982, and that not only are real wages already one percentage point behind growth in labor productivity, but also that workers have had to accept the erosion of real wage levels.[3] This applies particularly to Ireland, Italy, and Spain in 1995 (see Table 1).

In almost all the countries of Europe, trade unions have sought in recent years to help overcome unemployment, and thus to contribute to

TABLE 1

NOMINAL AND REAL WAGE GROWTH IN 1995-96 AND FORECASTS FOR 1997 IN WESTERN EUROPE, THE UNITED STATES, AND JAPAN (%)

Country	Nominal[1]			Real[2]		
	1995	1996	1997f	1995	1996	1997f
Austria	3.8	2.9	2.4	1.5	0.8	0.5
Belgium	2.5	1.6	2.6	0.8	−0.4	0.5
Denmark	3.6	4.1	3.8	1.5	2.1	1.4
Finland	4.7	4.0	3.2	4.5	3.1	1.6
France	2.3	2.2	2.2	0.7	0.4	0.8
Germany	3.6	2.6	2.5	1.6	0.8	0.8
Greece	12.7	11.1	9.2	3.1	2.4	2.2
Ireland	1.1	4.0	4.2	−0.9	2.0	1.9
Italy	5.2	6.2	4.1	−0.6	2.2	1.2
Luxembourg	3.8	3.4	3.7	1.7	1.7	1.6
Netherlands	2.0	1.0	2.3	1.1	−0.9	0.3
Norway	2.8	2.2	4.3	0.4	0.9	1.8
Portugal	5.3	5.8	5.0	1.1	2.4	1.9
Spain	3.0	3.9	3.2	−1.6	0.3	0.3
Sweden	3.1	6.6	4.3	0.4	4.8	1.9
Switzerland	1.4	1.5	1.9	0.1	0.8	0.7
UK	2.9	3.3	4.1	0.3	0.7	1.7
EU 15	3.4	3.4	3.2	0.4	0.8	0.9
US	3.5	3.5	3.5	2.7	1.1	0.8
Japan	1.2	2.5	1.1	1.6	2.2	0.0

1. Nominal compensation per employee; total economy.
2. Real compensation per employee, deflator private consumption; total economy.

Sources: *EC Economic Forecasts 1996-1998,* Autumn 1996; and OECD, *Economic Outlook* (Paris: OECD, December 1996).

social cohesion, by adopting a distinctly moderate collective bargaining policy. At the same time, they have been under considerable pressure from employers' associations, and in part from governments, which have pushed for wage reductions and more flexible working conditions. A comparison of European collective bargaining policy must consider the substantial differences among the various systems that govern industrial relations. Among other things, the government's role and function in income policy agreements, in which it establishes the legislative framework conditions, is vitally important in collective bargaining policy. In particular, three variants can be distinguished in the EU: an interventionist income policy placing restrictions on free collective bargaining (e.g., in Belgium); a reduction in the possibilities for influence through collective bargaining via neoliberal deregulation (e.g., in Great Britain); and the trend toward neocorporatist regulation, in other words, the coordination of economic and social policy with collective bargaining (e.g., in the Scandinavian countries, the Netherlands, and, to a certain extent, Italy).[4]

The minimum wage is gaining importance in the wake of demands by employers and trade associations that labor costs be forced down further and of the clear increase in low wage working conditions that create the working poor. In Europe, minimum wage agreements are based on either legislatively mandated or collectively agreed on regulations. However, trade unions differ in their assessment of minimum wage systems. For example, although the Trade Union Congress has long called for a legal minimum wage and the Austrian trade union confederation has been calling for a minimum wage of 10,000 schillings since the beginning of the 1990s, German trade unions are, in general, highly skeptical of such systems, in part because of their tendency to encroach on free collective bargaining.

"UNFAIR WAGES" IN EUROPE

In Europe, the debate on low pay was stimulated by the EC in 1990, when it commissioned an international group of experts to conduct an inventory of "unfair pay" in Europe.[5] The reference point was the standard set by the Council of Europe's 1960 European Social Charter, which stated that no wage paid should be below 68 percent of the national average wage. The working group of experts defined three thresholds of unfairness: 50 percent, 66 percent, and 80 percent of the corresponding national average earnings, the so-called average wage. The 50 percent threshold corresponds to the legal minimum wage level in France, which, however, is below the level of social welfare in Germany. Other supranational organizations, including the EC, have adopted this threshold as the official criterion for income poverty.

The 66 percent threshold largely corresponds to the statutory portion of unemployment compensation provided—relative to the latest net monthly earnings—in the Netherlands, the Scandinavian countries, and

Germany. The experts looked at the income situations only of those employed on a full-time basis, to avoid national differences and problems in comparing part-timers and the marginally employed. Despite the numerous methodological problems at the detailed level, including those related to the availability of corresponding statistical data, the working group of experts clearly demonstrated the problem of the working poor (see Table 2). Although this is not a relevant political consideration in Belgium, Denmark, and France because of these countries' statutory minimum wage provisions, countries such as Greece and Ireland show significantly high values. According to this study, in Europe, on average, about one-fourth of those in full-time employment receive only 80 percent of the average wage. This is a surprisingly high proportion, and it would be even higher if the working group had used as its point of reference for the poverty threshold the average income of males employed full time rather than the average income of both men and women employed full time. This would have highlighted the wage discrimination against women in terms of both equal pay for equal work and access to jobs.[6] Substantial differences also emerge when individual economic sectors are examined.

As a whole, the study showed that the trade unions in the EU member states cannot prevent obviously unfair pay or the creation of a working poor. This fact raises two questions: To what extent will trade unions be able to prevent social division—the "two-thirds society"—between the employed and the unemployed; and will they be able to counteract the trend toward social segregation among the workforce?

FROM A PASSIVE TO AN ACTIVE LABOR MARKET POLICY

The European Trade Union Confederation (ETCU) and its member organizations, among other groups, have repeatedly pointed out that under the terms of the future European monetary union, the EU's employment and labor market policy must be strengthened. They have further argued that although the EU's adoption of employment policy priorities was a first step, much more needs to be done. In the context of the intergovernmental conference in Amsterdam in 1997 held to revise the Maastricht Treaty, the ETUC called for the inclusion in the treaty of an employment chapter, and this was achieved despite considerable reservations.[7] Fostering a high level of employment is already among the goals enumerated in the EU Treaty (Article 2), but from a trade union view this general goal falls far short as an adequate response to the depth of structural change in European labor markets. Unions believe that confining employment and labor market policy to the national level is no longer sufficient given the conditions of the European internal market and the future monetary union. Trade unions have good reason to fear that the advancing globalization of goods and capital markets will exacerbate the frantic rush by states to win production and capital locations through national deregulation policies and a reduction in

TABLE 2

LOW PAY IN THE EUROPEAN COMMUNITY, 1990

	Percentage of Full-Time Workers Earning Less than:			
	50% Overall Median[1]	66% Overall Median	80% Overall Median	Minimum Wage/Median
Belgium	0%	5%	19%	66%
Denmark	0	0	1	NA
France	0	14	28	61
Greece	10	16	26	70[3]
Ireland	10	18	30	NA
Italy	9	15	25	NA
Netherlands	5	11	24	77
Portugal	5	12	31	74
Spain	9[2]	19	32	60
UK	7	20	35	NA
West Germany	6	13	25	NA

1. The overall (males and females together) median wage in each case is taken from the earnings survey used to obtain low pay figures. The data and coverage of the surveys vary across countries (see Centre d'Etude des Revenues et de Coûts [CERC], *Les Bas-Salaires en Europe,* EG-Dokument V1018/91-FR [Brussels, 1991]).
2. 42% of the median wage.
3. 70% of the average wage.

Sources: CERC, 1991; and S. Bazen and G. Benhyoun, "Low Pay and Wage Regulation in the European Community," *British Journal of Industrial Relations,* Vol. 30 (1992), p. 623.

social security costs, thereby helping to heighten social deprivation and exclusion. If this form of competition is to be prevented and a contribution made to overcoming the crisis in European labor markets, an economic policy geared exclusively to monetary goals is inadequate. Much more important for coping with mass unemployment in Europe are a coordinated economic and employment policy and tax coordination, which will end social dumping and the unfair distribution of income. An active labor market policy and innovative regulations to reform labor market relationships in Europe are also required.

The structural changes in labor markets have clearly shown that in the classical welfare state concept of the EU member countries, it is increasingly difficult to prevent poverty and establish social cohesion and fairness with respect to incomes. The traditional Keynesian approaches to restoring full employment are increasingly becoming unsuited to the new conditions. Given the emergence of distinctly different labor markets, a question arises about the conditions under which full employment and thus social cohesion can be achieved in the future. Clearly, problems can no longer be solved by falling back on classical concepts of income transfer during temporary periods of unemployment.[8] The EC realized this long ago and achieved a partial victory at the European summit of heads of state and government in December 1994, when it adopted its so-called employment policy guidelines. At the summit, it was officially recognized for the first time that the employment and labor market policy instruments of the member states alone were no longer sufficient to cope with labor market problems. The employment policy priorities adopted at the summit seek to:

1. improve employment opportunities for workers by promoting investment in vocational training;

2. raise the employment intensity of growth;

3. reduce nonwage labor costs, which in individual EU member states amount to more than 40 percent;

4. improve the effectiveness of an active labor market policy; and

5. create more effective measures on behalf of groups particularly affected by unemployment.

The "Essen Guidelines" helped to support efforts at the national and European levels to reduce unemployment and reform labor market policy tools. However, the experience in various EU member states has shown that employment policy priorities can be misused to legitimize the extensive deregulation of labor markets and social insurance systems.[9] As a result of the pressure of the huge unemployment level, the jobless and lower income groups in particular can expect to find themselves shouldering new burdens that will lead to an increasingly unfair overall distribution.

EUROPEAN INSTRUMENTS TO REDUCE REGIONAL DISPARITIES AND PROMOTE SOCIAL COHESION

Along with an active labor market and employment policy, social and structural policies are greatly important for the creation of social cohesion and the reduction of unemployment and poverty. Everywhere in Europe, deep-rooted structural changes in labor markets have led to the considerable need for social policy reform.[10] A primary deficiency of

European integration to date is the EU's lack of competence in the social security area. Yet one of the primary characteristics of the European social model is the obligation of the member states at the national level to combat poverty and to correct excessive income differentials by means of taxes and transfers. The impact of social transfers on poverty in the EU member states is considerable. It has been estimated that without such transfers, about 40 percent of all households in Europe would fall beneath the poverty threshold, whereas because of transfers, this figure is reduced to 15 percent.[11]

The EU's structural policies are particularly important for the creation of social cohesion in Europe. When the Treaty of Rome was signed in 1957, provision was made for a European social fund designed to support continuing training measures and geographic mobility of European unemployed workers. Significant changes to this provision were introduced with the Single European Act (1987) and the Treaty on European Union (1993, the Maastricht Treaty). The chapter on economic and social cohesion, first introduced by the Single European Act, represented the treaty's basis for the reform of the European structural funds. To promote the policy of European cohesion, the EU currently has four structural funds: the European Regional Development Fund (ERDF), the European Social Fund (ESF), the European Agricultural Guidance Fund (EAGF), and the financial instrument for fisheries guidance.

The ERDF, established in 1975, is intended to promote the economic potential of the economically weak regions of Europe and contribute to the creation of lasting employment. The ERDF's resources were increased significantly from 35 billion European Currency Units (ECUs) for the 1989-93 period to more than 80 billion ECUs for the 1994-99 period. For the period 2000-05, a further significant increase is foreseen, expressly targeted to employment promotion measures.

The ESF is mainly intended to combat long-term unemployment and improve the employment opportunities of young people.

The EAGF is the most important fund in terms of resources, accounting for almost one-half of the total EU budget in 1994. The Common Agricultural Policy was originally based chiefly on support for agricultural produce and was traditionally justified by the argument that the transfer of incomes from the richer inhabitants to the poorer rural population produced positive social effects. In fact, however, 80 percent of the transfers go to the 20 percent of the most profitable farms whose incomes are frequently higher than average nonagricultural incomes.[12]

The fisheries instrument, with 1.9 percent of the total EU budget, plays a subsidiary role.

The measures conducted under all the European structural funds are concentrated in the following areas:

- development and structural adjustment of regions suffering a development lag;

- conversion of areas affected by the decline of traditional industries;

- measures to facilitate the incorporation of young people and the long-term unemployed into the labor market;

- forward-looking and preventive measures to assist workers in adapting to economic structural change; and

- fostering adjustment of the agriculture and fisheries sectors and development and structural adjustment in rural areas.

The Maastricht Treaty also established a cohesion fund designed to support transportation infrastructure and environmental projects in Greece, Spain, Ireland, and Portugal.

The EU structural funds ultimately serve to transfer resources from the richer member states to the poorer ones, with the aim of promoting adjustment to structural change and employment in Europe. The contribution thus made to social cohesion and reduction of income disparities and poverty should not be underestimated; yet these instruments have proved unable to make any significant inroads in the unemployment situation. In its first report on cohesion in 1996, the EC rightly pointed out that the existence of high unemployment rates and the increasing spread of poverty undermine the European social model.[13] In the framework of the forthcoming reform of the structural funds, discussions are taking place on more accurately targeting the utilization of these funds and on measures to increase their effectiveness in the employment sphere. At a time when public budgets are in crisis throughout Europe, a substantial increase in funding levels is not likely. The EU's structural policy will also be confronted with additional problems in the context of the forthcoming eastward enlargement of the EU, which will widen regional disparities even more.

CONCLUSIONS

New poverty and the working poor are no longer descriptions confined to developing countries or to the situation in the United States. As a result of radical and far-reaching structural changes in European labor markets, the EU is faced with permanently high levels of unemployment and 50 million people already reduced to poverty.

In recent years, not only have European trade unions had to accept losses in real earnings, but also they have become increasingly helpless to prevent poverty among sections of the workforce.

As European integration proceeds and gains momentum, national employment and labor market policies are no longer sufficient, nor are they likely to succeed. To complement these national policies, a European employment strategy must be devised. Initial moves in this direction are a first response, but they fall short. To effectively combat income inequality and poverty, an active European labor market policy must be an important goal.

In narrowing gaps among different regions in Europe, the European structural funds play an important role. However, they have made only a modest contribution to social cohesion. Preservation and further development of the social model can succeed only if a social dimension is incorporated into the process of European integration.

NOTES

1. European Commission, *Employment in Europe* (Luxembourg, 1995).

2. Commission of the European Communities, White Paper, *Growth, Competitiveness, Employment. The Challenges and Ways Forward into the 21st Century* (Luxembourg, 1993).

3. European Trade Union Institute (ETUI), *Collective Bargaining in Western Europe 1995-1996* (Brussels, 1996).

4. See M. Mesch, ed., *Sozialpartnerschaft und Arbeitsbeziehungen in Europa* (Wein, 1995); and F. Traxler, "Entwicklungstendenzen in der Arbeitsbeziehungen Westeuropas. Auf dem Weg zur Konvergenz?" in Mesch, *Sozialpartnerschaft und Arbeitsbeziehungen.*

5. Centre d'Etude des Revenues et de Coûts (CERC), *Les Bas-Salaires en Europe,* EG-Dokument V1018/91-FR (Brussels, 1991).

6. C. Schäfer, "Europa sucht einen gerechten Lohn," *WSI-Mitteilungen,* Vol. 12 (1991), p. 711.

7. However, it was not possible to reach an understanding on concrete goals and instruments, and these were discussed at an extraordinary employment summit held in November 1997.

8. R. Hoffmann, "Is Full Employment Possible? Some Theses for Further Debate," *Labour Market and Job Creation Policies in Europe,* ETUI Report No. 56 (Brussels, 1996).

9. D. Foden, "From Essen to Madrid—Growth and Employment," in *European Trade Union Institute Yearbook 1995,* ed. E. Gabaglio and R. Hoffmann (Brussels: ETUI, 1996).

10. A. Bosco and M. Hutsebaut, *Social Protection in Europe: Facing up to Changes and Challenges* (Brussels: ETUI, 1997).

11. European Commission, *Erster Kohäsionsbericht (vorläufige Fassung)* (Brussels, 1996).

12. Ibid.

13. Ibid.

Chapter 11

U.S. Income Inequality in a Cross-National Perspective: Why Are We So Different?

◆

by Timothy M. Smeeding

INCREASINGLY, THE RICH NATIONS of the world face a common set of social and economic issues: the cost of population aging; a growing number of single parent families; the growing majority of two-earner families; increasing numbers of immigrants from poorer nations; and, in particular, rising economic inequality generated by skill-based technological change, international trade, and other factors. All of these nations have also designed systems of social protection to shield their citizens from the risk of a fall in economic status due to unemployment, divorce, disability, retirement, and death of a spouse. The interaction of these economic and demographic forces and social programs generates the distribution of disposable income in each of these nations.

The experiences of nations in dealing with issues of economic and social inequality is the subject of this chapter. Because of the emergence and availability of cross-nationally comparable data bases, the experiences of rich nations in coping with the growth of market income inequality can be directly compared. Such comparisons may help in understanding how the United States is similar to and different from other nations. It may also help in tracing these differences to their economic, demographic, and policy-related sources. The institutions put in place in other nations to help mitigate the forces of market-driven economic inequality are also of interest. Cross-national research has taught that every nation must design its own set of social policies tempered by its institutions, values, culture, and politics. But it has also shown that important features of policy design can be learned by looking to other nations that seem to be doing a better job in combating social injustice and the poor outcomes of market-based economic inequality than does the United States. It will be seen that policies designed to generate economic equality need not result in lower rates of economic growth or increased economic inefficiency. In fact, a set of policies to help combat growing economic inequality is available to the United States. What is needed is the leadership to make these opportunities a reality.

This chapter begins by asking why should we care about economic inequality? How do both large and widening differences between the top and the bottom of the income (and economic well-being) distribution affect socially important outcomes? The parameters that are used here to measure economic inequality and their strengths and weaknesses are briefly outlined and then analyzed. It will be seen that the United States tolerates a very high degree of economic inequality, that it differs most from other nations in the relative and absolute income position of its low income families, and that income inequality in the United States has continued to increase at a rapid rate.

The explanations of these differences are then examined, with the finding that both the proportion of workers with low wages and the relative generosity of social programs help explain the economic position of low income families in rich nations. The chapter concludes by suggesting a package of policies designed to remedy the poor economic position of those at the bottom of the U.S. income distribution.

The results pulled together here come from a number of recent publications examining the cross-national facts of economic inequality in the United States and elsewhere. Although my coauthors in these works helped compile much of this evidence, I assume full responsibility for its treatment in this context.[1] While differences exist in my mind (and those of my coauthors) as to the exact nature and consequences of rising economic inequality, I am taking this opportunity to push the issues of "so what," "why," and "what can be done about it." In this context, it is my normative treatment of the issues and weighing of the evidence that is presented in this chapter, not theirs.

WHY SHOULD WE CARE ABOUT ECONOMIC INEQUALITY?

An economist's first reaction to increased economic inequality is "Has economic inequality actually increased?" and second, "So what? Why should one be concerned about economic inequality, or does inequality generate social evils?"

The first "evidential" question is much easier to answer than the second question. Virtually no serious empirical economist denies that economic inequality in America (and in most other rich nations) has increased. Inequality in earned income, in market income (earnings, property income, and private pensions), and in aftertax and transfer disposable income has increased in America and elsewhere.[2] Over the past 15 to 25 years, consumption and expenditure inequality has increased along with income inequality in America,[3] as has inequality in total compensation—wages, salaries, and benefits[4]—and inequality in the wealth distribution.[5] This inequality has also spread to living conditions, housing, and neighborhood patterns.[6]

This is not to say that opinions do not differ on the extent of the increase in inequality or on its implication for policy. Much of the increased inequality has been accomplished because the former middle classes have moved up in the income distribution, leaving others behind. The extent to which individuals and households actually saw their real incomes decline depends on the measure of inequality, time period, and price deflator.

Estimates range from 35 percent[7] to 10-15 percent.[8] My work with Greg Duncan and Willard Rodgers suggests that about 25-30 percent of those who left the middle class in the 1980s and early 1990s fell from the middle class into poorer economic circumstances, while 70-75 percent reached a higher economic plane.[9]

Moreover, although all of us would argue that economic growth and low unemployment rates are good for the poor as well as for the rich, there is little credible evidence that this increase in inequality is purely cyclical and not secular. Finally, accurate and unbiased studies of income and earnings mobility over time and across nations have reached two robust conclusions: Economic mobility is no greater in the United States than in other nations, and economic mobility in the United States has not increased with rising inequality and, in fact, may have fallen in recent years.[10] The literature also differs as to the policy implications of increased economic inequality. Some, but not all, argue that the distributional "winners" should compensate the "losers."[11]

With the answer being "yes," economic inequality in America has secularly increased in recent decades (albeit with a cyclical component), it is fair to ask the second question, "So what?" For the past several years, teams of social and behavioral scientists have been hard at work on this question. One problem seems to be indifference in public policy to the general issue of inequality, largely because it is an abstract statistical concept.[12] However public opinion reacts, there is a growing body of research that goes beyond public opinion to try and assess the measurable relationship between economic inequality and other important social goods. While conclusive answers to "so what" are still difficult to find, the evidence reviewed here is very recent and growing. A recent medical journal reports that high and increasing economic inequality is highly correlated with high and increasing mortality.[13] The potential link between income inequality and poor health seems to be declining social cohesion and lack of shared social goals.[14] Declining social cohesion has many correlates: declining investment in human capital (such as in education or health care) in low income areas; increasing social distrust manifested by declining confidence in government and in one another; increased rates of property crime and violence in low income areas; and impaired functioning of democracy, as seen by voting patterns and related evidence.[15]

At the same time that there is widening social distance between the incomes of the rich and the poor, there is a parallel increase in the residential concentration of the rich and the poor.[16] Left to fester, these inequalities will produce lower rates of economic growth and an increasing draw on public resources for prisons, police services, and other remedial public social services with a high social and economic cost. Simply put, if the rich and the poor share no common economic and social reality, there will be little or no agreement on common social goals or vehicles for achieving these goals. The geographic and political breadth of the United States may already attest to this lack of shared goals, as shown by the growing sentiment and actuality of the devolution of social and health programs from the federal government to the states. But inequalities within states and local jurisdictions themselves suggest that these differences go beyond national geography and also operate at state and local levels of government.[17]

While models have yet to separate cause from effect, the growing regularity of these correlations between U.S. economic inequality and poor social outcomes is cause for concern. Too much inequality can be bad for the United States as a society. Not only are absolute measures of income and their growth important, but also too great a social distance between the top and the bottom of the income distribution may be associated with poor social outcomes.

The cross-national evidence on patterns of economic inequality, poor health, and other outcomes across nations is even less well established. Some authors find a strong negative link between cross-national patterns of income inequality and mortality, but others are less convinced.[18] Even more recently, the assumed positive relationship between economic inequality and economic growth has been brought into question.[19]

Although the international evidence is spotty, it may well be that very recent changes in economic inequality have not yet shown their effects on important social phenomena such as health status, economic growth, and social exclusion. One reason for not finding such patterns is that not all rich nations have experienced a substantial widening of income inequality; to be sure, none have yet reached the overall level of U.S. inequality.

MEASURING ECONOMIC INEQUALITY: THE BASICS

There are currently no international standards for income distribution that parallel the international standards used for systems of national income accounts. Hence, researchers need to decide what they want to measure and how far they can measure it on a comparable basis. The Luxembourg Income Study (LIS), which underlies much of this chapter, offers the reader many choices of perspective in terms of country, income measure, accounting unit, and time frame. But its relatively short time frame (1979-93 for most nations, but 1968-95 for five countries) and small number of observation periods per country (three to five periods per country at present) currently limit its usefulness for studying longer-term trends in income distribution. This section explains the choices made here in the use of the LIS.

Attention is focused on the distribution of disposable money income—income after direct taxes and including transfer payments. Several points should be noted:

- Income rather than consumption is taken as the indicator of resources, although both theoretical and empirical arguments may favor use of the latter.

- The definition of income falls considerably short of a comprehensive definition, typically excluding much of capital gains, imputed rents, home production, and most income in kind (with the exception of near-cash benefits such as food stamps).

- No account is taken of indirect taxes or of the benefits from public spending (other than cash and near-cash transfers) on, for example, health care, education, or most housing subsidies.

- The period of income measurement is in general the calendar year, with income measured on an annual basis (although evidence from the United Kingdom relates to annualized weekly or monthly income).

Thus, variables measured may be less than ideal, and results may not be fully comparable across countries. For example, one country may help low income families through money benefits (included in cash income), whereas another will provide subsidized housing, child care, or education (which is not taken into account). Although a recent study finds that the distribution of housing, education, and health care benefits reinforces the general differences in income distribution for a subset of the western nations examined here,[20] there is no guarantee that these relationships hold for alternative countries or methods of accounting.[21] Still, this study shows that countries that spend more for cash benefits tend also to spend more for noncash benefits. Because noncash benefits are more equally distributed than cash benefits, levels of inequality within countries are lessened, but the same rank ordering of these countries with respect to inequality levels that is found here using cash alone persists when noncash benefits are added in. Further, although income, not consumption, is used as the basis for the comparisons because of the relative ease of measurement and comparability of the former, there is evidence that consumption inequalities are similar to income inequalities in major European nations.[22]

Market income—which includes earned income from wages and salaries and self-employment, cash property income (but not capital gains or losses), and other private cash income transfers (occupational pensions, alimony, and child support)—is the primary source of disposable income for most families. To reach disposable income, governments add public transfer payments (social retirement, family allowances, unemployment compensation, and welfare benefits) and deduct personal income tax and Social Security contributions from market income. Near-cash benefits—virtually equivalent to cash (food stamps in the United States and housing allowances in the United Kingdom and Sweden)—are also included in the disposable income measure used here.

The question of distribution "among whom" is answered among individuals. When disposable income inequality is assessed, however, the unit of aggregation is the household: The incomes of all household members are aggregated and then divided by an equivalence scale to arrive at individual equivalent income. For the most part, the household—all persons sharing the same housing unit regardless of familial relationship—is the common unit of analysis. However, for Sweden and Canada, more restrictive nuclear family (Sweden) and economic family (Canada) definitions of the accounting unit are necessary.[23]

The approach adopted here, based in large part on data from the LIS, overcomes some, but not all, of the problems of making comparisons across countries and across time that plagued earlier studies. Some problems, e.g., the use of data from different types of sources, remain. But all of the data are drawn from household income surveys or their equivalent, and in no case are synthetic data used.

One major advantage of the LIS is the availability of microdata. The aim of the LIS project has been to assemble a single data base containing survey data from many countries that are as consistent as possible. Access to the microdata make it possible to produce results on the same basis, starting from individual household records, and to test their sensitivity to alternative choices of units, definition, and other concepts. It is therefore possible to make any desired adjustment for household size. Aggregate adjustments, such as that from pretax (market income) to post-tax (disposable) income, are not necessary, although in some cases imputations are necessary at the household level. The data all cover, at least in principle, the whole noninstitutionalized population. Data have also been provided by two major nations not yet members of the LIS, Japan and New Zealand. In both, national experts at their central statistical offices calculated income inequality measures under the supervision of the LIS staff.[24] The rest of the calculations were made by the author and the LIS project team.

While the aim of the LIS project is to increase the degree of cross-national comparability, complete comparability is not possible, even if we were to administer our own surveys in each nation. Comparability is a matter of degree, and all that one can hope for is to reach an acceptably high level. In economic and statistical terms, the data are noisy, but the ratio of signal to noise is still quite high. Ultimately, readers must decide the acceptability of the evidence before them. For the benefit of the skeptics, most of the cross-national results provided here have been reviewed by a team of national experts—statisticians, social scientists, and policy analysts—prior to their publication by the Organization for Economic Cooperation and Development (OECD) and in other forums. Because the LIS data are ultimately available to the research community at zero economic cost, researchers are free to repeat these calculations themselves.

WHERE DOES THE UNITED STATES STAND?

The LIS data sets are used to compare the distribution of disposable income in 22 nations in about 1990.[25] The focus in this chapter is on relative income differences (see Chart 1).[26] Four inequality measures are used: the

CHART 1

DECILE RATIOS AND GINI COEFFICIENTS FOR ADJUSTED DISPOSABLE INCOME[1]

(Numbers given are percent of median in each nation and Gini coefficient)

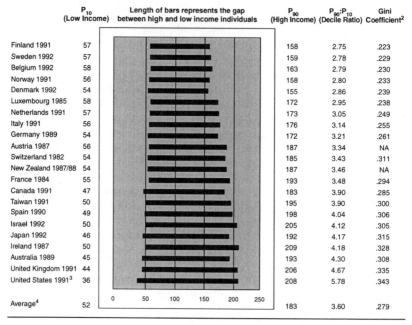

	P_{10} (Low Income)	Length of bars represents the gap between high and low income individuals	P_{90} (High Income)	$P_{90}{:}P_{10}$ (Decile Ratio)	Gini Coefficient[2]
Finland 1991	57		158	2.75	.223
Sweden 1992	57		159	2.78	.229
Belgium 1992	58		163	2.79	.230
Norway 1991	56		158	2.80	.233
Denmark 1992	54		155	2.86	.239
Luxembourg 1985	58		172	2.95	.238
Netherlands 1991	57		173	3.05	.249
Italy 1991	56		176	3.14	.255
Germany 1989	54		172	3.21	.261
Austria 1987	56		187	3.34	NA
Switzerland 1982	54		185	3.43	.311
New Zealand 1987/88	54		187	3.46	NA
France 1984	55		193	3.48	.294
Canada 1991	47		183	3.90	.285
Taiwan 1991	50		195	3.90	.300
Spain 1990	49		198	4.04	.306
Israel 1992	50		205	4.12	.305
Japan 1992	46		192	4.17	.315
Ireland 1987	50		209	4.18	.328
Australia 1989	45		193	4.30	.308
United Kingdom 1991	44		206	4.67	.335
United States 1991[3]	36		208	5.78	.343
Average[4]	52	0 50 100 150 200 250	183	3.60	.279

1. Adjusted disposable income includes all forms of cash income net of direct tax using the household as the unit of aggregation and adjusting for household size differences using a square root equivalence scale.
2. Gini coefficients are based on incomes that are bottom coded at 1 percent of disposable income and top coded at 10 times the median disposable income.
3. For United States 1994: P_{10} equals 34, $P_{90}{:}P_{10}$ ratio equals 6.42, and the Gini coefficient is .368 (author's calculations).
4. Simple average.

Sources: Gottschalk and Smeeding, "Cross-National Comparisons of Earnings"; Smeeding, "America's Income Inequality"; Japanese data from T. Ishikawa, Ministry of Welfare; New Zealand data from Atkinson, Rainwater, and Smeeding, *Income Distribution in OECD Countries*, Chap. 4.

ratio of the income of the person at the bottom 10th percentile (P_{10}) to the median; the ratio of the income of the person at the top 90th percentile (P_{90}) to the median; the ratio of the income of the person at the 90th percentile to the person at the 10th percentile—the decile ratio (a measure of social distance); and the Gini coefficient.[27]

Relative Differences in Inequality Across Nations

As Chart 1 shows, in the United States, the low income person at P_{10} in 1991 had an income 36 percent of the median. In contrast, a high income person at P_{90} had an income 208 percent of the median. The U.S. decile ratio was 5.78, meaning that the income of the high income person was almost six times the income of the low income person, even after adjusting for taxes, transfers, and family size.[28] In contrast, the average low income person had 52 percent of the income of the middle person in the average country, and the average rich person had 183 percent as much. The decile ratio showed an average social distance between rich and poor of 3.6 times P_{10}.

Countries fall into clusters, with inequality the least in Scandinavia (Finland, Sweden, and Norway) and northern Europe (Belgium, Denmark, Luxembourg, and the Netherlands). Here, P_{10}'s average 57 percent of the median, and decile ratios range from 2.75 to 3.05. Central and southern Europe come next (Italy, Germany, Austria, Switzerland, and France), with decile ratios from 3.14 to 3.48. New Zealand and Canada are mixed in here as well. Taiwan, Spain, Israel, Japan, and Ireland follow, with decile ratios from 3.90 to 4.18. Finally come the English-speaking countries of Australia (4.30), the United Kingdom (4.67), and the United States (5.78).

The United States has the highest decile ratio largely because of its very low relative incomes at the bottom of the distribution. The closest ratios to the U.S. P_{10} value of 36 are the United Kingdom (44), Australia (45), Japan (46), and Canada (47). The only other nation with a value below 50 is Spain (49). At the top of the distribution, incomes in the United States are not so different from those in other high inequality nations. The U.S. P_{90} of 208 is below that in Ireland (209) and close to that in Israel (205) and the United Kingdom (206).

While percentile ratios as measures of social distance have some obvious appeal (e.g., insensitivity to top coding and ease of understanding), they have the disadvantage of focusing on only a few points in the distribution and lack a normative basis. Chart 1 presents an alternative Lorenz-based summary measure of inequality, the Gini coefficient. Using this measure, country rankings change little—inequality is still lowest in Scandinavia, then central Europe, southern Europe, and Asia, with the English-speaking countries having the highest inequality and the United States the highest among these.

In sum, there is a wide range of inequality among rich nations. Measures of social distance and overall inequality indicate that the United States has the most unequal distribution of adjusted household income among all 22 countries covered in this study.[29] The Scandinavian and Benelux countries have the most equal distributions, with the United Kingdom coming closest to the degree of inequality found in the United States. Where the United States differs most from other nations is in the lowest part of the income distribution. American low income families are at a distinct disadvantage compared with similarly situated families in other nations.

Absolute Differences in Income Inequality Across Nations

Because countries differ substantially in terms of real gross domestic product (GDP) per capita, most authors have made comparisons across nations in nominal or relative terms, i.e., U.S. or Swedish low income units relative to U.S. or Swedish median income. Measures of real or absolute income differences across nations are much more difficult because they require comparisons of purchasing power of currencies across nations. One problem is that the purchasing power parities used to compare real levels of GDP per capita or total consumption (including government spending on health, education, and transportation) across nations are not designed for adjusting measures of disposable personal income such as those examined here. Nonetheless, such comparisons are at least implicitly made by analysts who argue that the higher the average standard of living in a particular nation, the better off are its citizens. For example, because U.S. real GDP per capita in 1993 was $24,750 compared with, say, $17,750 in the United Kingdom, $15,230 in Finland, $18,050 in the Netherlands, and $18,070 in Italy, the United States is, "on average," better off than these nations.[30] It is interesting to ask how far that average advantage carries when the wider dispersion in overall distribution in the United States is taken into account. What analysts have implicitly assumed is that the higher U.S. average standard of living extends to all levels of the income distribution.

This question is considered by converting the median incomes of a set of rich nations on which the percentile points in Chart 1 are based into real 1991 U.S. dollars using the Penn World Tables' purchasing power parities[31] in Chart 2. Then, median, high, and low incomes as a fraction of the U.S. median are recomputed. The decile ratio from Chart 1 is also repeated. Because both P_{10} and P_{90} have been adjusted by the same purchasing power parity, the decile ratio is unchanged.

The real dollar gaps between the United States and other nations in Chart 2 are much closer at the bottom end of the scale than those in Chart 1 because almost all of the nations shown in Chart 2 are "poorer" than the United States in terms of real GDP per person. Stated differently, both low and high disposable incomes as a percent of the U.S. median income fall in most nations. On average, a low income person now has a real income that averages 44 percent of the U.S. median compared with 52 percent of the person's own median (compare with Chart 1). As is often claimed, the United States has the highest median ("average") standard of living of the countries compared here based on adjusted median income (with the exception of Canada). The rankings of nations at the 50th percentile are therefore similar to those found when GDP per capita is used.[32]

However, the wider distribution of U.S. incomes means that low income individuals living in households at the P_{10} level in the United States still had lower living standards than did similarly situated persons in almost all of the 15 other nations shown here, the United Kingdom being the

CHART 2

REAL INCOME DISTRIBUTION: DECILE RATIO COMPARISONS

(Numbers given are percent of U.S. median income in 1991 U.S. dollars)[1]

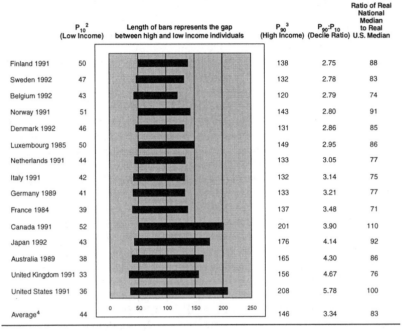

	P_{10}[2] (Low Income)	Length of bars represents the gap between high and low income individuals	P_{90}[3] (High Income)	$P_{90}:P_{10}$ (Decile Ratio)	Ratio of Real National Median to Real U.S. Median
Finland 1991	50		138	2.75	88
Sweden 1992	47		132	2.78	83
Belgium 1992	43		120	2.79	74
Norway 1991	51		143	2.80	91
Denmark 1992	46		131	2.86	85
Luxembourg 1985	50		149	2.95	86
Netherlands 1991	44		133	3.05	77
Italy 1991	42		132	3.14	75
Germany 1989	41		133	3.21	77
France 1984	39		137	3.48	71
Canada 1991	52		201	3.90	110
Japan 1992	43		176	4.14	92
Australia 1989	38		165	4.30	86
United Kingdom 1991	33		156	4.67	76
United States 1991	36		208	5.78	100
Average[4]	44	0 50 100 150 200 250	146	3.34	83

1. Unit of aggregation is the household, and units are weighted by the number of persons in the household. Incomes are adjusted by E = 0.5 where adjusted disposable income (DPI) = actual DPI divided by household size(s) to the power E: Adjusted DPI = DPI/s^E.
2. Relative income for individuals who are below 90 percent of the individuals in the country and more affluent than 10 percent of the individuals in the country. Numbers give real income (1991 U.S. dollars) as a percent of the U.S. median.
3. Relative income for individuals who are more affluent than 90 percent of the individuals in the country and below 10 percent of the individuals in the country. Numbers give real income (1991 U.S. dollars) as a percent of the U.S. median.
4. Simple average, excluding United States.

Source: Author's calculations using LIS data base.

exception. Even though the median American enjoyed a standard of living far above the median German (whose disposable income per equivalent adult was only 77 percent as high), Belgian (77 percent as high), or Swede (83 percent as high), low income Americans—at P_{10}—had living standards that were 13 percent below those of low income Germans, 17 percent below

low income Belgians, and 24 percent below the average income of the bottom quintile Swede. Only British, French, and Australians had real incomes that were near or below those of Americans at the bottom end of the income distribution.

Real income comparisons move in both directions, of course. At the other end of the scale, high income Americans enjoyed real living standards far above those experienced in other nations. At the P_{90} level, the real income of Americans was 42 percent more than the average incomes of the rich in the other nations studied (208 versus 146).

Although it would be argued that economic well-being in the most developed countries is most crucially a function of the individual's relative position in the distribution of income, real levels of living are also important in comparing income and well-being. Such comparisons allow differences in income distribution to be balanced by differences in real overall spendable income. The claim that "America enjoys the highest standard of living in the world" must be evaluated along with the equally valid claim that America enjoys the greatest level of real income inequality in the postindustrialized world—with America's rich being far better off than the rich in other nations and its poor not as well off as the poor in other nations.

Low absolute levels of living may also have great social costs. For example, the highly negative effects of a low absolute standard of living for young children is now well established.[33] Young American children living in households with incomes at 75 percent of the U.S. poverty line (i.e., roughly the P_{10} level) or below are at severe risk of poor health, subsequent poor educational performance, and, more generally, diminished abilities and achievements. And the LIS data show that among families with children, real economic status at P_{10} is below that of all of the other nations shown here.[34] Hence, the social costs of low absolute incomes for families with children may be quite high.

In closing, the crudeness of the purchasing power parity ratio when applied to the disposable after-tax income concept must be reiterated. Because countries differ in how they finance goods such as health care and education, and because they differ in the extent to which specific types of consumption are tax subsidized (e.g., owned versus rented housing), these purchasing power parities are less than ideal for adjusting disposable income for total control over resources—standards of living—across countries. The real income measures above should therefore be seen as measures of net spendable income rather than as measures of total consumption, the largest difference between the two concepts being goods and services such as health care, child care, and education, which are provided at different prices and under different financing schemes in different nations. To the extent that other nations' low income citizens need to spend less out of pocket for these goods than do Americans, America's low income citizens are at an even larger real income disadvantage compared with their peers in comparable high income nations.

TRENDS IN INEQUALITY

Do the differences in inequality in countries in the OECD in the late 1980s and early 1990s reflect convergence to a common level of inequality, or are the less equal countries (the United States, the United Kingdom, and Australia) becoming even less equal? The answers can be found by comparing recent trends in inequality (from 1979 onward). Because the LIS data cover only two to four data points in each nation, published data from other sources are used to assess the trend in income inequality.[35] While differences in units, income measures equivalence adjustments, and other factors in different studies make it difficult to compare levels of inequality across these studies, the trends will be comparable as long as surveys and inequality measures remain constant within countries over time.

The recent empirical evidence on trends in income inequality in different nations is summarized in Chart 3. Countries are listed in order of yearly percentage changes in disposable income inequality (as measured by the change in the Gini coefficient) from largest to smallest change. Also shown is the absolute yearly change in the Gini coefficient over this same period.[36]

The largest percentage changes in income distribution occurred in the three countries that also experienced large increases in earnings inequality—Australia, the United States, and the United Kingdom—and in the three countries with small increases in inequality of labor market income—Denmark, Sweden, and the Netherlands. Although household income inequality increased in several countries, the degree and the timing of changes were markedly different. In the United States, the largest increases in inequality occurred in the early 1980s and continued into the early 1990s. In the United Kingdom, income inequality fell through the mid-1970s, but the Gini coefficient rose by more than 30 percent between 1978 and 1991 and has remained roughly constant since. This is almost double the increase over a similar period in the United States and more than double the decline in the United Kingdom from 1949 to 1976.[37] In Sweden, all of the increases occurred since 1989; in Denmark, they occurred during the late 1980s; and in the Netherlands, from the mid-1980s to the mid-1990s. While the large relative change in the Gini in the United Kingdom might be ascribed to the fact that it started from an average base Gini in 1979, the absolute increase in inequality is also larger in the United Kingdom than in any other nation. The Swedish, Danish, and Dutch distributions had relatively high percentage changes in their Ginis in part because they began from a lower base Gini. But Sweden also experienced a high absolute change equal to that found in the United States. Still, the Dutch, Danish, and Swedish income distributions have remained considerably more equal than those in either the United States or the United Kingdom, as Chart 1 showed. Denmark and the Netherlands have displayed a much smaller absolute increase in their Ginis than have the United States, Sweden, Australia, and the United Kingdom.

Japan, Taiwan, and Germany form another group of countries with

CHART 3

TRENDS IN DISPOSABLE INCOME INEQUALITY AS MEASURED BY THE CHANGE IN THE GINI COEFFICIENT

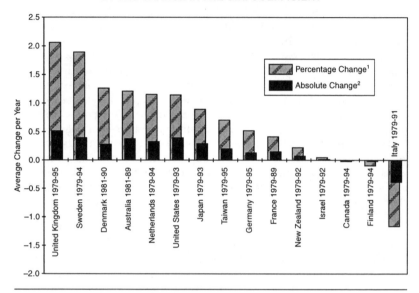

1. Average percentage change per year equals the percentage change in the Gini coefficient over the time frame indicated divided by the number of years in the interval.
2. Average absolute change per year equals the absolute change in the Gini coefficient over the interval multiplied by 100 and divided by the number of years in the interval.

Source: Gottschalk and Smeeding, "Empirical Evidence on Income Inequality."

moderate increases in family income inequality. What is remarkable about the other six countries is that they have so far experienced little or no increases in the dispersion of family income. In Italy, measured income inequality has declined substantially since 1979. Increases in disposable family income inequality have been much less widespread than increases in inequality of individual earnings or of household market income (earnings of all members plus other market sources such as interest, dividends, and rents), suggesting that taxes and transfers muted some of the market-driven changes in inequality over this period.[38] Indeed, detailed studies of other nations such as Canada suggest that even very large countries can enjoy a relatively low level of income inequality if they pursue the proper policies.[39]

There also appears to be no clear relation between the trend over the 1980s and the overall level of inequality at the start of the period. Inequality increased both in the United States, with a high level of inequality even before the increase, and in Sweden, Denmark, and the Netherlands, which started from much lower levels of inequality in the 1980s. Inequality fell by 10 percent in Italy, but rose by an even larger amount in the United Kingdom, two European Community (EC) nations that occupied intermediate positions in the mid-1980s. Nor is there a consistent country group story. Among the Nordic countries, Sweden and Denmark experienced a rapid rise in inequality in the early 1990s, whereas Finland did not. In Europe, there were large secular increases in inequality in the United Kingdom, Denmark, and the Netherlands but smaller increases in Germany and France. Canada experienced no measurable increases in inequality of household income, while the United States experienced much larger increases, despite similar changes in earnings inequality.[40] Only in Japan and Taiwan were there similar changes in similarly situated nations over roughly the same period.

Whether the other countries will follow the trends in the United States, the United Kingdom, Australia, and Sweden is an open question. There is increased pressure from high unemployment and rising earnings inequality in most of the nations discussed here,[41] as well as very recent signs that they are having predictable effects in some nations (e.g., the Netherlands). However, creative employment policy, tax and transfer policy, and other factors (e.g., increased labor force participation by married women) have so far prevented these market influences from affecting the distribution of disposable income in many other nations.

WHY IS THE UNITED STATES SO DIFFERENT?

As has been shown, the United States has the highest overall level of income inequality among the 22 nations studied here. It has also been shown that income inequality has increased in the United States and in several other nations. The question that must now be addressed is not an easy one: Why is the United States different?

The story of why there are differences in levels and trends in income inequality is necessarily incomplete because of the confluence of market, demographic, institutional, and policy forces and because of behavioral changes on the part of individuals, families, and households. The inclusion of multiple income sources received by multiple individuals thwarts attempts to identify the causal links that lead to variations across countries and over time in the distribution of total post-tax and transfer family income.[42] There is ample evidence that family members consider all sources of income available to the family in deciding not only how much each member might work in a market setting, but also how to structure living arrangements. Moreover, governments themselves react differently to market income changes through changes in redistribution (tax and transfer) policy and through other policies (e.g., macroeconomic policy or micro policies such as government employment). This leads to decision-making processes that are much too complex to be treated in a unified causal framework at this time.

The "why" question can be unraveled in part by concentrating on the largest point of difference between the United States and the other nations observed here, the ratio of the incomes at the bottom of the distribution to the median, or P_{10}. Previous research leads to the suggestion that this difference is attributable to two factors—relatively low wages in the United States compared with other nations, and the relative weakness of the U.S. income support system for families with children and for the aged at these income levels.[43] These relations are assessed here by comparing the P_{10}'s from the LIS with recent OECD data on both low wages and social expenditures, rather than basing them solely on the LIS database.[44]

Chart 4 presents a simple linear regression of P_{10} (the 10:50 ratio) from Chart 1 on the share of full-time workers earning less than two-thirds of median national earnings. Because earnings make up about 70 percent of all household income, they should have a strong effect on inequality. In fact, there is a strong and statistically significant relationship: Low income is highly correlated with the frequency of low wage workers. The United States and Australia lie below the line and Canada above it, indicating that something other than market income forces is driving the relationship in these three nations. Moreover, earlier research has shown that cross-national patterns of poverty and P_{10} are much better explained by low wages than by unemployment rates.[45] Hence, low wages are an important factor in predicting low relative incomes across nations.

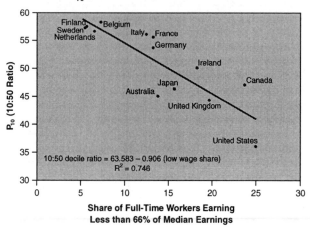

CHART 4

P_{10} (10:50 RATIO) AND LOW WAGE

Sources: OECD, *Employment Outlook, July 1996;* Smeeding, "America's Income Inequality"; and author's calculations.

A second explanatory factor for P_{10} is the level of social spending across nations. In every nation, the distribution of disposable income is more equal than is the distribution of market income due to government tax and transfer policy. Large percentages of otherwise low income households in the countries studied receive one-half or more of their disposable incomes from government transfers.[46] National income and employee payroll taxes also tend to have a progressive effect on the income distribution in these nations.[47] Following the same strategy, we regress P_{10} on total social expenditures as a fraction of GDP for the 13 nations for which there are consistent data on social spending (Chart 5). Again, there is a strong and significant relationship with the United States far below the line, indicating that its social transfers should be related to a higher P_{10} ratio than what is observed. I take this as a sign that U.S. social transfers are less well targeted to low income households than those in other nations. The United Kingdom seems also to share this feature.

Of course, both social transfers and low wages may explain the U.S. P_{10} position, and the regression shown in Appendix Table A-1 (see page 216) indicates that this is indeed the case. Both low wages and social transfers significantly affect low income status, with the coefficient on wages being larger than that on transfers. I interpret this to mean that low wages are perhaps a more important determinant of low P_{10} than are transfers. But both are significant and important determinants of income inequality at the bottom end of the distribution.

CHART 5

P_{10} (10:50 RATIO) AND TOTAL SOCIAL TRANSFERS

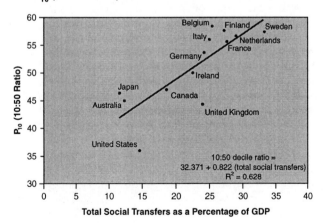

Sources: Smeeding, "America's Income Inequality"; OECD, *New Orientations;* Gottschalk and Smeeding, "Cross-National Comparisons of Earnings"; and author's calculations.

Turning briefly to explanations of trends in inequality across nations, I would argue that changes in earned income inequality appear to be the prime force behind changes in market income inequality during the 1980s in the nations studied here.[48] With earnings at or above roughly 70 percent of market income in most modern nations, this is to be expected. Other market forces (such as capital income) and nonmarket forces, both demographic and social, also affect market income inequality, though to a lesser degree. In fact, due to the relatively short period over which the trend in inequality is being measured (1979 to 1990 or shortly thereafter), demographic factors such as growing numbers of single parents or population aging have little affect on the trends found here. Changes in labor market incomes appear to be the prime factor driving inequality trends in rich nations.

Again, market income changes may not tell the whole story. By the mid-1980s, more than 25 percent of all households in major OECD nations depended on something other than earnings as the primary source of their incomes. In nations such as the United Kingdom, the Netherlands, and Sweden, this figure reached 30 percent of income.[49] The redistributive effects of government may therefore be important in explaining trends in inequality as well as the level of inequality.

However, my reading of the evidence indicates that the trends in disposable income inequality mirror the trends in earned income inequality in most nations.[50] In some countries, especially in Finland, but also in Canada and Germany, government redistribution appears to have muted the trend in market income inequality. But these nations are in the minority. In most other nations, the effect of taxes paid and transfers received were largely offsetting to the changes in the distribution of pretax and transfer incomes. This would occur automatically in countries with progressive tax and transfer systems, and the bulk of this effect is likely to be from these rather than from other sources.[51] Thus, the effect of taxes and transfers on the trend in inequality cannot be ignored. However, social policy via taxes and transfers seems to be much more important in explaining differences in the level of income inequality across nations than in explaining the trend in inequality. Hence, I conclude that it is market-driven forces, largely wages but perhaps also most recently income from capital (interest, rents, and dividends) that is driving the observed trend in disposable income inequality in most rich nations.

WHAT CAN THE UNITED STATES DO ABOUT INCOME INEQUALITY?

Clearly, there are features of other nations' social policy structures that would produce better outcomes for U.S. low income households should these be implemented. But not all such features are transferable to the United States. Moreover, U.S. policy solutions need to be made in the context of the federal budget, recent welfare reform legislation, and other features of the contemporary U.S. policy situation. With these factors in mind, short-term changes in U.S. policy can be inexpensive and better targeted to the populations most in need of assistance—low wage workers and at-risk families with children who by and large need to exist on low wage earnings. These groups are growing rapidly, and to the extent that the recently enacted welfare reform legislation is successful, the future working poor will dominate the welfare poor even among single-parent families.

The first and foremost policy innovation in the U.S. toolbag is the Earned Income Tax Credit (EITC). Europeans, Scandinavians, Australians, and Canadians all see the EITC as America's contribution to the social policy arena. Given a strong labor demand, the ability of the EITC to help otherwise working poor families avoid poverty is seen as a way to make work pay at the bottom of the distribution. But the EITC alone is not enough to make a large difference in labor market-generated inequality, and there is limited support to further increase the generosity of this single instrument.

Additional policies need to be pursued to raise the incomes of low wage working families with children. Virtually every nation other than the United States has some form of family allowance or child tax credit built into its tax transfer system. These subsidies are usually independent of parents' income levels (at least until far above the median income, e.g., Canada's system). They can be implemented through the tax code at fairly low cost. If the United States targeted them to working poor families alone, they could be enacted in the form of an expanded and refundable child care tax credit. Alternatively, children's personal income tax exemptions could be turned into children's tax credits and made refundable, again helping low income earners realize a higher net income than their earnings alone would allow. These policies, run through and by the Internal Revenue Service and the income tax withholding system, can be targeted to low income earners outside the welfare system. Politically this has great advantages. Welfare has been reformed, and there is no reason to open this stigmatizing can of worms again until the country has assessed the impacts of what has been done, both positive and negative. The solution for working people is to make work pay, and the tax system is the way to do this.

Single parents and older women living alone are two additional groups that need assistance outside the work arena. Single parents have but one earner (and generally one parent) to provide for their families. Modest levels of guaranteed child support (e.g., $2,000 for each first child and $1,000 for each additional child) could be provided in cases where absent parental support is not forthcoming due to low wages or inability to work. The single parent would have to provide a child support order and comply with other program rules (e.g., the welfare-to-work rules in a given state), but then they would be eligible for this stipend. Lastly, there is still a substantial elderly poverty problem for older single women, largely widows, compared to that found in other nations. The low cost solution is to provide a larger survivor benefit and a lower initial couple benefit through Social Security.[52]

The above are all short-term policies that are relatively inexpensive and that can be accomplished within the parameters of current efforts to maintain a balanced federal budget. A more expensive long-term policy strategy is to invest in workers by raising the skill levels of those from the least advantaged backgrounds. Policies here run the gamut from pre-school investments to better elementary and secondary schools to expanded subsidies for higher education for disadvantaged students.[53] It also includes studying the school-to-work transition process in Germany and other nations where employer-subsidized skill-based training is more successful than in the United States.[54] While a comprehensive human capital-building policy strategy is undeniably expensive, the cost of not pursuing this agenda may be even higher.[55]

SUMMARY AND CONCLUSION

A wide range of levels of income inequality is found across the nations studied. The range of inequality among OECD nations is very large, and the United States has the highest level of inequality owing in particular to the distance between its low income households and the median U.S. household. Real income differences also matter. The wider degree of income inequality found in America offsets its overall wealth to such a degree that low income Americans have a standard of living below those found in almost all other rich nations. Income inequality in several key rich countries has been increasing over the past 15 years. The largest percentage increases have been found in the United Kingdom, followed by Sweden and Denmark. The largest absolute changes have been in the United Kingdom, Sweden, and the United States. Thus, the United States, which had the most unequal income distribution in 1979, also had the most unequal distribution in 1994, with inequality growing rapidly through the mid-1990s.

Both low wages and low social spending help to explain the relative and absolute poor living standards of low income Americans. Believing that the winners should compensate the losers, I have outlined remedies for these problems, both short and long term. Other nations (e.g., Canada) have shown that market-based inequalities can be successfully addressed if there is a collective will to do so. What is lacking is not the road map, but rather the political leadership to sponsor progressive legislation such as that suggested here and to see it passed into law and implemented.

NOTES

The author would like to thank Anthony Atkinson, Peter Gottschalk, Lee Rainwater, and Peter Stoyko for their help in assembling the evidence on cross-national patterns of inequality that underlie this article. An earlier version is available as Luxembourg Income Study (LIS) Working Paper No. 157. Katherin Ross and Esther Gray provided excellent assistance in preparing the paper. The opinions expressed here are those of the author only.

1. My recent work with A.B. Atkinson and L. Rainwater, *Income Distribution in OECD Countries: Evidence from the Luxembourg Income Study* (Paris: Organization for Economic Cooperation and Development [OECD], 1995); P. Gottschalk and T.M. Smeeding, "Cross-

National Comparisons of Earnings and Income Inequality," *Journal of Economic Literature*, Vol. XXXV (June 1997); and P. Gottschalk and T.M. Smeeding, "Empirical Evidence on Income Inequality in Industrialized Countries," in *The Handbook of Income Distribution*," ed. A.B. Atkinson and F. Bourguignon (Amsterdam: North Holland Press, 1997) have helped assemble the data that underlie this essay. Also, my own recent work has provided some of the background material. See T.M. Smeeding, "America's Income Inequality: Where Do We Stand?" *Challenge* (September/October 1996); and Smeeding, "Financial Poverty in Rich Countries," paper prepared for the United Nations Human Development Report, Syracuse University, April 1997, mimeo.

2. S. Danziger and P. Gottschalk, *America Unequal* (New York: Russell Sage Foundation, and Cambridge: Harvard University Press, 1995); Gottschalk and Smeeding, "Cross-National Comparisons of Earnings"; and Gottschalk and Smeeding, "Empirical Evidence on Income Inequality."

3. D. Johnson and T.M. Smeeding, "Measuring the Trends in Inequality of Individuals and Families: Income and Consumption," paper presented to the American Economic Association, New Orleans, January 6, 1997.

4. J.S. Little, "The Impact of Employer Payments for Health Insurance on the Premium for Education and Earnings Inequality," *New England Economic Review* (May/June 1995), pp. 25-40.

5. E. Hurst, M. Luch, and F. Stafford, "Wealth Dynamics of American Families, 1984-1994," University of Michigan, Survey Research Center, August 12, 1996, mimeo.

6. P. Jargowsky, "Take the Money and Run: Economic Segregation in U.S. Metropolitan Areas," *American Sociological Review* (1996); and D. Massey, "The Age of Extremes: Concentrated Affluence and Poverty in the Twenty First Century," *Demography*, Vol. 33, No. 4 (November 1996), pp. 395-412.

7. L.A. Karoly, "Anatomy of the United States Income Distribution: Two Decades of Change," Santa Monica, CA, RAND Corporation, September 1995, mimeo.

8. R.V. Burkhauser et al., *Where in the World Is the Middle Class? A Cross-National Comparison of the Shrinking Middle Class Using Kernel Density Estimates*, Cross-National Studies in Aging Program Project Paper No. 26, All-University Gerontology Center, Maxwell School (Syracuse, NY: Syracuse University, October 1996).

9. G. Duncan, T.M. Smeeding, and W. Rodgers, "W(h)ither the Middle Class? A Dynamic View," in *Poverty and Prosperity in the USA in the Late Twentieth Century*, ed. D. Papadimitriou and E. Wolff (New York: St. Martin's Press, 1993), pp. 240-271.

10. For a summary of this evidence, see R. Aaberge et al., *Income Inequality and Income Mobility in the Scandinavian Countries Compared to the United States* (Turku, Finland: Abo Akademi University, 1995); and P. Gottschalk, "Inequality, Income Growth and Mobility: The Basic Facts," *Journal of Economic Perspectives* (1997).

11. R.B. Freeman, *When Earnings Diverge: Causes, Consequences, and Cures for the New Inequality in the U.S.* (Washington: National Policy Association, 1997); Danziger and Gottschalk, *America Unequal*; and Smeeding, "America's Income Inequality."

12. R. Lowenstein, "Public Indifference to Income Inequality," prepared for the MacArthur Foundation Meeting on the Cost of Inequality, Boston, May 3, 1996.

13. G.A. Kaplan et al., "Income Inequality and Mortality in the United States," *British Medical Journal*, Vol. 312 (1996), pp. 999-1003; and B. Kennedy, I. Kawachi, and D. Prothrow-Smith, "Income Distribution and Mortality: Cross-Sectional Ecological Study of the Robin Hood Index in the United States," *British Medical Journal*, Vol. 312 (1996), pp. 1004-1007.

14. I. Kawachi and B. Kennedy, "Health and Social Cohesion: Why Care About Income Inequality?" *British Medical Journal* (1997); and I. Kawachi et al., "Social Capital, Income

Inequality and Mortality," *American Journal of Public Health* (1997).

15. Kawachi and Kennedy, "Health and Social Cohesion"; and Massey, "The Age of Extremes."

16. Massey, "The Age of Extremes"; and Jargowsky, "Take the Money and Run."

17. Massey, "The Age of Extremes."

18. G.B. Rodgers, "Income Inequality as Determinants of Mortality: An International Cross-Section Analysis," *Population Studies*, Vol. 33 (1979), pp. 343-351; P. Saunders, *Poverty, Income Distribution and Health: An Australian Study*, Report and Proceedings No. 128 (Social Policy Research Centre, University of New South Wales, August 1996); I. Wennemo, "Infant Mortality: Public Policy and Inequality—A Comparison of 18 Industrialized Countries, 1980-85," *Sociology of Health and Illness*, Vol. 15 (1993), pp. 429-446; R.G. Wilkinson, "Income Distribution and Mortality: A 'Natural' Experiment," *Sociology of Health and Illness*, Vol. 12 (1990), pp. 391-412; R.G. Wilkinson, "Income Distribution and Life Expectancy," *British Medical Journal*, Vol. 304 (1992), pp. 165-168; and R.G. Wilkinson, *Unhealthy Societies: The Afflictions of Inequality* (London: Routledge, 1996).

19. R. Benabou, "Inequality and Growth," in *NBER Macroeconomics Annual, 1996*, ed. B. Bernanke and J. Rotemberg (Cambridge: MIT Press, 1996).

20. T.M. Smeeding et al., "Poverty, Inequality and Family Living Standard Impacts Across Seven Nations: The Effect of Noncash Subsidies," *Review of Income and Wealth*, Vol. 39, No. 3 (1993), pp. 229-256.

21. W. Gardiner et al., *The Effects of Differences in Housing and Health Care Systems on International Comparisons of Income Distribution*, Welfare State Programme Discussion Paper No. 100, STICERD (London: London School of Economics, 1995).

22. K. deVos and A. Zaidi, "Inequality in Consumption vs. Inequality of Income in the EC," The Netherlands: University of Leiden, 1996, mimeo.

23. For additional details, see B. Buhmann et al., "Equivalence Scales, Well-Being, Inequality and Poverty: Sensitivity Estimates Across Ten Countries Using the Luxembourg Income Study (LIS) Database," *Review of Income and Wealth*, Vol. 34 (1988), pp. 115-142 ; and Atkinson, Rainwater, and Smeeding, *Income Distribution in OECD Countries*, Chap. 2.

24. For Japan, results compiled by T. Ishikawa, data runs conducted by the Ministry of Welfare, November 26, 1996. For New Zealand, runs conducted by P. O'Brien, Statistics New Zealand, November 1994.

25. Gottschalk and Smeeding, "Cross-National Comparisons of Earnings"; and Smeeding, "America's Income Inequality."

26. The relative inequality patterns correspond roughly to the results found in Atkinson, Rainwater, and Smeeding, *Income Distribution in OECD Countries*, who in most cases used LIS data from earlier years.

27. The Gini coefficient ranges from 0, perfect equality, to 1, perfect inequality.

28. We use U.S. evidence for 1991 because it is the year closest to the other years shown. More recent U.S. evidence for 1994 indicates even more inequality. See note 3 to Chart 1.

29. Of all the LIS nations, only Russia has a higher decile ratio than the United States. Even in Russia, the P_{10} is 35, not much different from the U.S. value of 36. In Russia, the decile ratio is 6.84, and the Gini coefficient is 393. See Smeeding, "America's Income Inequality."

30. World Bank, *The World Bank Atlas 1995* (Washington: World Bank, 1995).

31. R. Summers and A. Heston, "The Penn World Trade (Mark 5): An Expanded Set of International Comparisons, 1950-1989," *Quarterly Journal of Economics* (1991), pp. 327-368.

32. For example, *The World Bank Atlas 1995.*

33. See Duncan, Smeeding, and Rodgers, "W(h)ither the Middle Class?"

34. L. Rainwater and T.M. Smeeding, *Doing Poorly: The Real Income of American Children in a Comparative Perspective,* Luxembourg Income Study Working Paper No. 127, Center for Policy Research, Maxwell School (Syracuse, NY: Syracuse University, 1995).

35. Gottschalk and Smeeding, "Cross-National Comparisons of Earnings," and "Empirical Evidence on Income Inequality." The author particularly wishes to thank Peter Stoyko for his help in gathering these data.

36. Percentage and absolute changes are both important. Percentage change may be misleading in cases such as the Netherlands and Denmark, where the base Gini is much lower than in other nations. Because we had data for different periods in different nations, we standardized by dividing by the number of years over which we measured change. The raw data that underlie these changes are presented in Gottschalk and Smeeding, "Empirical Evidence on Income Inequality."

37. A. Atkinson, "Bringing Income Distribution in from the Cold," Presidential Address to the Royal Economic Society, Oxford University, 1996, mimeo; and Karoly, "Anatomy of the United States Income Distribution."

38. Gottschalk and Smeeding, "Cross-National Comparisons of Earnings"; Gottschalk and Smeeding, "Empirical Evidence on Income Inequality"; and Smeeding, "America's Income Inequality."

39. K. Banting and C. Beach, eds., *Labour Market Polarization and Social Policy Reform* (Kingston, ONT: School of Policy Studies, Queens University, 1995); D. Card and R.B. Freeman, eds., *Small Differences That Matter* (Chicago: University of Chicago Press, 1993); and M. Hanratty and R. Blank, "Down and Out in North America: Recent Trends in Poverty Rates in the U.S. and Canada," *Quarterly Journal of Economics,* Vol. 10 (1993), pp. 233-257.

40. Card and Freeman, *Small Differences That Matter;* and Banting and Beach, *Labour Market Polarization.*

41. OECD, *Employment Outlook, July 1996* (Paris: OECD, 1996).

42. Gottschalk and Smeeding, "Cross-National Comparisons of Earnings"; and Atkinson, "Bringing Income Distribution in from the Cold."

43. Rainwater and Smeeding, *Doing Poorly;* Gottschalk and Smeeding, "Cross-National Comparisons of Earnings"; T.M. Smeeding, L. Rainwater, and B.B. Torrey, *Going to Extremes: The U.S. Elderly in an International Context,* Luxembourg Income Study Working Paper No. 89, Center for Policy Research, Maxwell School (Syracuse, NY: Syracuse University, 1993); and Smeeding, "America's Income Inequality."

44. OECD, *New Orientations for Social Policy,* Social Policy Studies No. 12 (Paris: OECD, 1994); and OECD, *Employment Outlook, July 1996.*

45. Smeeding, "Financial Poverty in Rich Countries."

46. Atkinson, Rainwater, and Smeeding, *Income Distribution in OECD Countries.*

47. Gottschalk and Smeeding, "Cross-National Comparisons of Earnings."

48. Ibid.

49. Atkinson, Rainwater, and Smeeding, *Income Distribution in OECD Countries.*

50. Gottschalk and Smeeding, "Cross-National Comparisons of Earnings."

51. How many of these changes came from explicit policy changes compared with changes in the economic behavior of households is an important question that remains to be answered.

52. R.V. Burkhauser and T.M. Smeeding, *Social Security Reform: A Budget Neutral Approach to Reducing Older Women's Disproportionate Risk of Poverty*, Policy Brief 2, Center for Policy Research, Maxwell School (Syracuse, NY: Syracuse University, 1994); and T.M. Smeeding, "Reshuffling Responsibilities in Old Age: The United States in a Comparative Perspective," Luxembourg Income Study Working Paper No. 153, Center for Policy Research, Maxwell School (Syracuse, NY: Syracuse University, February 1997).

53. Freeman, *When Earnings Diverge.*

54. F. Blau and L. Kahn, "Gender and Youth Employment Outcomes: The U.S. and Germany, 1984-1991," paper presented to the Sloan Conference on Labor Market Inequality, Madison Wisconsin, February 28, 1997.

55. Children's Defense Fund, *Wasting America's Future* (Washington, 1996).

Appendix

Table A-1

Inequality, Low Wage Workers, and Social Transfers, 1989-92

Country	Year	10:50 Decile Ratio	% Low Wage Workers	Total Social Transfers	Nonaged Social Transfers
Australia	1989	45.0	13.8	12.2	3.3
Belgium	1992	58.2	7.2	25.4	8.6
Canada	1991	47.0	23.7	18.8	7.6
Finland	1991	57.5	5.9	27.1	13.3
France	1984	55.4	13.3	27.8	9.0
Germany	1989	53.6	13.3	24.1	7.9
Ireland	1987	50.0	18.2	22.5	10.2
Italy	1991	56.0	12.5	25.0	3.2
Japan	1992	46.4	15.7	11.6	1.8
Netherlands	1991	56.8	6.6	29.0	13.1
Sweden	1992	57.4	5.2	33.1	14.4
United Kingdom	1991	44.2	19.6	24.0	8.1
United States	1991	36.0	25.0	14.6	3.5

10:50 ratio = 50.372 − 0.633 (low wage) + 0.416 (total social transfers)
| *standard error:* | (5.874) | (0.175) | (0.173) | $R^2 = 0.839$ |
| *t-statistic:* | (8.576) | (−3.611) | (2.396) | |

10:50 ratio = 59.535 − 0.793 (low wage) + 0.310 (nonaged social transfer)
| *standard error:* | (4.723) | (0.195) | (0.311) | $R^2 = 0.769$ |
| *t-statistic:* | (12.607) | (−4.058) | (0.999) | |

Sources: Decile ratios, author's calculations from LIS database; low wage, all but Ireland, OECD, *Employment Outlook, July 1996,* Table 3.2; social transfer, OECD, *New Orientations,* Table 1b; Belgium social transfer data are from 1991; Canada, Japan, Sweden, and U.S. social transfer data are from 1990.

TABLE A-2

DECILE RATIOS AND GINI COEFFICIENTS
FOR ADJUSTED DISPOSABLE INCOME[1] BY ETHNICITY

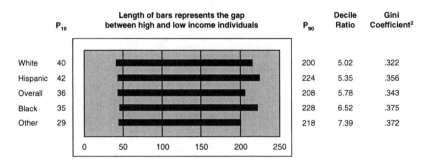

	P_{10}	Length of bars represents the gap between high and low income individuals	P_{90}	Decile Ratio	Gini Coefficient[2]
White	40		200	5.02	.322
Hispanic	42		224	5.35	.356
Overall	36		208	5.78	.343
Black	35		228	6.52	.375
Other	29		218	7.39	.372

	P_{10}	P_{50}	P_{90}	P_{10}:P_{50}	Difference	P_{90}:P_{50}	P_{90}:P_{10}	N	Percent
White	7,145	17,917	35,871	40	160	200	5.02	197,792	75.05
Black	3,822	10,913	24,910	35	193	228	6.52	32,339	12.27
Hispanic	4,732	11,314	25,336	42	182	224	5.35	24,106	9.15
Other	5,281	17,928	39,023	29	188	218	7.39	9,302	3.53
Overall	5,876	16,320	33,950	36	172	208	5.78	263,539	100.00

1. Adjusted disposable income includes all forms of cash income net of direct tax using the household as the unit of aggregation and adjusting for household size differences using a square root equivalence scale.
2. Gini coefficients are based on income that are bottom coded at 1 percent of disposable income and top coded at 10 times the median disposable income.

Source: Author's calculations using LIS data base.

PART V
POLICY RESPONSES

Introduction

◆

by Isabel Sawhill
Senior Fellow, The Brookings Institution

THREE MAIN QUESTIONS need to be addressed in terms of policy responses to the increase in income disparity. First, "What should be our policy objectives?" Many believe that our key objective should be shoring up the bottom of the distribution, not necessarily redistributing income across the spectrum.

Second, "What should be the menu of policy options to deal with the problem?" Briefly, the major policy options or major categories in which they fall are: first, investing in education and training, including early childhood development and workforce training throughout the life cycle; second, redistributing income through taxes and transfers or other publicly provided benefits—in other words, shoring up the social safety net; third, encouraging, mandating, or bargaining for a different set of pay and benefit practices on the part of employees that could include changing the sharing of risks and rewards in the workplace; fourth, protecting U.S. labor markets from competition through trade restrictions or immigration restriction; and fifth, doing nothing or very little on the grounds that inequality of rewards in U.S. society drives people to work harder and to invest in their children's education and skills or on the grounds that the market will correct itself.

The third question that we need to address is "Why has this country chosen its current policy stance?" In Chapter 2, Janet Yellen emphasizes that we should not discount the importance of current policies, including the current social safety net, in reducing poverty and inequality. There are some who argue that current policies are exacerbating economic disparity as the result of the recent welfare bill and of budget cuts that are disproportionately affecting low income families and communities. Regardless of viewpoint, I would argue that in addition to a diagnosis of the problem and a discussion of the various policy options for dealing with it, we need a better understanding of the effects of current public policies.

Chapter 12

Is the New Income Inequality the Achilles' Heel of the American Economy?

◆

by Richard B. Freeman

CHAPTER 3 (BY THIS AUTHOR) PRESENTED the facts about increasing income disparity in the United States. This chapter addresses why we should be concerned about the widening distribution. Rather than directly presenting an argument that rising income disparity is perhaps *the* economic problem of our time, the discussion that follows examines and rebuts the five main reasons often given in debate by those who downgrade the importance of economic inequality as a major concern for the U.S. economy.

1. High income disparity simply reflects high mobility and opportunity and is thus something to applaud rather than lament.

To be sure, inequality is intrinsically related to mobility. If everyone were paid the same, inequality would be zero. In such a world, no one could improve their earnings through hard work, good ideas, or luck. No one would have a financial incentive to invest in skills or to take risks. If someone found an opportunity to produce and earn more, inequality would increase. At least one person would be better off and no one worse off, surely a better situation than if there were no inequality. More likely, the new discovery would benefit most of society. For instance, if a new form of transportation were invented, say, a flying automobile, almost everyone would benefit (except, of course, the newly outmoded car and airplane companies).

One way to determine if inequality has increased largely because of more opportunity is to follow the earnings of individuals for several years. Studies that do this find that a considerable proportion of inequality, possibly one-third, is variation in earnings over the life cycle. But this proportion has not changed over time, so the rise in inequality cannot be ascribed to it. Rather, studies find a secular rise in earnings instability for individuals in recent years.[1] Not only are differences in pay wider among individuals at a point in time, but also pay varies more for the same person over time. There is even a significant rise in consumption variability.[2]

Another way to explore mobility is to compare the probability that workers move among positions in the earnings distribution over a specified time period. At this writing, three studies, each using a different set of data, have looked at changes in U.S. earnings mobility over time with sufficient scientific care to yield valid results.[3] Two of the studies find that mobility has decreased.[4] One finds that it has been unchanged.[5] There is no evidence that the increase in inequality is due to a rise in mobility.

Many Americans view mobility in the United States as being massively greater than it is in Europe because America is a more open society. However, comparisons of mobility between the United States and western Europe show only modest country differences in the proportion of workers who change positions in the earnings distribution.[6] For example, between 1986 and 1991, 51 percent of American full-time wage and salaried workers moved from one quintile (fifth) in the U.S. distribution to another quintile. This exceeded mobility in Germany, Sweden (where 47 percent moved one quintile position), Italy (where 49 percent moved), and France (where just 43 percent moved), but it did not exceed mobility in Denmark and the United Kingdom (where 52 percent moved) or Finland (where 56 percent moved).[7] What distinguishes the United States is not so much mobility from one percentile of the distribution to another as the extent to which mobility affects earnings. Because the American earnings distribution is exceptionally wide, any given movement has a greater effect on earnings in the United States than elsewhere. For example, if an American moves from the 10th decile to the median, he or she will more than double his or her earnings, whereas a Swede moving from the 10th decile to the median obtains less than a one-third increase in earnings. When mobility is measured in this manner, the United States has greater upward and downward earnings mobility than other advanced countries.

In sum, evidence on earnings and on transitions between positions in the earnings distribution shows that the widening of the U.S. distribution is not "spuriously" due to increased opportunities.

2. The fall in real earnings is exaggerated because of defects in the Consumer Price Index (CPI).

Measures of nominal wages deflated by consumer prices may understate the growth of real earnings in the United States. The principal problem is that the CPI and other price deflators do not fully measure improvements in the quality of goods. If these indices overstate inflation, dividing them into nominal earnings understates the growth of real earnings. How much this biases the CPI is a matter of debate. The index is one of the most carefully developed statistical series in the United States, and the Bureau of Labor Statistics (BLS) improves it almost every year. Still, some experts believe that the CPI overstates inflation by as much as 1.5 percent per year.[8] If this were true, average real wages would have risen in the past two decades rather than having fallen. If, on the other hand, the CPI overstates inflation by, say, 0.3-0.5 percent per year, real wages would still have fallen for the average male worker.

Regardless, the fact remains that compared with the past, the trend growth rate in real earnings has fallen dramatically. Improvements in the CPI have presumably reduced mismeasurement of prices over time, which implies that the understatement of real earnings growth is less now than in the past. If better price data were available, the break in the trend growth rate of real wages would presumably be more severe. Using the CPI deflator, I obtained a pre-1973 growth rate of real wages of 2 percent a year compared with a change of –0.5 percent from 1973 to 1995—a decline of 2.5 percentage points. If the CPI were mismeasured by 2.0 percent in earlier periods and 1.5 percent per year recently, the drop in the growth of properly measured real wages would be from 4.0 percent to 1.0 percent—a decline of 3.0 percentage points.

In any case, real wage growth has stagnated in the U.S. relative to real wage growth in other advanced countries, all using CPI-style price deflators. In every Organization for Economic Cooperation and Development (OECD) country except the United States, wages deflated by national price indices have risen in the past two decades. For example, in the 1980s, real hourly compensation for production workers in manufacturing increased by 2.6 percent per year in the United Kingdom, 1.6 percent in Japan, 0.9 percent in France, and 1.3 percent in Germany, while it fell in the U.S.[9] The BLS estimates of average annual compensation of all workers in manufacturing show an increase in real earnings from 1973 to 1996 in the U.S. of 0.5 percent per year compared with 2.0 percent in Japan and 3.2 percent in the United Kingdom (see Table 1). There is nothing intrinsic in CPI deflators to produce declining or stagnating real wages. They never did until the 1980s and 1990s and then only in the U.S.

TABLE 1

AVERAGE YEARLY PERCENTAGE CHANGE IN REAL ANNUAL COMPENSATION IN MANUFACTURING, 1973-96

United States	0.5%
Japan	2.0
France	2.2
Germany	2.9
Italy	2.5
United Kingdom	3.2

Source: Table 14 in the U.S. Department of Labor, "International Comparisons of Manufacturing Productivity and Unit Labor Cost Trends, 1996," News, USDL: 97-285 (Washington: Bureau of Labor Statistics, August 15, 1997).

3. Rising earnings disparity is the necessary price the United States pays for job creation.

If decreasing wages for the low skilled had created a job boom for those workers, it could be argued that increased inequality has been, on net, positive for them. However, the employment of low skilled workers has not increased absolutely or relative to that of high skilled workers, but has instead decreased. From the 1970s through 1990, annual hours worked of men in the bottom deciles of the earnings distribution dropped, while hours worked of men in the upper deciles were stable or rose (see Chapter 3, Chart 3, page 31).

Comparing employment rates for less skilled workers in the United States and Europe further highlights the fact that the U.S. 1985-95 jobs miracle bypassed less educated men. In the early 1990s, employment-to-population rates for out of school 20-24 year olds were lower in the United States than in most advanced OECD-Europe countries despite lower relative pay in the United States.[10] In 1988, American men with less than four years of high school were less likely to be employed than European men with comparable low levels of schooling.[11] Further, these figures understate the problem faced by less educated young American men because many are jobless but are incarcerated for committing crimes and thus are not counted in the employment statistics.

If the great American jobs miracle has not benefited low skilled men, who have been the main beneficiaries? The answer is women. The employment-to-population rate for women rose from 54.5 percent in 1985 to 58.9 percent in 1995. In contrast, the employment-to-population rate for men was 70.9 percent in 1985 and 70.8 percent in 1995. That the gain in employment of women was accompanied by an increase in the pay of women relative to men—the only case in which a lower paid group rose in the earnings distribution—argues against any simple "cut pay, create jobs" interpretation of the U.S. jobs boom.

4. The problem will cure itself through economic growth and low unemployment.

Before the 1980s-90s experience, most economists would have endorsed this proposition. Throughout U.S. history, healthy growth of national product and jobs has improved the economic situation of the lower paid. But it is hard to sustain this belief when the nation has experienced nearly two decades of significant economic growth and expansion of employment, yet income disparity has gotten worse, not better. For perhaps the first time in U.S. economic history, growth is not an economic cure-all.

However, growth through the mid-1990s was accompanied by historically high levels of unemployment. Although the U.S. unemployment record in the post-1981 recession period looked good compared with that of Europe, it still represented an upward creep in unemployment from the 3-4 percent levels of the 1950s and 1960s. Macroeconomists claimed that the natural rate of unemployment had risen and that the United States simply had to live with 6 percent or so joblessness. The Federal Reserve would have to engineer mild recessions if unemployment fell further. If this were the case, the growth scenario would have little plausibility because unemployment rates of 6 percent or so imply much larger unemployment among low skilled workers and thus the absence of any market pressure on employers to increase their pay.

But, and not for the first time, macroeconomists seem to have erred. From 1995 to 1997, the drop in unemployment rates to 6 percent, then to 5 percent, and then below 5 percent with no inflation suggests that the natural rate is an extremely slippery measure. Whenever macroeconomists try to explain why it is what it is, the rate changes. A growing economy with rates of joblessness in the range of 4-5 percent, or maybe even less, can by itself raise the pay of low skilled workers.[12] In fact, the earnings of low decile workers rose from 1995 to 1997 as the jobless rate fell, though the increase in the minimum wage may be a more important factor in this change than the drop in unemployment. Still, if the United States can maintain a low rate of joblessness for an extended period of time and avoid a major recession, the market can be expected to raise the real earnings of the low paid, albeit slowly, with no additional policy intervention. But there is a long way to go, and the next recession may prove that these gains are ephemeral—cyclic upticks rather than any change in trend.

5. The problem will cure itself through increased investments in schooling.

The increased differential in the pay of college and university graduates relative to less educated workers has caused enrollments in institutions of higher education to grow rapidly in the 1980s and 1990s. Between 1980 and 1993, the proportion of 18-19 year olds enrolled in school rose from 46 percent to 62 percent, while the proportion of 20-21 year olds enrolled in school rose from 32 percent to 43 percent.[13] Blacks, who had especially high dropout rates from high school and low academic achievement scores, have improved in both areas, despite the problems of the inner cities where many live. Increases in the supply of educated workers will alleviate the rise of inequality by providing upward mobility to some, by reducing the number of the less educated seeking work, and by increasing the demand for less skilled workers whose jobs complement those of the more skilled.

Therefore, the question is not whether the labor market will reduce inequality, but whether it will do so sufficiently quickly and powerfully. I suspect that the market correction will reverse only part of the increase in inequality in the next decade because the requisite flood of college graduates seems too large.[14] Thus far, even with increasing numbers of graduates in the 1990s, the relative pay of the more educated has yet to fall. For some less educated people, moreover, having additional educated workers with whom to compete will exacerbate rather than ameliorate their economic plight. As more and more college graduates seek clerical and other jobs traditionally held by high school graduates, where will the latter find work?

Finally, I know of no evidence that the large rise in inequality within educational or occupational groups is reversible through greater investments in schooling. There is nothing about investing in education that can alter the structure of "winner take all" occupations or industries. Because so much of the increase in income disparity has occurred within narrowly defined groups of workers with roughly similar skills, it is difficult to believe that additional investments in skill will cure the income disparity problem.

CONCLUSION: ACHILLES' HEEL OR WHAT?

The widening of the distribution of earnings and incomes is significantly affecting the United States. An economy in which workers are sharply divided by income must operate differently from one dominated by a large, confident middle class. However, because the huge widening of the earnings distribution is a recent phenomenon, it is not certain whether the new disparity will have major consequences for the U.S. economy or simply be another bump in the road.

The clearest consequence of increased disparity is that people in the lower parts of the income distribution are poorer than they otherwise would be. Being poor in the United States is a meager and deprived economic existence.[15] One-fourth of the poor fail to meet rent or mortgage payments at least once during a year; one-third fail to pay utility bills during a year; 1 in 11 have services cut off by the gas, electric, or oil company; and 1 in 6 have their telephone disconnected. The poor are more likely than other Americans to live in crime-prone neighborhoods and to be victims of crime; their children are more likely to have health problems and trouble in school. The very poor risk homelessness. When people are on a financial edge, changes in earnings that may seem modest to higher income Americans can be critical to how they live.

The widening of the income distribution has already had adverse effects on the economic well-being of many children. Historically, poverty has been concentrated among the elderly and children, particularly those living in single-parent families, largely because neither group worked. In 1970, the rate of poverty for the elderly was 25 percent; for children, it was 15 percent. For both groups, the rate of poverty was trending downward. In ensuing years, Social Security and private pensions reduced the poverty rate among the elderly to 12 percent in 1993. In contrast, the poverty rate among children rose to 22 percent in 1993—a figure that exceeds child poverty rates in most other advanced countries. In the 1990s, American children in the lowest quintile of the income distribution have been absolutely poorer (using purchasing power parity currency adjustments to convert foreign currencies into dollars) than low income children in 15 other advanced countries. At the other end of the distribution, U.S. children in the top quintile families have markedly higher real incomes than the top quintile children in other countries.[16]

The widening of the earnings distribution contributes directly to child poverty because the sharpest loss in real incomes has been for young people just beginning their working lives. For example, in 1993, people in families headed by someone under age 25 had incomes roughly one-third less than those of similarly aged people in 1973. Moreover, to the extent that the widened distribution has helped fuel the rise of the single-parent home, it has also indirectly added to child poverty.

Another potential cost of inequality is a growing prison and jail population and a costly criminal justice system. A staggering number of American men are involved in crime: By 2000, roughly 3 percent of the male workforce will be incarcerated, and about 9 percent will be under the supervision of the criminal justice system. These numbers are a decimal point away from comparable statistics in other countries. Mass incarceration may explain why the crime rate stabilized in the 1980s and fell in the 1990s, although it is still too high. But incarceration is an incredibly expensive way to control crime. Incarcerating a criminal costs about as much per year as sending someone to Harvard. In 1995, the state of California budgeted more money for prisons than for higher education. A society that spends more on prisons than on universities is a society in trouble.

There is no smoking gun linking crime to falling real wages or employment opportunities for the less skilled, but the economic logic is clear: Whatever makes legitimate work less attractive makes crime more attractive. While it is not clear why the crime rate has remained high despite the number of criminals incarcerated, it is clear that the real earnings of low skilled young men most prone to crime fell in the 1980s and 1990s and that most of these men recognize they can do better on the street than in legitimate work.[17]

Continued homelessness is another likely consequence of high inequality. When the homeless burst on the scene in 1981-82, the Reagan administration saw them as a temporary problem that would disappear with economic recovery, a reasonable but erroneous expectation. When the economy recovered, homelessness remained. The bulk of the homeless are from low skilled, low wage groups whose employment and earnings prospects have deteriorated. Many cannot earn enough to rent even the lowest quality housing. Moreover, as the income distribution widens, fewer middle class families are moving to better housing and thereby freeing older dwellings for the poor.[18] Inequality is likely to adversely affect the family structure as well. Falling earnings and job prospects for young men is as antifamily a "policy" as one can imagine. If a young man cannot earn enough to support a family, he will not do so, though he may still father a child. He may become involved in crime.

Hundreds of thousands of children in single-parent homes in the United States have fathers in jail or prison. Millions of children receive little or no child support from fathers whose real earnings have trended downward. If low skilled young men had better earnings prospects, would they be more responsible participants in a family? Of course. Though again, how many would change their behavior is uncertain.

Some medical experts suggest that inequality has harmful health consequences. Mortality is inversely related to income and education, and the relation has grown pronounced in the United States since about 1960.[19] States with more unequal distributions of income by some metrics have higher mortality rates.[20] Poor families are less likely than other families to inoculate their children against diseases.[21] Teenagers from poor communities are more likely to be homicide victims. But cross-section relationships cannot be generalized to changes over time. Until changes in inequality or changes in the real incomes of low paid Americans are linked to changes in health status, the claim that the divergence of earnings has adversely affected the nation's health is problematic. Perhaps the increased disparity in death rates by economic status is due to the widening disparity in incomes, or perhaps other factors are at work.

Broader Consequences of Income Inequality

Economists have studied the effects of inequality on the growth of GDP per capita—the single best indicator of economic performance and the development of markets—and have found that growth across countries is inversely related to inequality.[22] East Asian countries with low inequality such as South Korea and Taiwan have grown more than countries with highly unequal distributions such as many in Latin America. Why? Some speculate that in societies with high levels of inequality, people fight over the distribution of national output rather than work to increase national output. As the divide between bosses and employees grows, many employees come to view business unfavorably and may be attracted to policy interventions harmful to the national product. Moreover, without a perfect capital market in which individuals can borrow on their future earnings, inequality reduces the chances for the poor to invest in education and skills. In addition, when a large segment of the workforce lacks skills, their inefficiency may adversely affect the performance of the skilled who rely on them for some tasks. The engineer or scientist who works with highly competent technicians or craftworkers will have higher productivity than the one who works with poorly trained or illiterate workers.

A more unequal earnings distribution benefits businesses that provide goods and services to the super-rich and those that cater to the new poor. In contrast, the businesses that produce for the middle class will face smaller markets. Consumer credit defaults may rise, as many individuals find themselves unexpectedly sliding down the earnings distribution. Saving by citizens, already low, may fall or fail to rise to provide the funds needed for investment. Because businesses adjust to market opportunities, one potential outcome is more Neiman Marcuses and more Wal-Marts—a division in retailing that mirrors the division in the earnings distribution. Similarly, in terms of the use of labor, the division between good employers and bad employers could grow. Already sweatshops have returned to the United States, and many major firms contract cleaning services to small enterprises that pay low wages and offer few benefits.

More speculatively, a widening income distribution may increase social tensions, reduce stability, and create opportunities for demagogues of diverse bents. Animus against CEOs, Wall Street, free trade, and the like is one logical consequence of rising inequality. Animus against immigrants or ethnic groups other than one's own may grow. Policies to aid disadvantaged groups lose appeal. If Pat Buchanan's "peasants with pitchforks" take to the streets, in which direction will they turn?

To look at the problem from an even wider perspective, American democracy has been premised on a reasonable degree of equality among citizens. Whether that democracy can function as well when incomes are highly unequal as when they are more equally distributed is an open question. If people believe that the well-to-do or special moneyed interests control politics, why should they bother to vote or to commit themselves to the democratic process? In the 1994 mid-term elections, just 27 percent of those with incomes under $15,000 a year voted—down from 34 percent four years earlier.

This list of costs—crime, insecurity, family, business decisions, political attitudes—is neither exhaustive nor definitive. Some costs may be larger than expected; others may be smaller. Riots and urban disorder have occurred spasmodically in U.S. history, usually when the expectations of the impoverished or discriminated against have exceeded their rate of progress in society and usually to the surprise of most observers. Racial tensions are often fueled by economic insecurity and feelings of being left out or left behind.

What should worry Americans most about the new disparity, however, is not disorders by people in the lower rungs of the income distribution, but acceptance of the new inequality by the better-off in society. The United States may be on the road to a stable but divided economy in which the division of society into the well-off and the poor is accepted as the way things are. I have used the phrase "apartheid economy" to describe this scenario—an economy in which the rich live aloof in their suburbs and expensive apartments with little link to the poor in their slums or to the declining middle class struggling to keep its head above water.[23] People have a remarkable capacity to adjust to social and economic situations that they once viewed as intolerable such as homelessness and inner-city poverty. Perhaps the answer to the Achilles' heel question should be twofold: There is a risk that rising disparity will prove to be the Achilles' heel of the U.S. economy, but there is an even greater risk that it will not be such a burden and will produce a viable society and economy that, although less desirable than one with less disparity, is simply accepted.

It would be great to report that American-style capitalism offers the model for economic advancement in the 21st century. The U.S. economy has many strengths on which to build. But until America figures out how to remedy the problem of rising income disparity, this weakness will betray the promise of the American dream to all too many average citizens and employees.

NOTES

1. Peter Gottschalk and Robert Moffitt, "The Growth of Earnings Instability in the U.S. Labor Market," *Brookings Papers on Economic Activity*, Vol. 2 (1994), pp. 216-254.

2. Susan Dynarski and Jonathon Gruber, "Earnings Variability and Family Living Standards," Massachusetts Institute of Technology, 1997, mimeo.

3. A fourth study is unfortunately based on largely erroneous analysis (Michael Cox and Richard Alm, "By Our Own Bootstraps: Economic Opportunity and the Dynamics of Income Distribution," *Federal Reserve Bank of Dallas Annual Report*, 1995, p. 4). This study shows huge movements of Americans from the bottom parts of the earnings distribution to the top parts of the distribution. The authors find a massive degree of mobility, far beyond that found in any other study. For instance, they claim that only 5.1 percent of people in the lowest 20 percent of the earnings distribution remain there 16 years later, while 29 percent rise to the top decile. The main reason behind this finding is the inclusion of teenagers and students, who have low earnings at the outset of their careers but high earnings later on. The average income in this study's lowest 20 percent in 1975 is just $1,153, which could not conceivably hold for adult workers. See Peter Gottschalk, "Notes on 'By Our Own Bootstraps,'" Boston College, April 22, 1996, mimeo.

4. Moshe Buchinsky and Jennifer Hunt, "Wage Mobility in the United States," NBER Working Paper 5455 (February 1996); and Maury Gittleman and Mary Joyce, "Earnings Mobility and Long-Run Inequality: An Analysis Using Matched CPS Data," *Industrial Relations*, Vol. 35, No. 2 (April 1996), pp. 180-196.

5. Richard V. Burkhauser, "Income Mobility and the Middle Class," reports little change in U.S. mobility between the 1970s and 1980s (paper presented at the American Enterprise Institute Seminar on Understanding Income Inequality, Washington, D.C., April 15, 1996); and Exhibits F and G, using the Panel Study of Income Dynamics. See also Gottschalk and Moffitt, "The Growth of Earnings Instability."

6. Organization for Economic Cooperation and Development (OECD), *Employment Outlook, July 1996* (Paris: OECD, 1996).

7. Ibid.

8. Boskin Commission (the informal name given to the Advisory Commission to Study the Consumer Price Index) Report (Washington: December 1996); and Matthew Shapiro and David W. Wilcox, "Mismeasurement in the Consumer Price Index: An Evaluation," NBER Working Paper 5590 (May 1996).

9. OECD, *Historical Statistics, 1960-1989* (Paris: OECD, 1991).

10. OECD, *Employment Outlook, July 1994* (Paris: OECD, 1994), Table 1.20.

11. OECD, *Employment Outlook, July 1989* (Paris: OECD, 1989), Chap. 2, Annexes 2A and 2B.

12. Richard B. Freeman, "Labor Market Tightness and the Declining Economic Position of Young Less Educated Male Workers in the United States," in *Mismatch and Labour Mobility*, ed. F. Padoa-Schippa (Cambridge, ENG: Cambridge University Press, 1991).

13. U.S. Bureau of the Census, *Statistical Abstract of the United States, 1996* (Washington: U.S. Government Printing Office [GPO], 1997), Table 234.

14. John Bishop, "Is the Market for College Graduates Headed for a Bust? Demand and Supply Responses to Rising College Wage Premiums," *New England Economic Review* (Special Issue, May/June 1996), pp. 115-136.

15. Maya Federman et al., "What Does It Mean to Be Poor in America?" *Monthly Labor Review,* Vol. 199, No. 5 (May 1996), pp. 3-17.

16. Lee Rainwater and Timothy M. Smeeding, "Doing Poorly: The Real Income of American Children in a Comparative Perspective," Luxembourg Income Study Working Paper No. 127 (April 1995).

17. Richard B. Freeman, "Why Do So Many Young American Men Commit Crimes and What Can We Do About It?" *Journal of Economic Perspectives*, Vol. 10, No. 1 (Winter 1996).

18. Brenden O'Flaherty, *Making Room: The Economics of Homelessness* (Cambridge: Harvard University Press, 1996).

19. Gregory Pappas, Susan Queen, Wilbur Hadden, and Gail Fisher, "The Increasing Disparity in Morality between Socioeconomic Groups in the U.S., 1960 and 1986," *New England Journal of Medicine*, Vol. 329, No. 2 (July 8, 1993), pp. 103-109.

20. Bruce Kennedy, Ichiro Kawachi, and Deborah Prothrow-Smith, "Income Distribution and Mortality: Cross-Sectional Ecological Study of the Robin Hood Index in the United States," *British Medical Journal*, Vol. 312 (1996), pp. 1004-1007.

21. U.S. Department of Health and Human Services, *Trends in the Well-Being of America's Children and Youth: 1996* (Washington: GPO, April 1996).

22. Roland Benabou, "Inequality and Growth," in *NBER Macroeconomics Annual, 1996,* ed. Ben Bernanke and Julio Rotemberg (Cambridge: MIT Press, 1996).

23. Richard B. Freeman, "Toward an Apartheid Economy?" *Harvard Business Review* (September-October 1996).

Chapter 13

To Narrow the Gap, Focus on the Process

◆

by John T. Joyce

THE GROWING GAP in income and wealth in the United States is not simply between the rich and the poor. The heart of the matter is that the gap is between the finance community, and its witting or unwitting partners in corporate management, and the rest of society, with the poor's plight worsening faster than the rest. This development is not fully measured in dollars and cents. The income and wealth differential represents not a flaw in America's market economy, but a failure of American democracy—"a" failure, not yet "the" failure, but nonetheless a very dangerous failure.

The disparity in the distribution of wealth and income is so dangerous because it is only one manifestation of the failure of democracy; it just happens to be the one that people are focusing on now. Attention will at some point move on to focus on, but not long enough to solve, unemployment, underemployment, employment insecurity, declining real wages, and, probably without identifying them as related to economic causes, crime, drugs, inadequate housing, a growing population without medical care, and a host of other symptoms of a society disintegrating around the edges.

These problems are not the fault of one political party, one administration, or even one specific set of policies. But the problems are not mere happenstance. They flow from making public policy decisions by attaching paramount importance to one set of interests. They flow from the fact that the United States does not have economic decisionmaking structures that give an effective voice to all the stakeholders in those decisions.

DICTATING ECONOMIC POLICY

More and more, one community in the United States—the finance and investment community—has been in a position to dictate economic policy for everyone else. Not surprisingly, the members of that community have done what people in such a position always do—they have made the key decisions in their own favor.

The solution is not to demonize the investment community. Morally, its members are no worse than anyone else, and they do play a vital role in the U.S. economy. The solution is to break their financial hammerlock on industry and on the nation and, concurrently, to build the structures that democratically bring into play the interests of the rest of society.

The mind-set that shareholders are the only true risk takers must be changed. This old shibboleth goes against common sense and economic reality. All kinds of groups—managers, communities, and workers—make real investments in enterprises, investments that have worth only if the company succeeds. The concept of economic democracy stems from the logic that all risk-taking stakeholders need a role in decision-making.

The investment community did not conspire to bring about this situation. Some members just stumbled on new incantations from the book of electronic wizardry and coupled them with some "mumbo jumbo" market formulas and adventurism forbidden until the Reagan administration. The result has been to free the investment community to spin out of control. The American public, Congress, and the investment community itself know this is true, but no one is doing anything to remedy the situation.

PROGRESSING TO THE NEXT STAGE OF DEVELOPMENT

Yet the remedy is not a radical one requiring revolution. What is required is to see that things already in place at the industry level, the national level, and the global level progress to their next stage of development.

At the industry level, the fabric of collective bargaining in the United States must be rebuilt. The law expressly declares that the national policy should encourage the "practice and procedure" of collective bargaining. Why? Not because of labor's political clout in the New Deal or to appease well-meaning reformers, but to end the industrial violence that had been racking the nation since 1865 and to move society to a more just and democratic concord.

The National Labor Relations Act, in fact, is a social contract between labor, management, and government in which all three parties agreed to put aside baseball bats, guns, and other means of coercion to settle their differences at the bargaining table. The contract worked reasonably well through the end of the Depression, when revolution was a distinct possibility, through the Second World War, and through the tremendous postwar economic expansion that lasted until about the mid-1960s.

Today, however, management and government are in breach of that social contract. If a determined employer uses every legal loophole—loopholes that have been attached to the contract without labor's consent since World War II—there is no way a labor union can legally achieve the lawful objectives of working people. Labor law in the United States has therefore lost its moral imperative. The only reason to obey the law is to avoid paying a fine or going to jail. That creates a profoundly unstable situation.

The constraints on collective bargaining must also be removed. Collective bargaining can be revitalized only if it is made generally and freely available instead of being confined merely to those with the economic muscle, the abnormal passion, and the perseverance required to overcome all the legal and illegal obstacles that employers can put in the way of organizing efforts.

Furthermore, collective bargaining can no longer be narrowly constricted to a zero sum game about negotiating who gets how much of the existing economic pie. Collective bargaining must address strategic-level issues of corporate or industry policy. Doing so would enable labor and management to work to make a bigger pie and would give workers a voice in the decisions that determine how many jobs there will be and how good those jobs will be. With a measure of security established at the strategic level, labor and management could then move toward replacing rigid working rules with a cooperative problem-solving process aimed at making the workplace both more productive and more satisfying for workers.

Collective bargaining at the industry level, however, even with some obvious impediments removed, will not be able to fully develop in a larger public policy vacuum. A frame of reference must be provided by a macroeconomic decisionmaking body, representing all stakeholders in the U.S. economy, and a national collective bargaining coordinating mechanism. The two could be part of the same national economic structure, meeting with and chaired by or reporting to the President on a monthly or quarterly basis.

The Carter administration had the right strategy in mind with the National Accord. Had the Accord established roots and grown, it could have developed along the lines of its counterparts in western Europe to include representatives not only of labor and management, but of the professional and agricultural communities as well. Lacking such a macroeconomic structure, the United States will be unable to achieve the level of economic growth needed to adjust over time the present gross disparity in income and wealth without social divisiveness and economic inflation.

While such a structure is necessary, it is not sufficient. The United States must also establish a more rational framework for global trade and finance, one that adds labor standards and the impact of global trade and finance on working people to the considerations addressed by the World Trade Organization (WTO). In short, what is needed is a strengthened International Labor Organization with a newly defined mission relating to global trade and finance and having coequal status with the WTO and the World Bank.

A NEW REASON TO BOTHER

A major impediment to creating a more democratic economic decision-making system seems to be a "Why bother?" attitude among policymakers and policyshapers. In politics, in government, and in the academic community, the view seems to be that since working people have already tolerated so much abuse, they will continue to tolerate more.

It is time to let union members know that efforts to reform the economic decisionmaking process through political action do not work because of this why bother attitude. It is time to give policymakers and policyshapers a new reason to bother.

It has been said that the public is slow to speak, but that when it does speak, it shatters the eardrums. Those who have ears to hear know the decibels are rising. Those who have eyes to see know why it is happening. Those who have brains to think must begin cooperating on a solution or get a good pair of earplugs. And those who choose earplugs should be prepared to watch America lose, and lose badly, in a global economic competition. That race will go to the nations that maintain their social cohesion.

Chapter 14

Growing Economic Disparity in the U.S.: Assessing the Problem and the Policy Options

♦

by Lynn A. Karoly

"AMERICA UNEQUAL" AND THE "NEW INEQUALITY" are only two of the many terms used to describe the growing income and wage gap that has been a major aspect of the U.S. economic landscape for the past two decades or more.[1] The rise in economic inequality first captured the attention of analysts and journalists in the early 1980s, and it has continued to draw scrutiny from academic researchers, policymakers, and the public. Attention has been devoted to characterizing the pattern of growth at the top and the bottom of the economic ladder as well as to identifying the causal factors responsible for the dramatic shift in the distribution of economic well-being in the past 20 years. These issues have been examined on two fronts: the widening income gap between rich and poor, and the growing disparity in wages between high paid and low paid workers.[2]

Increasingly, the role for policy in addressing the widening income and wage gap has garnered attention. For example, in the 1997 *Economic Report of the President*, the Council of Economic Advisers devotes an entire chapter to growing economic inequality that concludes with a brief discussion of the role of government policy. The report identifies the Earned Income Tax Credit (EITC), increases in the minimum wage, and investments in education and training as the package of options worth considering.[3] At the other end of the political spectrum, arguments are common in favor of strong economic growth, the use of traditional redistributive tax or transfer policies, or a reliance on private market forces to provide self-correcting mechanisms.[4] The goal of this chapter is to provide some context for identifying policy objectives in light of the nature of the distributional shifts and to provide a framework for thinking about the range of policy options available given those objectives.

Before the policy options are discussed, it is necessary to understand the phenomenon of rising income and wage inequalities in the United States since 1973. The next section highlights both the salient features of the distributional changes and current understanding of the causes of these trends. This background provides the basis for the discussion of policy options that follows. Rather than identifying a single policy lever or combination of specific strategies, this chapter presents a menu of policy options that differ in their ability to achieve three possible policy objectives, to have an impact sooner or longer into the future, and to directly influence the wage or income distribution.

THE PHENOMENON OF RISING ECONOMIC INEQUALITY

When considering policy options to address the growing inequality in the United States, it is important first to set the stage: What is the phenomenon that policy must address? To answer this question, this section reviews the most important aspects of the distributional changes in the past two decades and current understanding of the causes of these trends. This section will not delve into many of the subtleties of the changes that have been experienced or the details of the debate that continues among academics regarding the relative contributions of different causal factors; many of these issues are discussed elsewhere in this volume. Instead, the objective here is to lay a foundation for considering what might be done to address the changes that have been seen. This section approaches the distributional changes from two vantage points—the distribution of income among all individuals in the population and the distribution of wages among workers.[5]

Family Incomes: A Break from the Historical Past

Several features of the changing distributional landscape since 1973 are most striking. One phenomenon that marks a difference between recent decades and the immediate post-World War II period is the stagnation in median family income. By official U.S. Bureau of the Census statistics, real median family income grew an average of 2.8 percent per year between 1947 and 1973. Between 1973 and 1989, real growth in family median income averaged only 0.5 percent per year. When the definition of the income unit is expanded to include one-person families (individuals living alone or with nonrelatives), even these modest gains in real income disappear. Real gains in median income among families or individuals appear only when declines in family size are accounted for (that the typical family today is smaller than in the past means that the income is spread over fewer members). Even then, the gains are modest, with only a 14 percent real gain in median adjusted family income among persons between the business cycle peak years of 1973 and 1989, equal to about 0.8 percent average real growth per year.[6]

The stagnation of incomes at the middle of the income ladder has been accompanied by another significant change from the historical past: a rise in the income gap between rich and poor. Regardless of the distributional metric, disparities have widened over the past three decades as the growth in real income has been more rapid the higher the point in the income distribution. To illustrate these changes, Chart 1 shows my estimates of the change in the distribution of individual well-being for

CHART 1

**ABSOLUTE PERCENTILES OF ADJUSTED FAMILY INCOME
AMONG PERSONS, 1973-95**

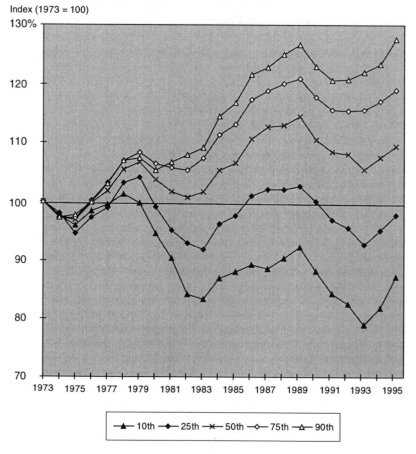

Note: Adjusted family income is pretax family money income relative to the family's poverty line.

Source: Author's calculations using March 1974 to March 1996 Current Population Survey (CPS).

the entire U.S. population between 1973 and 1995 as measured by adjusted family income. The chart plots the trend in real income (adjusted for inflation) at five points in the income scale: the 10th and 25th percentiles capturing trends in the lower ranks of the income ladder; the 50th percentile or median representing the income growth for the person at the middle of the distribution; and the 75th and 90th percentiles reflecting the experiences of individuals at the top of the income scale. Table 1 provides an additional assessment of the patterns by summarizing the growth trends over various subperiods for the 10th, 50th, and 90th percentiles, as well as the trends in three ratios: 90th to 10th percentile, 90th to 50th percentile, and 50th to 10th percentile. The overall income gap is reflected in the first ratio, the 90:10 gap. The second ratio captures changes in the shape of the top half of the income distribution, whereas the third ratio captures changes in the bottom half of the distribution.

Several points are illustrated by Chart 1. If all points in the income scale experience real growth, the trend lines at each point in the distribution would slope upward and would move together (since they are all indexed to equal 100 in 1973). In contrast, real income losses are reflected in a downward-sloping trend line. The most striking feature of

TABLE 1

TRENDS IN ABSOLUTE AND RELATIVE PERCENTILES OF ADJUSTED FAMILY INCOME, 1973-95

	Absolute Percentile			Relative Percentile		
	10th	50th	90th	90th-10th	90th-50th	50th-10th
Level						
1973	0.96	2.84	6.03	6.3	2.1	2.9
1979	0.96	3.03	6.47	6.7	2.1	3.2
1989	0.89	3.25	7.63	8.6	. 2.3	3.6
1995	0.84	3.11	7.69	9.1	2.5	3.7
Percentage Change						
1973-95	−12.7	9.4	27.4	46.0	16.5	25.4
1973-79	− 0.3	6.7	7.3	7.7	0.6	7.0
1979-89	− 7.4	7.2	17.8	27.2	9.9	15.7
1989-95	− 5.5	−4.3	0.8	6.6	5.3	1.2
1979-83	−16.3	−4.7	1.7	21.5	6.7	13.8
1983-85	5.6	4.8	6.9	1.2	2.0	− 0.7
1985-89	4.8	7.3	8.4	3.4	1.0	2.4
1989-93	−14.3	−7.8	− 3.7	12.4	4.4	7.6
1993-95	10.3	3.7	4.6	− 5.1	0.9	− 5.9

Note: Adjusted family income is pretax family money income relative to the family's poverty line.

Source: Author's calculations using March 1974 to March 1996 CPS.

the chart is that the trend lines grow apart over time, so that by 1995, the 90:10 income gap stands at a ratio of 9.1 compared with 6.3 in 1973. (The gap peaked in 1993 at 9.6.) A comparison of the trends at each percentile point of the income scale confirms that income growth over this period was steadily higher the higher the ranking on the income scale.[7]

If the only distributional change over this period was faster income growth at the top of the income scale, there might be little to be concerned about. But the changes over this period are marked not only by relative losses at the bottom of the income ranks, but by absolute declines as well. In 1995, as seen in Chart 1, an individual at the 25th percentile had about the same income adjusted for family size as the individual at the 25th percentile in 1973. All people to the right of that individual experienced real income growth compared with their counterparts two decades earlier, while those to the left experienced real income declines. In other words, the poorest 25 percent of the U.S. population in 1995 were worse off measured by adjusted family income than the bottom 25 percent of the population in 1973. When the income gap peaked in 1993, one had to go to the 40th percentile of the income scale to find individuals who were better off in real terms than their counterparts at the same point in the income scale two decades earlier.

Chart 1 suggests that the income gap has begun to narrow as the economic recovery has continued in recent years. Since 1993, real income growth has recovered at the bottom of the income ranks, although the peak attained in 1989 has yet to be regained. The same is true at the 50th and 75th percentiles. At the same time, the more rapid real growth at the 90th percentile has resulted in a 1995 level that just exceeds the previous peak in 1989. Consequently, the overall income gap, as well as the spread between the 90th and 50th percentiles and the 50th and 10th percentiles, still exceeds the levels attained in earlier business cycle peaks since 1973 (see Table 1).

Although the conventional wisdom for some time was that business cycle recoveries were associated with flat or declining levels of inequality, the economic expansion of the 1980s is an exception to that rule. Income disparities widened between 1983 and 1989, a significant break from the historical pattern of a narrowing of the income gap during periods of economic growth. Will the most recent recovery repeat that experience? As Table 1 shows, the pattern of absolute and relative income growth across the income scale between 1993 and 1995 does differ from what occurred between 1983 and 1985. In the first few years after incomes at the bottom of the scale reached their lowest absolute level in 1983, income growth through 1985 was modest and less rapid compared with incomes at the top (5.6 percent at the 10th percentile compared with 6.9 percent at the 90th percentile). In contrast, since the trough attained in 1993, incomes through 1995 recovered more rapidly at the bottom than at the top (10.3 percent at the 10th percentile contrasted with 4.6 percent at the 90th percentile). With a long enough expansion, incomes at the bottom of the scale could again regain lost ground and close part of the gap with the upper percentiles. Even so, it is important to note that even when incomes peaked in 1989, after the longest postwar peacetime expansion, the 10th percentile was still 7 percent below the 1973 level in real terms, while the 25th percentile gained only 2 percent in real terms over the same period.

During the past two decades or more, few groups in the population have been immune from the distributional shifts. In fact, the income trends evident in Chart 1 and Table 1 are replicated for most other demographic groups, indicating that inequality has grown within as well as between population groups in the past two decades. For example, similar patterns of rising income disparities are evident for whites, African Americans, and Hispanics.[8] In all cases, income grew fastest at the higher income percentiles and slowest at the lower income percentiles, indicating an increase in dispersion within each group. Since African American and Hispanic families have lower incomes on average, they were particularly hard hit by the overall rise in inequality.

Although inequality grew within most demographic groups, comparisons across groups show that some were clear winners during this period.[9] The most fortunate included families headed by individuals with more education and with two potential earners. Another often overlooked group of gainers was the elderly, a group that managed to reduce its concentration at the bottom of the income ladder through steady real income growth on average. If there were winners, there also had to be losers. The latter consisted primarily of traditionally disadvantaged groups—the young, the least educated, and families with a single head. On average, these groups experienced the largest real income losses and were increasingly concentrated in the lower ranks of the income scale.

A few other features in the changing distributional landscape are worth noting. First, this perspective on the widening income gap focuses on a measure of adjusted family income that excludes taxes and in-kind benefits. Alternative measures of the distributional changes based on more comprehensive measures of annual income (e.g., after accounting for in-kind benefits and taxes) show similar trends.[10] Thus, tax and transfer policies have done little to offset the trends observed in pretax incomes nor have changes in these sources of income contributed to the trends. When annual consumption is used as the metric of economic well-being, there is also a comparable rise in disparity over time.[11] Second, careful studies of changes in income mobility based on longitudinal data reveal that longer-run or lifetime measures of inequality have also risen over this same period.[12] Thus, there has been no increase in economic mobility to offset the rise in annual income inequality. Finally, the patterns summarized here for the United States are replicated in many other developed economies, although the United States stands out among most countries, with one of the highest levels of inequality overall and with greater relative declines at the bottom of the income scale.[13]

Workers' Wages: A Similar Story

So far, the focus of this chapter has been on the widening income gap measured in terms of adjusted family income. It is worth emphasizing that these patterns are echoed in equally striking changes in the U.S. wage structure during this period. These patterns are carefully summarized in a recent review by Freeman.[14] Table 2 offers additional evidence of these patterns, based on trends in hourly wages for men and women, measured for the same time period and at the same three points in the distribution as Table 1.

What has happened to the distribution of wages (see Table 2) can be readily summarized. With few exceptions, "wage distribution" can be substituted for "income distribution" in the preceding discussion. In other words, (1) real median wages have declined (since 1979 for men) or stagnated (since the late 1980s for women); (2) the wage gap has widened as wages at the top of the scale grew faster than median wages, and wages at the bottom of the scale fell more rapidly (for men) or grew more slowly (for women) than wages at the middle; (3) real wages have declined in absolute terms since 1979 for most of the male wage distribution and for the bottom half of the female wage distribution; and (4) inequality among workers has increased due both to widening gaps among workers with different characteristics (e.g., education, experience) and to growing disparities within similarly defined groups of workers.

As with family income, there is some evidence that the most recent economic downturn and subsequent recovery differs from the pattern observed in the early 1980s (see Table 2). For men, for example, the 1993-95 period is marked by a slight narrowing of the 90:10 gap, largely because of very modest growth at the bottom of the wage scale in contrast to continued declines at the middle and upper ranks. A decade earlier, the recovery was marked by a growing 90:10 gap because of a nearly symmetric pulling apart of the top and bottom from the middle. For women, the pattern after 1983 and 1993 is growth in inequality for two years, although the more recent pattern is more modest compared with the 1980s. In neither the male nor female wage distribution is there evidence of a rapid turnaround in the economic fortunes of lower wage workers.

As with the income distribution, there are other ways to slice the data that still produce similar results. For example, adding fringe benefits to the measure of labor compensation not only fails to diminish the trend, it actually accentuates the growing gap as fringe benefits grow most rapidly in prevalence and value among more highly paid workers.[15] Data from longitudinal studies also show that lifetime earnings inequality has risen over the same period, so economic mobility is not a countervailing force.[16] Finally, similar patterns are evident in wage trends for other developed countries, although the United States exhibits the largest real wage declines, especially for men.

TABLE 2

TRENDS IN ABSOLUTE AND RELATIVE PERCENTILES
OF HOURLY WAGES, 1973-95 (1995 $)

(a.) Male Workers

	Absolute Percentile			Relative Percentile		
	10th	50th	90th	90th-10th	90th-50th	50th-10th
Level						
1973	6.80	13.37	24.45	3.6	1.8	2.0
1979	6.71	13.66	24.62	3.7	1.8	2.0
1989	5.86	12.41	24.80	4.2	2.0	2.1
1995	5.49	11.62	24.88	4.5	2.1	2.1
Percentage Change						
1973-95	−19.3	−13.1	1.8	26.0	17.1	7.6
1973-79	− 1.3	2.2	0.7	2.0	− 1.4	3.5
1979-89	−12.7	− 9.2	0.7	15.3	10.9	4.0
1989-95	− 6.3	− 6.4	0.3	7.1	7.1	−0.1
1979-83	−12.7	− 5.7	0.3	14.8	6.4	8.0
1983-85	− 1.4	0.2	2.7	4.1	2.5	1.5
1985-89	1.4	− 3.8	− 2.2	− 3.5	1.7	−5.1
1989-93	− 7.2	− 5.3	0.8	8.6	6.5	2.0
1993-95	0.9	− 1.1	− 0.5	− 1.4	0.6	−2.0

(b.) Female Workers

	Absolute Percentile			Relative Percentile		
	10th	50th	90th	90th-10th	90th-50th	50th-10th
Level						
1973	4.80	8.44	15.26	3.2	1.8	1.8
1979	5.82	8.58	15.78	2.7	1.8	1.5
1989	4.76	9.07	18.36	3.9	2.0	1.9
1995	4.84	8.92	19.17	4.0	2.1	1.8
Percentage Change						
1973-95	0.8	5.7	25.6	24.6	18.9	4.8
1973-79	21.3	1.7	3.4	−14.7	1.7	−16.2
1979-89	−18.2	5.7	16.3	42.3	10.1	29.3
1989-95	1.7	−1.7	4.4	2.7	6.2	− 3.3
1979-83	−10.1	0.0	4.4	16.1	4.4	11.3
1983-85	− 5.2	0.9	4.8	10.5	3.8	6.4
1985-89	− 4.0	4.7	6.4	10.8	1.6	9.1
1989-93	3.8	0.6	4.2	0.4	3.7	− 3.1
1993-95	− 2.0	−2.2	0.2	2.2	2.4	− 0.2

Source: Author's tabulations derived from Lawrence Mishel, Jared Bernstein, and John Schmitt, *The State of Working America, 1996-1997* (Armonk, NY: M.E. Sharpe for Economic Policy Institute, 1996).

How Did These Changes Come About?

While there is little controversy over the basic facts that the U.S. economy has experienced a rise in the income and wage gap in recent decades, there is less agreement about the causes of these dramatic changes. Identifying the factors responsible for the observed trends is an important first step toward determining whether policy can attenuate or reverse the trends, assuming it is decided that this is a desirable goal. For example, if changes in the income or wage distribution are associated with the baby boom, a demographic phenomenon largely beyond the control of policymakers, there may be little room or justification for intervention. On the other hand, changes in the income distribution may themselves be a direct result of policy changes, in which case the distributional impact of these policies needs to be recognized and quantified.

The observed distribution of income or wages is the result of a complex set of factors, including the opportunities that individuals face, their decisions given those opportunities, and a set of public and private institutions that helps determine how society's output is allocated across families and individuals. The consensus that has emerged from the recent literature is that there is no single culprit, no smoking gun, that explains the growth in either income or wage inequality. Rather, a confluence of factors—all operating in the same direction and possibly interacting with each other—have pushed income and wage distributions toward greater inequality. Whereas in the past, many of these trends may have been influencing the distribution, some would have also served to widen the wage or income gap, while others would have been working toward more equality. More recently, the balance of factors shifted so that most operated in the same direction.

Explanations for Widening Family Income Disparities

In sorting through the possible explanations for changes in the income distribution among individuals, it is convenient to rely on three broad categories of explanations: demographic changes, changes in family formation, and changes in the sources of income. The first set of explanations covers factors such as population aging or shifts in ethnic composition that might be expected to change the composition of families in the population toward more high or low income families. The second category captures shifts in the processes that result in the formation of families, the units that, it is assumed, pool their incomes to enhance the economic well-being of all family members. Finally, within families, there may be a change in the composition or distribution of income sources, such as earned income, capital income, or public transfers that results in the observed distributional changes. The contribution of each of these factors is summarized briefly below.[17]

Demographic Shifts

Demographic shifts have been singled out as possible causes of both the changing income structure and the changing wage structure. In the past two decades, the population has grown steadily older, education levels of family heads have increased, and the share of minorities in the population has expanded. Even in the absence of other changes in family structure or sources of income, these demographic shifts may have affected the overall income distribution if the composition of the population shifted toward groups with more disparate incomes on average or toward groups with higher levels of inequality. In fact, my research shows that these changes have played, at most, a small role. The age and education shifts actually have served to dampen the rise in inequality rather than to increase it. The growing share of minorities in the population explains at most 10 percent of the rise in family income inequality.

Changes in Family Structure

More important in the past two decades, significant changes in family structure have occurred. More individuals—from 6 to 11 percent—are living alone or with nonrelatives, so they do not pool their income. The number of female-headed families has also increased, representing 11 percent of the population compared with 8 percent two decades ago. At the same time, traditional husband-wife families with a working wife, once in the minority, now make up 60 percent of these families. These three factors could increase the number of low income and high income families. Indeed, by one accounting method, these family structure changes explain about 25 percent of the rise in family income inequality. There is also evidence that the process of family formation is changing, with greater assortative mating. In other words, husbands and wives are becoming more similar, particularly in their earnings capacity. The matching of husbands and wives based on their earnings potential is also related to the third class of explanations.

Changes in Income Sources

The distribution of family income also depends on changes in the distribution of the various sources of income such as earnings from the labor market, capital income, or public transfers. Since most family income comes from earnings, strong links would be expected between changes in the distribution of labor market earnings and family inequality. In fact, the data bear this out. First, the rise in inequality among men explains a sizable share of the increase in family income inequality, about one-third of the increase. Second, working wives have also played a role in the growing income gap. In the past two decades, the likelihood of being ranked higher on the income ladder has become increasingly associated with being in a family with two potential earners. At the same time, the earnings of husbands and wives have become more highly correlated. While in the past a person in a family with a working male head was less likely than average to receive labor earnings from a working wife, today that relationship has been reversed. In families with a highly compensated male earner, an individual today is more likely than average to receive income from a well-paid female earner.

Explanations for the Growing Wage Gap

As the discussion of family income bears out, there is a direct link between rising wage inequality among men and rising family income inequality. This link is to be expected given that male earnings are a significant source of income for most U.S. families. What factors can explain the widening wage gap among workers? Here again, it is convenient to group the causal factors into three categories that, by most accounts, can be credited with equal blame: supply-side factors, demand-side factors, and changes in wage-setting institutions. These three groups of explanations encompass those factors that affect the supply of workers of different skill, the demand for workers based on their characteristics, and the set of nonmarket forces that intervene to determine the wage structure.[18]

Supply-Side Factors

A number of factors operated on the supply side of the labor market that contributed to widening disparities, particularly between groups of workers defined by skill or other characteristics. One notable change in the 1980s was the relative decline in the growth in demand of the supply of college-educated workers, a response that was consistent with the lower rates of return to education evident in the 1970s, but that was not able to meet the subsequent growth in demand for high skilled workers in the 1980s. The increased supply of lower skilled workers as the result of immigration flows further aggravated the relative mismatch between supply and demand on the basis of worker skill.

Demand-Side Factors

The supply-side changes were accompanied by a number of relative demand shifts. One longer-run trend has been the changes in the industrial composition of the workforce as the services-producing sector has grown relative to the goods-producing sector. Although wage disparities widened within most industries, the shifts in the sectoral composition of employment can explain part of the rising wage disparities in the past two decades. Two other factors have received even more attention by economists and are associated with a larger share of the impact. The first is the shifts in demand driven by the growth in international trade during the 1980s. Although most economists agree that this factor has played a role, there is still no consensus on the relative importance of globalization in the changing wage structure. More weight is consistently given to technological change as a source of increased demand for more skilled workers, although direct evidence of the importance of technology is harder to come by. Instead, technology is often the residual factor that can explain any remaining effect after the other supply- and demand-side explanations have been exhausted.

Wage-Setting Institutions

In addition to market forces, nonmarket factors have also influenced the recent wage structure changes. Two are most prominent. First, there has been a steady and substantial decline in the fraction of the workforce that is unionized. In their role as wage-setting institutions, unions have been found to both raise average wages and reduce wage dispersion among organized workers. Thus, a reduction in unionization rates could be expected to have an effect on overall wage inequality. A number of studies bear out this prediction. By most accounts, the decline in unionization rates can explain some of the rise in male wage inequality. A second factor is the erosion of the real value of the minimum wage. The absence of a steady real wage floor partly explains why real wages fell so dramatically for unskilled workers during the 1980s.

In the end, efforts at parsing out the percentage share due to any one factor—either for income or for wage distribution changes—is somewhat artificial given the likely interactions among different factors. These interactions are potentially complex and difficult to sort out and, at present, are relatively less well understood. For example, declining rates of marriage and increased rates of single motherhood—labeled here as family structure changes—may derive in part from the poor labor market prospects of men, especially those with low education levels. Thus, the labor market changes that alone would increase the income gap also lead to changes in family formation that further increase income disparities.

The bottom line, in terms of causes, is to recognize that this situation did not occur overnight and that no one factor can be singled out to explain these trends. The trends derive in part from fundamental changes in the economic environment, such as changing industry structure, globalization, or technological change. Part of the explanation lies in changes in individual and family decisions—for example, the rise in female-headed families or the increase in female labor force participation. Some of these individual choices may themselves be influenced by the economic environment, while others have their roots in independent social or cultural trends.

POLICY OPTIONS TO ADDRESS THE NEW
ECONOMIC INEQUALITY

If the trend toward more inequality in the distribution of income and wages continues, what measures are available to policymakers to counteract it? Unfortunately, finding a single policy lever that can quickly or even eventually reverse the significant distributional changes experienced by the United States in recent decades is unlikely. Rather, any reversal of the trend is likely to be a gradual process with modest, often unsteady gains. Policy changes themselves may play a role. Other self-correcting factors may also have an impact. In the same way that a number of market and nonmarket forces operated alone and in conjunction with each other to drive the growing income and wage gap, so too will the direct and interactive effects of an array of self-correcting factors and policy levers. Thus, in the discussion that follows, a menu of policy options is presented with different objectives in mind. These objectives are presented first to frame the discussion of the options.

Possible Goals of Policy Intervention

Three potential policy goals should be highlighted: to narrow the income or wage gap; to raise the absolute standard of living at the bottom of the income or wage scale; and to minimize the impact of the economic dislocation associated with the distributional changes. The first two objectives concern more static notions of income distribution, while the third emphasizes possible dynamic implications.

As noted in the previous section, the distributional changes have been marked by a growing gap between the top and the bottom of the income and wage ladders as well as by real absolute declines among those in the lower ranks. One objective for policy intervention is to narrow the overall income or wage gap, i.e., to select policies that are likely to have the greatest impact on narrowing the disparities that have evolved in recent decades. This objective may be achieved by increasing the growth rate of income or wages at the bottom of the scale relative to the top, by slowing the growth rate of income or wages at the top relative to the bottom, or by a combination of the two. As discussed below, traditional government tax and transfer policies are one way to attain this objective by redistributing income from the upper to the lower ranks of the income scale.

A second potential policy goal is to raise the absolute standard of living for those at the bottom ranks of the wage or income distribution, with or without a corresponding compression in the overall distribution. To attain the first goal, the shape of the distribution must change; the second goal emphasizes the location of the distribution. Rising inequality accompanied by real economic gains for all is likely to create less concern than when growing disparities are accompanied by real declines in the standard of living for the least well off. Policies that stimulate more economic growth, as discussed below, may work toward attaining this objective; if all incomes grow with economic expansion, faster growth at the top is not as alarming.

A third potential policy goal is to reduce the negative impact of economic dislocation, for example, from job loss or family breakup. Recent research has demonstrated that the consequences of downward mobility are more severe in the United States than in other countries that have a more extensive social safety net.[19] Families and individuals doing relatively well today may still not feel secure given the uncertainty of their employment or family situation. Options that may help in this area include making health insurance and pension benefits more portable to minimize the consequences of job loss and to encourage productive job turnover; providing private or public sector opportunities or incentives for life-long learning through worker education and training; and reducing the economic consequences for women and children of family breakup through measures such as greater enforcement of child support payments.

In addition to considering the objectives of policies designed to influence the distribution of income or wages, other dimensions should be factored in. First, policies may differ in the extent to which they are most likely to have a more immediate impact (usually because they are very interventionist in nature) or whether they are likely to take time to have an impact (typically because they rely on changes in individual or employer behavior brought about by incentive-based measures rather than mandates). It may be desirable to identify a mix of strategies that will have both short- and long-run effects.

Another feature that differentiates the various policy options is the extent to which they are likely to directly affect the wage distribution or the income distribution. Typically, policies directed toward wage distribution focus on labor market forces or institutions, while policies directed toward income distribution affect labor supply, the distribution of other income sources (e.g., transfers, in-kind benefits, and taxes), or family formation. Policies designed to compress the wage gap may have the added benefit of reducing income disparities, given the link between wage and income inequalities identified in previous studies.[20] Thus, policies that address the widening wage gap should have immediate or eventual spillovers on income distribution.

A Menu of Policy Options

Given the unlikely situation of finding a single magic bullet to attain the policy objectives discussed above and the possible interest in achieving multiple objectives simultaneously, it seems most fruitful to consider a range of policy options. Table 3 presents a summary of the policy levers that will be discussed here and notes whether they are most likely to achieve one or more of the objectives listed above, whether their impact will be felt in the short run or will take time to accumulate, and whether

TABLE 3

A MENU OF POLICY OPTIONS

| | Objective | | | Initial Impact | |
	Narrow Gap	Protect Bottom Rank	Minimize Shocks	Short Run vs. Long Run	Wage vs. Income Gap
Macroeconomic					
Pro-growth	?	✓		Short run	Income
Fiscal policies					
Tax progressivity	✓	✓✓		Short run	Income
EITC	✓	✓✓		Short run	Income
Transfer payments	✓	✓✓	✓✓	Short run	Income
Labor market					
Union strength	✓	✓		Long run	Wage
Minimum wage		✓✓		Short run	Wage
Promote low skill demand		✓✓		Long run	Wage
Portable benefits			✓✓	Short run	Wage
Human capital investments					
Education	✓	✓✓	✓✓	Long run	Wage
Training/retraining	✓	✓	✓✓	Long run	Wage
Early childhood	✓	✓✓		Long run	Wage
Family decisionmaking					
Child support			✓✓	Short run	Income

Note: ✓ = weaker role; ✓✓ = stronger role.

the effect will operate primarily through the income or the wage distribution. The menu of options is grouped in the following broad categories: macroeconomic policies; fiscal policies; labor market policies; human capital investment policies; and family policies. The first two categories represent more traditional approaches to addressing distributional changes. Policies that fall in the remaining three categories are more likely to be controversial and less certain in terms of their ultimate impact on income or wage distributions.

Macroeconomic Policies

A prescription for more economic growth does not guarantee, as in the past, that the income gap or the wage gap will narrow. As discussed in the previous section, the expectation that periods of economic prosperity are accompanied by a stable income or wage distribution or even a narrowing of the income or wage gap did not hold true during the 1980s. Rather, income and wage inequality continued to widen during the long expansion from 1983 to 1989. However, the conventional wisdom that a rising tide lifts all boats may still have some merit, at least for family income. The 1980s expansion and recent recovery in the 1990s suggest that periods of strong, sustained growth can improve the absolute level of well-being at the lower tail of the income distribution, even if the relative disparities do not decline (see the percentile trends for 1983-85, 1985-89, and 1993-95 reported in Table 1). But the differential impact of the business cycle on income and wage distributions (contrast Tables 1 and 2) suggests that recent economic recoveries have boosted families' income not through faster wage growth at the bottom, but by other mechanisms such as increased employment rates and longer worker hours.

At least for the income distribution, pro-growth policies should not necessarily be dismissed. While this approach may not be adequate to meet the first policy objective of narrowing the income gap (and may even lead to the opposite effect), it may contribute toward the second goal of shoring up the absolute standard of living for those at the bottom of the income scale. Moreover, a strong economy can also have an impact relatively quickly, although the recent recovery suggests that income gains at the bottom of the distribution are slow to materialize after the trough of a recession. A strong, sustained economic expansion is more likely to have the desired impact. However, this optimism applies only to the income distribution; if recent experience is borne out in the future, there is less reason to expect that strong growth will necessarily boost the wages of the least skilled workers, much less narrow the wage gap.

Fiscal Policies

Tax and transfer policies are one of the primary vehicles for redistributing income, typically from the top to the bottom of the income scale. (There is little role for the tax and transfer system to directly affect the wage distribution, unless the EITC is considered a wage subsidy.) The current U.S. tax structure already plays a prominent role in reducing income disparities, primarily through the federal income tax, by higher tax rates at the top of the income scale that finance transfer payments to the bottom. Other taxes, mainly the Social Security payroll tax, have the opposite effect. For example, in 1995, the Gini coefficient among U.S. households before the tax and transfer system was accounted for (i.e., for pretax money income) was 0.509.[21] (The Gini coefficient is a commonly used summary measure of inequality that ranges from 0 [perfect equality] to 1 [perfect inequality]. An increase in the Gini coefficient indicates greater disparity in the distribution of income.) Accounting for the payroll tax, the Gini coefficient increased 1 percent to 0.514, indicating greater inequality due to the regressivity of the payroll tax. When the federal income tax was accounted for, the Gini coefficient fell 5 percent, to 0.490, confirming the progressivity of the federal income tax. The Gini coefficient fell an additional 1 percent when the EITC was factored in and 1 percent again when state income taxes were included. The net effect of payroll tax, federal income tax, the EITC, and state income tax was a 6 percent reduction in inequality. Likewise, both nonmeans-tested and means-tested cash and in-kind transfer payments further reduced disparities in post-tax money income. The combined effect of all transfer payments was an additional 18 percent reduction in inequality in post-tax money income. Two-thirds of the reduction in inequality due to transfer payments was attributable to nonmeans-tested government transfers, consisting largely of Social Security payments, but also including unemployment compensation, workers' compensation, and educational assistance.

There is little scope for changes in tax and transfer policies to have an even greater impact than they already do in reducing income disparities. This is because the primary source of the increase in income disparity in the past two decades has been growing inequality in pretax money income, mainly earnings from the labor market. Various simulations of substantial changes in the tax and transfer system, including the EITC, show little chance of producing a sizable reduction in inequality. For example, Gramlich et al. used 1991 data to simulate a set of progressive changes in the tax system, including increasing the top marginal tax rate from 28 to 50 percent and doubling the EITC.[22] But these extremely progressive policy changes would have had only a modest effect in reducing the Gini coefficient toward levels attained in the early 1980s.

Although state and federal tax and transfer policies may be unable to substantially reduce income disparities further, the first goal, such policies can provide a mechanism for attaining the second goal—providing a safety net to shore up the incomes of families and individuals at the bottom of the income distribution. Moreover, these policies can have an immediate impact on the income levels of the least fortunate. The EITC, for example, is an excellent vehicle for improving the well-being of those at the bottom of the income ladder even if it results in only a small reduction in overall inequality.[23] The EITC is a refundable tax credit for the working poor of up to 40 percent of earnings, depending on family size. Expansions in 1990 and 1993 increased the number of families affected so that 18 million families benefited from the credit in 1996.[24] In 1995, the EITC is estimated to have moved approximately 3.4 million people above the poverty line, a 7 percent reduction in the poverty rate.[25] Cash and in-kind transfer payments, particularly those that are means tested, also play a role in boosting the economic well-being of those at the bottom of the income ladder.

Tax and transfer policies have another advantage in that they can minimize the negative impact of transitory shocks. Thus, for example, workers' compensation, disability insurance, and unemployment compensation provide benefits during periods when income would otherwise drop due to injury, disability, or job loss. Welfare benefits in the form of Aid to Families with Dependent Children, Supplemental Security Income, food stamps, and Medicaid provide means-tested benefits when resources are low, either on a transitory or a more permanent basis. While these programs have recently been criticized as creating a population dependent on public benefits, they have always played a critical role as a mechanism of short-run assistance in periods of job loss, family breakup, poor health, or other economic dislocations. The recent changes in welfare policy implemented through the 1996 Personal Responsibility and Work Opportunity Reconciliation Act are likely to continue to preserve the transitory aspect of these assistance programs, albeit for a more limited segment of the U.S. population.

Labor Market Policies

As the discussion in the section "The Phenomenon of Rising Economic Inequality" shows, a number of important structural changes are responsible for the widening wage gap. Policies to address these changes in economic fundamentals are likely to be more controversial and less certain in terms of their impact on wage and income distributions. Nevertheless, these strategies deserve serious attention because of the significance of the distributional changes and the inability to completely rely on traditional macroeconomic or redistributive policies.

Collective bargaining has been one mechanism used in the past to promote wage growth among blue collar and some white collar workers and to reduce the wage gap between unionized and nonunionized workers. Given that the decline in the fraction of workers covered by a collective bargaining agreement has played a part in widening the wage gap, one approach would be to encourage stronger collective bargaining activity compared with the recent past. This outcome may itself be a natural response by lower paid workers to the declines in real wages they are experiencing. Alternatively, labor law reform and changes in company behavior may promote greater collective bargaining activity or at least greater cooperation between labor and management in setting wage and benefit policies.[26] Changes in the level and nature of union activity are likely to be slow in coming, so that the payoff in terms of the wage structure may be some time in the future.

Another market institution that has played at least a part in widening the wage gap and the absolute decline in real wages for the least skilled has been the fall in the real value of the minimum wage. Even with the stagnation in wages of the average worker during the 1980s, the minimum wage also declined in relative terms. Increases in the minimum wage would obviously reverse that trend, and recent national and state legislation has moved in that direction. The minimum wage is less than perfect in targeting low income families, as many minimum wage workers are secondary earners in high income families.[27] There are also possible disemployment effects, although most recent studies conclude these are likely to be modest.[28] On balance, a moderate increase in the minimum wage should provide a higher floor on income and wage distributions, even if it does little to arrest the growth of wages at the top of the scale. Moreover, the minimum wage combined with the EITC can be an effective type of insurance for low wage workers.[29] For example, the EITC does not apply to low wage single individuals or couples without children, whereas the minimum wage does not differentiate by family composition. Also, the potential labor supply disincentives implied by the EITC phaseout are not an issue with the minimum wage.

One characteristic of the labor market in recent years has been the mismatch between demand and supply of labor by skills, with demand for high skilled labor outpacing supply and thereby bidding up wages for the more educated, experienced, or trained workers. Conversely, the problem can be restated as too low a demand for or too high a supply of the least skilled. To remedy this mismatch, one approach would be to adopt policies that promote demand for the least skilled or that reduce their supply. Education and training policies are discussed below in the context of human capital investments, but they are also a mechanism to reduce the supply of the low skilled workforce. To the extent that immigration trends have added to the supply of low wage workers, curbs on immigration flows or composition would be another strategy in this area, although there is little reason to expect dramatic effects.[30] Alternatively, the supply of low wage workers in traded goods industries is another source placing downward pressure on low skilled U.S. workers. More restrictive trade policies would be a logical response and have been cited in some quarters as an appropriate strategy. However, there is strong evidence that protectionist policies are extremely costly relative to the benefits they produce.[31]

On the demand side, tax credits or subsidies could be offered to employers to hire low wage workers, or the public sector could generate more demand through public works programs.[32] These strategies have demonstrated some success in the past, although they are likely to take time before improvements in low skill wages are evident.[33] These strategies are also drawing attention as a way to promote the transition from welfare to work under the new welfare reform law. In fact, the influx of lower skilled workers from the welfare population is likely to place further downward pressure on wages for the least skilled, necessitating even larger programs to stimulate demand for low wage workers than would otherwise be the case.

The labor market in recent years has also been characterized by greater instability in both earnings and employment.[34] Workers who lose their job not only face reductions in money earnings (which may be replaced in part by unemployment insurance), but they also risk losing important benefits such as pension accruals and health insurance for themselves or their families. Thus, it is worth considering policy levers that can help reduce the negative impact of job dislocations, the third goal. Human capital investment strategies are discussed next as a way to boost skill levels and to facilitate job transitions in the face of demand shifts. Other options to help employment transitions include portable health insurance and pension benefits. The former objective has been achieved in part by the 1985 Consolidated Omnibus Budget Reconciliation Act (COBRA) and the 1996 Health Insurance Portability and Accountability Act (HIPAA, also known as the Kassebaum-Kennedy legislation). While COBRA and HIPAA guarantee the right to continue employer coverage at the group rate for 18 months and then to purchase private health insurance coverage without pre-existing conditions, the price on private policies beyond the 18-month COBRA continuation period will not be constrained in many states.

Human Capital Investment Policies

The rise in demand for skills, the dominant characteristic of the U.S. labor market in the past two decades, has led most analysts to conclude that greater investment in human capital is the approach to remedying the widening income and wage gap. With few exceptions, this strategy tops the list of prescriptions offered by parties across the political spectrum. For some, such investments will be the natural outgrowth of current market forces that have elevated the return to skills to historically high levels. In fact, there is evidence of a private sector response in the increasing rates of college attendance for most demographic groups since the early 1980s. An increase in the supply of college graduates will eventually dampen the current gap in wages between more and less educated workers, provided the supply response is sufficiently large.

In the event that the private sector is not able to respond sufficiently or there are barriers for some individuals to respond to market incentives, there would be a role for government policy in expanding educational opportunities. This role includes investments in resources devoted to primary and secondary schooling to increase the quality of schooling as well as to increase graduation rates. Investments in higher education are also appropriate, although with private sector returns to additional schooling already so high, the need for actual tax credits or subsidies of schooling costs may be reduced. Instead, expansion of student loan programs to facilitate investments in more schooling is appropriate to overcome the credit constraints facing many individuals who would benefit from greater educational investments. For noncollege-bound youth, efforts to ease the school-to-work transition through occupational-specific training in secondary school and better linkages to employers can prepare young people for the world of work and for a workplace that demands more skills at the time of job entry. Obviously, such investments are likely to take time before the impact on wage or income distributions is evident.

While educational investments can target the human capital acquisition of today's children and youth, today's workers also face the demands of a more dynamic and demanding work environment. For these workers and future generations of workers who can no longer expect to spend an entire career in a given occupation or industry, opportunities for worker training and retraining are essential. But the evidence is mixed that the payoffs will be large, especially for the least skilled.[35] Opportunities for continued training or life-long learning may be even more beneficial for future cohorts, provided they enter the labor market better trained at the outset of their career and can therefore benefit from additional educational investments. Opportunities for training or re-training can also ease the consequences of job loss and promote productive job turnover.

Yet another approach is to consider human capital investments even before the traditional period of school entry. An increasing body of evidence points to the beneficial effect of early childhood investments during infancy and the preschool years. This stage of early childhood represents a unique period of human development and is important for preparing children for subsequent learning, as well as for developing the social and emotional skills required in adulthood. Investments at these stages include promoting improved parenting, better health and nutrition, high quality child care, and improved cognitive and emotional development. In some cases, these investments can be shown to be cost-effective when provided to all children. In other cases, targeted interventions can be shown to produce savings to government that more than outweigh their costs.[36] Such programs, which can be justified in their own right, also may ultimately influence the distribution of wages and income by promoting greater human capital acquisition, particularly among the disadvantaged. In addition, targeted early childhood investments may break the relatively high degree of correlation between the outcomes of children and their parents in the United States, thereby promoting greater intergenerational income mobility.

Family Policies

Some of the forces driving the widening income gap derive from shifts in individual behavior related to family decisionmaking. Decisions of whether, when, and whom to marry, whether to have children and how many to have, and which family members will work in the labor market have changed in response to a variety of economic and social forces. Generally, there has been little support or pressure for the government to somehow influence or intervene in these decisions, although various tax, transfer, and other policies can indirectly provide incentives or disincentives for family behavior.[37] Nevertheless, there may be a role for government policy to strengthen or mitigate other forces that have a bearing on family decisionmaking.

Tax and transfer policies were discussed above as one mechanism to reduce the economic consequences of family breakup, as well as directly affecting the income gap or economic well-being of low income families.

In addition to providing public transfers, the government can play a greater role in ensuring that appropriate private transfers also take place. Thus, efforts to promote the determination of paternity in cases of out-of-wedlock childbearing and to mandate and enforce child support payments by noncustodial parents can minimize the need for government transfers and ensure a regular source of support for children in single-parent families.[38] Steps in this direction have received greater support in recent years, including new provisions in the 1996 Personal Responsibility and Work Opportunity Reconciliation Act. In addition to providing short-run benefits, such policies may promote more responsible decisionmaking about family formation and childbearing.

A Two-Pronged Approach

The policy menu outlined here presents a range of strategies, from reliance on the market's self-correcting influences to more activist government involvement. Is there a single strategy that can be relied on, or can an optimal strategy mix be designed? My judgment is that no single policy approach will, on its own, achieve any or a combination of the three policy goals discussed. However, there is not enough information to identify the mix of strategies that would be the most successful in meeting a given policy objective or combination of objectives. Moreover, even if it were possible, other policies may indirectly counteract any direct measures aimed at influencing income and wage distributions, while others may indirectly benefit the trends.

For this reason, I would argue for a two-pronged approach. First, consider policies that can be justified solely on distributional grounds or that, in addition to attaining other policy goals, are likely to have a spillover distributional effect in the desired direction. Second, identify the likely distributional impact of other policy changes that are motivated by different policy objectives but that may have positive or negative externalities on the distribution of income or wages. To the extent that significant negative distributional consequences are likely to arise from a given policy, it may be appropriate to consider additional measures to reduce the negative effects. Examples include decisions regarding trade policy or major reforms in social welfare policy such as Medicare or Social Security. Policy changes in these areas may be made with other objectives in mind, but the distributional consequences also need to be considered, with mitigating steps taken if necessary.

In determining the best or most desirable strategy mix, three additional features need to be incorporated. The first is that any progress toward achieving the three objectives discussed here should come from both private sector and public sector initiatives. At one extreme is the "do nothing" argument that would let the market take care of itself. At the other end is the suggestion that a series of strategies should be adopted that would entail significant government involvement in the operations of U.S. labor and product markets. However, the political will to rely solely on the government to attain these objectives does not exist; nor is the pure do nothing strategy adequate given the negative short- and long-run consequences of falling economic well-being at the bottom of the income ladder. Thus, a private-public sector partnership is likely to be the most attractive. In some cases, changes in private sector decisionmaking, by individuals or firms, may be a response to market forces. For example, there is an increased interest by employers in the quality of schooling received at the secondary level to the extent it affects the quality of the workforce, with some firms making investments in improving school quality in their local communities. In other cases, private sector initiatives may derive from public sector encouragement through subsidies or mandates. Examples include greater investment in worker training through tax credits or subsidies to private employers.

Second, a strategy mix should focus on the short run and the long run. The present state of affairs did not happen overnight, so most of the policies that would be adopted are likely to take considerable time before there is any payoff. It is important not to lose sight of this fact, particularly in terms of strategies that involve human resource investments, whether in early, primary, secondary, or postsecondary education, in training, or in other aspects of human capital such as health. The fiscal impacts of such investments should be accounted for separately from spending that has a primarily consumption component. While waiting for long-run strategies to take hold, short-run options that shore up the economic safety net and improve the standard of living of the least fortunate can be emphasized.

Finally, given the linkages between income and wage distributions, policy interventions are more likely to be successful to the extent they address both the widening income gap and the growing wage disparity. Some argue that it is sufficient to address widening income inequality alone because this is the broadest metric of individual well-being. However, based on previous research, part of the growth in the income gap is due to widening wage disparity. Moreover, there are other linkages that are less well understood but no less likely to be important. For example, as discussed earlier, increased rates of single parenthood may be linked to reduced wage opportunities for lower skilled men. Without improvements in wage opportunities for a large segment of the male labor force, dramatic changes in family formation and family stability are less likely. Thus, efforts to address the labor market opportunities of the least skilled members of the labor force should not only improve wages at the bottom of the wage distribution, but should also have spillover benefits in terms of improvements in family incomes through higher rates of family formation, greater family stability, and higher rates of labor force participation.

CONCLUSIONS

The distributional changes in the United States in recent decades represent a fundamental shift in the allocation of economic resources as both income and wage disparities have widened and the level of real income and earnings at the bottom of the scale has declined. These shifts have taken place during economic downturns as well as periods of expansion, and they span the administrations of both Democratic and Republican Presidents. While current understanding of the drivers behind these changes is far from complete, no single culprit has been responsible for either the wage or the income shifts. Instead, multiple factors have been at work, with both direct and indirect effects on income and wage distributions. On the income side, demographic shifts, changes in family structure, and widening wage disparity have all played a role. Demand shifts, supply shifts, and institutional forces have been factors in the expanding wage gap. The confluence of factors over a sustained period, all operating in the direction of widening the income and wage gap, represents a shift from the pattern of a more stable income and wage distribution experienced in the postwar period up to the late 1960s.

Once the significance of the distributional shifts is recognized, the natural question is to ask what can or should be done about the rise in income inequality. Just as there is no single source behind the widening disparity, there is no single magic bullet that will turn around recent trends. Rather, a multipronged approach will be needed to bring about short- and long-run shifts in income and wage distributions. The policy menu discussed here offers a range of options, some that will operate somewhat rapidly and others that will take time before realizing payoffs. The options include a more traditional reliance on macroeconomic and fiscal policies, as well as initiatives targeting labor markets, human capital investments, and family decisionmaking. The various options differ in the extent to which they directly target either wage or income distributions and in the extent to which they are likely to obtain one of three policy objectives.

Even if there is little interest by policymakers or the public to directly address widening income and wage disparities, it is critical to take account of the distributional impact of other policies designed with other objectives in mind. Thus, in addition to assessing the fiscal implications or the impact on economic growth or economic efficiency, the distributional impact of any given policy change merits consideration. Some policies, justified on grounds other than distribution, will have beneficial externalities in terms of short- or long-run improvements in income or wage disparities. In fact, some of the policies discussed above may generate interest for reasons other than their beneficial distributional effects. Still other policies may have the opposite effect. In cases where policies may worsen the distributional trends described here, policymakers should consider measures to counteract the negative distributional implications. Failure to do so may add to the pressures pulling income and wage distributions apart or at the least may counteract any self-correcting influences at work.

NOTES

1. Sheldon Danziger and Peter Gottschalk, *America Unequal* (New York: Russell Sage Foundation, and Cambridge: Harvard University Press, 1995); and Richard B. Freeman, *When Earnings Diverge: Causes, Consequences, and Cures for the New Inequality in the U.S.* (Washington: National Policy Association, 1997).

2. For two recent reviews on these topics, see Lynn A. Karoly, "Anatomy of the U.S. Income Distribution: Two Decades of Change," *Oxford Review of Economic Policy*, Vol. 12 (1996), pp. 76-95; and Freeman, *When Earnings Diverge*.

3. Council of Economic Advisers, *Economic Report of the President, 1997* (Washington: U.S. Government Printing Office [GPO], 1997).

4. Council of Economic Advisers, *Economic Report of the President, 1992* (Washington: U.S. GPO, 1992).

5. For a discussion of the methodological issues associated with examining inequality on these two fronts, see Lynn A. Karoly, "The Trend in Inequality Among Families, Individuals and Workers in the United States: A 25-Year Perspective," in *Uneven Tides: Rising Inequality in America*, ed. Sheldon Danziger and Peter Gottschalk (New York: Russell Sage Foundation, 1993).

6. For purposes of this chapter, adjusted family income is pretax family money income divided by the poverty line. Because the poverty scales adjust for differences in family income relative to needs (based on family size), this metric implicitly accounts for differing income needs for families of different sizes. For a discussion of this approach and results based on alternative definitions, see Karoly, "The Trend in Inequality"; and Karoly, "Anatomy of the U.S. Income Distribution."

7. Karoly, "Anatomy of the U.S. Income Distribution."

8. Ibid.

9. Ibid.

10. Ibid.

11. David M. Cutler and Lawrence F. Katz, "Rising Inequality? Changes in the Distribution of Income and Consumption in the 1980s," *American Economic Review*, Vol. 82 (1992), pp. 546-551.

12. Thomas L. Hungerford, "U.S. Income Mobility in the Seventies and Eighties," *Review of Income and Wealth*, Vol. 39 (1993), pp. 403-417; Stephen P. Jenkins and Frank A. Cowell, *The Changing Pattern of Income Inequality: The U.S. in the 1980s*, University College of Swansea Department of Economics Discussion Paper Series, 93-10 (Swansea, UK: University College of Swansea, 1993); and Stephen J. Rose, "Declining Family Incomes in the 1980s: New Evidence from Longitudinal Data," *Challenge*, Vol. 36 (1993), pp. 29-36.

13. Anthony. B. Atkinson, Lee Rainwater, and Timothy M. Smeeding, *Income Distribution in OECD Countries: Evidence from the Luxembourg Income Study* (Paris: Organization for Economic Cooperation and Development, 1995).

14. Freeman, *When Earnings Diverge*.

15. Ibid.

16. Steven J. Haider, "Earnings Instability and Earnings Inequality in the United States: 1967-1991," unpublished manuscript, March 1997.

17. For additional discussion, see Karoly, "Anatomy of the U.S. Income Distribution."

18. For a recent, comprehensive review of the relative importance of each of the three sets of factors reviewed only briefly here, see Freeman, *When Earnings Diverge.*

19. Ibid.

20. See, for example, Lynn A. Karoly and Gary Burtless, "Demographic Change, Rising Earnings Inequality, and the Distribution of Personal Well-Being, 1959-1989," *Demography*, Vol. 32 (1995), pp. 379-405.

21. U.S. Bureau of the Census, *Money Income in the United States: 1995*, Current Population Reports, Series P-60, No. 193 (Washington: GPO, 1996).

22. Edward M. Gramlich, Richard Kasten, and Frank Sammartino, "Growing Inequality in the 1980s: The Role of Federal Taxes and Cash Transfers," in Danziger and Gottschalk, *Uneven Tides.*

23. Danziger and Gottschalk, *America Unequal.*

24. Council of Economic Advisers, *Economic Report of the President, 1996* (Washington: GPO, 1996).

25. U.S. Bureau of the Census, *Poverty in the United States: 1995*, Current Population Reports, Series P-60, No. 194 (Washington: GPO, 1996).

26. Freeman, *When Earnings Diverge.*

27. Michael W. Horrigan and Ronald B. Mincy, "The Minimum Wage and Earnings and Income Inequality," in Danziger and Gottschalk, *Uneven Tides.*

28. David Card and Alan Krueger, *Myth and Measurement* (Princeton: Princeton University Press, 1995).

29. Barry Bluestone and Teresa Ghilarducci, *Making Work Pay: Wage Insurance for the Working Poor*, Jerome Levy Economics Institute of Bard College, Public Policy Brief No. 28 (1996).

30. Freeman, *When Earnings Diverge.*

31. Ibid.

32. Danziger and Gottschalk, *America Unequal.*

33. Peter Gottschalk, "Public Sector Employment," in *Labor Demand Policies and Low-Skill Workers*, ed. Richard B. Freeman and Peter Gottschalk (New York: Russell Sage Foundation, 1997); and Larry Katz, "Wage Subsidies for the Disadvantaged," in Freeman and Gottschalk, *Labor Demand Policies.*

34. Freeman, *When Earnings Diverge.*

35. James J. Heckman, "Is Job Training Oversold?" *The Public Interest*, Vol. 115 (1994), pp. 91-115.

36. Lynn A. Karoly, Peter Greenwood, Susan S. Everingham, Jill Hoube, M. Rebecca Kilburn, C. Peter Rydell, and Matt Sanders, *Investing in Our Children: What We Know and Don't Know about the Costs and Benefits of Early Childhood Interventions* (Santa Monica, CA: RAND, forthcoming).

37. See, for example, Robert Moffitt, "Incentive Effects of the U.S. Welfare System: A Review," *Journal of Economic Literature*, Vol. XXX (1992), pp. 1-61.

38. Danziger and Gottschalk, *America Unequal.*

National Policy Association

◆

The National Policy Association (NPA) is an independent, private, nonprofit, nonpolitical organization that carries on research and policy formulation in the public interest. NPA was founded during the Great Depression of the 1930s when conflicts among the major economic groups—business, labor, and agriculture—threatened to paralyze national decisionmaking on the critical issues confronting American society. NPA is dedicated to the task of getting these diverse groups to work together to narrow areas of controversy and broaden areas of agreement as well as to map out specific programs for action in the best traditions of a functioning democracy. Such democratic and decentralized planning, NPA believes, involves the development of effective government and private policies and programs not only by official agencies but also through the independent initiative and cooperation of the main private sector groups concerned.

To this end, NPA brings together influential and knowledgeable leaders from business, labor, agriculture, and academia to serve on policy groups. These groups identify emerging problems confronting the nation at home and abroad and seek to develop and agree upon policies and programs for coping with them. The research and writing for the policy groups are provided by NPA's professional staff and, as required, by outside experts.

In addition, NPA's professional staff undertakes research and special projects designed to provide data and ideas for policymakers and planners in government and the private sector. These activities include research on national goals and priorities, productivity and economic growth, welfare and dependency problems, employment and human resource needs, and technological change; analyses and forecasts of changing international realities and their implications for U.S. policies; and analyses of important new economic, social, and political realities confronting American society.

In developing its staff capabilities, NPA increasingly emphasizes two related qualifications. First is the interdisciplinary knowledge required to understand the complex nature of many real-life problems. Second is the ability to bridge the gap between theoretical or highly technical research and the practical needs of policymakers and planners in government and the private sector.

Through its policy groups and its research and special projects, NPA addresses a wide range of issues. Not all NPA trustees or members of the policy groups are in full agreement with all that is contained in NPA publications unless such endorsement is specifically stated.

For further information, please contact:

National Policy Association
1424 16th Street, N.W., Suite 700
Washington, D.C. 20036
Tel (202) 265-7685 Fax (202) 797-5516
e-mail npa@npa1.org Internet www.npa1.org

NPA Officers and Board of Trustees

Selected NPA Publications

◆

The Contingent Workforce, by Richard S. Belous (1998), NPA #289.

"The Growth of Income Disparity," ed. James A. Auerbach and Richard S. Belous, *Looking Ahead* (Vol. XIX, No. 2-3, November 1997).

Trade Blocs: A Regionally Specific Phenomenon or a Global Trend? by Richard L. Bernal (48 pp, 1997, $8.00), NPA #287.

"The Rise of the Contingent Workforce: Growth of Temporary, Part-Time, and Subcontracted Employment," by Richard S. Belous, *Looking Ahead* (Vol. XIX, No. 1, June 1997).

Foreign Assistance as an Instrument of U.S. Leadership Abroad, by Larry Q. Nowels and Curt Tarnoff (30 pp, 1997, $15.00), NPA #285.

When Earnings Diverge: Causes, Consequences, and Cures for the New Inequality in the U.S., by Richard B. Freeman (80 pp, 1997, $12.00), NPA #284.

Change at Work. Coauthors: Peter Cappelli, Wharton School, University of Pennsylvania; Laurie Bassi, Georgetown University; Harry Katz, Cornell University; David Knoke, University of Minnesota; Paul Osterman, MIT; and Michael Useem, Wharton School, University of Pennsylvania. Commissioned by NPA's Committee on New American Realities (NAR), (288 pp, 1997, available from Oxford University Press, $27.00).

A Synopsis of Change at Work (40 pp, 1997, $8.00), NPA #283.

"The North American Workforce: Challenges and Opportunities for Education and Training," *North American Outlook* (Vol. 6, No. 3, March 1997).

The New World of Work, by Stephen Barley (78 pp, 1996, $15.00), NPA #280.

Aging and Competition: Rebuilding the U.S. Workforce, ed. James A. Auerbach and Joyce C. Welsh, with an Introduction by Robert B. Reich (280 pp, 1994, $17.50), NPA #273.

The Future of Labor-Management Innovation in the United States, ed. James A. Auerbach and Jerome T. Barrett (108 pp, 1993, $10.00), NPA #267.

Turbulence in the American Workplace, an NAR-commissioned study, available from Oxford University Press (270 pp, 1991).

European and American Labor Markets: Different Models and Different Results, ed. Richard S. Belous, Rebecca S. Hartley, and Kelly L. McClenahan (144 pp, 1992, $15.00), NPA #257.

Preparing for Change: Workforce Excellence in a Turbulent Economy, Recommendations of the Committee on New American Realities (32 pp, 1990, $5.00), NPA #245.

An NPA subscription is $100.00 per year. In addition to new NPA publications, subscribers receive *Looking Ahead,* a quarterly journal that is also available at the separate subscription price of $35.00. NPA subscribers, upon request, may obtain a 30 percent discount on other publications in stock. A list of publications will be provided upon request. Quantity discounts are given.

NPA is a nonprofit organization under section 501(c)(3) of the Internal Revenue Code.

NATIONAL POLICY ASSOCIATION
1424 16th Street, N.W., Suite 700
Washington, D.C. 20036
Tel (202) 265-7685   Fax (202) 797-5516
e-mail npa@npa1.org   Internet www.npa1.org